Library of
Davidson College

# RELIGION AND HUMAN AUTONOMY

# RELIGION AND HUMAN AUTONOMY

## HENRY DUMÉRY'S PHILOSOPHY OF CHRISTIANITY

*by*

### RENÉ FIRMIN DE BRABANDER

MARTINUS NIJHOFF / THE HAGUE / 1972

© 1972 by Martinus Nijhoff, The Hague, Netherlands
All rights reserved, including the right to translate or to
reproduce this book or parts thereof in any form
ISBN 90 247 1329 3

PRINTED IN THE NETHERLANDS

"Sorrow is knowledge: they who know the most mourn the deepest over the fatal truth, the tree of knowledge is not that of life."
Lord Byron: Manfred

"We are sinful not only because we have eaten of the Tree of Knowledge, but also because we have not yet eaten of the Tree of Life. The state in which we are is sinful, irrespective of guilt."
Franz Kafka: Reflections on Sin, Suffering, Hope and the True Way

# PREFACE

For most of its career philosophy of religion has been a controversial discipline: it has usually ended up becoming a substitute for what it set out to explain. Born out of the religious scepticism of the late seventeenth century it remained for many years what it was to Hume and Lessing: an instrument for criticizing rather than for interpreting faith. Gradually the hostility subsided, but not the tendency to reduce. Nearly each one of the great names in this area represents a theory that goes "beyond" faith. Phenomenology changed that situation. Conceived for accurate understanding of acts and meanings rather than for the building of vast syntheses, its method was more apt to yield understanding than criticism. Moreover, by distinguishing the ideal meanings from the psychic realities of the act, it chased its followers from the quagmire of psychic genesis, causal justification and rational "proof" of the religious object, and forced them to concentrate on the intentional terminus of the experience. Husserl's disciples immediately perceived the promise of the new method for the study of religion. Even before phenomenology was fully defined two of them started exploring the old terrain with the new tools. Students of religion also overcame their long-standing distrust of the tentacular science of philosophy now that it was finally becoming a malleable instrument. Thus we find such disparate figures as Hering and Scheler, Van der Leeuw and Eliade indebted to the same method. Undoubtedly phenomenology had blown a breeze of air into the stale attics of philosophy of religion.

Yet phenomenological analysis alone could never satisfy the philosophical mind in this area. Beyond the experience the philosopher is concerned with its ontological foundation. Most phenomenologists, with the illustrious exception of Husserl himself and some unorthodox, existentialist disciples, show little interest in leaving the phenomenon. Yet in the case of the religious experience such an investigation appears to be indispensable. For all its immanence the religious act is directed toward an intentional terminus which ultimately defies phenomenological analysis. The religious experience presents itself as intrinsically dependent upon a being other than the being of consciousness. To grasp the act's full meaning, then, the investigator must at some point come to grips with this trans-conscious existence. At this point all the difficulties of the past return. For a philosophy which is self-sufficient with respect to the transcendent and its relation to consciousness, remains unacceptable to the believer, apart from being a futile enterprise from a philosophical point of view. A God conceived "within the limits of reason alone" independently of the religious act, will always be a questionable metaphysical entity. Even if the philosopher were to deduce the existence of an infinite, perfect being, his conclusion would hardly be pertinent for what religious man adores.

One philosopher who perceived this difficulty with unusual clarity was Maurice Blondel. He refused to accept the self-sufficiency of modern philosophy, yet maintained the autonomous method essential to philosophy. To him philosophy is always removed from, and dependent upon, the living experience. Its task is to reflect upon this experience and to discover its logical coherence. In the area of religion this means that the philosopher must study the logical coherence of the various expressions of man's relation to the transcendent. Since reality as the metaphysician finds it, is essentially incomplete, the religious "hypothesis" which postulates a transcendent reality becomes a necessary object of investigation.

Duméry unites Blondel's insight with Husserl's method. It is not the least of his merits in the study of religion. Yet the synthesis which emerges differs substantially from either philosophy. The *henological* reduction which he postulates beyond Husserl's phenomenological reductions has no more in common with Husserl than with Blondel. In interpreting the mind's activity as ultimately a surge toward absolute unity beyond determination Duméry joins a very different tradition: Plotinus' speculation on the One which is both identical with the mind as the source of its activity, and transcendent to its subject-object opposition. Neoplatonism has long proven to be the most vital element in the religious thought of the West.

Though Duméry has captured the philosophical trends most fertile for the study of religion, he is not an eclectic. His work is deeply personal and addresses itself to problems of which his predecessors remained unaware. His particular concern is with the creative autonomy of man, without which no authentic freedom is possible. His search is for transcendence as the basis of human creativity, rather than as the source of preestablished values.

Regrettably (although perhaps not exceptionally) no critical study of this important continental philosopher existed in the English language. The present one will remedy this defect in a worthy fashion. René De Brabander's main qualities are lucid clarity and a sure grasp of Duméry's context. I hope his solid work will enjoy the reception which it deserves.

Louis Duprè

# TABLE OF CONTENTS

*Preface*     VII

*Introduction*     XIV

## CHAPTER I
### FREEDOM AND RELIGION

SECTION I:
Posing the problem     1

SECTION II:
Duméry's appraisal of Sartre's position on God and freedom     5

SECTION III:
Duméry's critique of Sartre's position on God and freedom     13

## CHAPTER II
### SEARCH FOR A METHOD TO BE USED IN THE PHILOSOPHICAL STUDY OF RELIGION

SECTION I:
Method of explication and method of confrontation     22
 a) Stating the problem     22
 b) The method of explication     25
 c) The method of confrontation     29

SECTION II:
Blondel's method of immanence and the philosophical study of religion     33
 a) Introducing the framework of the Blondelian thought     33
 b) The problem of the supernatural and the method of immanence     37
 c) How the principle of immanence can provide a method for the philosophical study of religion which escapes the pitfalls of immanentism and dualism     48

SECTION III:
Husserl's method of comprehension and Duméry's method of discrimination     52
 a) The method of Husserl and the service it renders to the phenomenology of religion     52

XII                TABLE OF CONTENTS

    b) Objections against Husserl's phenomenological method    56
    c) Duméry's method of discrimination: reflective and critical analysis    61

## CHAPTER III
### DUMÉRY'S RELIGIOUS PHILOSOPHY. THE SPIRIT AS CONSTITUTIVE EXIGENCY OF THE ABSOLUTE

SECTION I:
Transition from method to doctrine    66

SECTION II:
The irreducible relation of the spirit with God    72
    a) The God of living religion    72
    b) Plotinian translation and completion of Husserl's reductions    77
    c) Nature of the relation between the Absolute One and the spirit    82

SECTION III:
The spirit as creator of the world of determinations. The theory of the Act-Law    86
    a) The spirit as correlation of freedom and order    86
    b) Description of the relation between the act-law and the psyche: freedom and determinism, eternity and time    91
    c) Empirical consciousness and its universe: inverted expressions and projections of the system of spirits    98

## CHAPTER IV
### DUMÉRY'S PHILOSOPHY OF RELIGION: CRITIQUE OF THE CATEGORIES AND SCHEMES WHICH EXPRESS THE SPIRIT'S CONSTITUTIVE EXIGENCY OF THE TRANSORDINAL ONE

SECTION I:
The scheme of transcendence and the category of the Absolute    105
    a) Scope of the reflective critique in general and of the critique of the attributes in particular    105
    b) Henological redemption of the scheme of transcendence and the category of the absolute    109
    c) Henology and negative theology    113

SECTION II:
Interpretation of the category of grace and the scheme of the supernatural    117
    a) Is there a philosophical problem of grace and how can philosophy deal with it?    117
    b) Discriminative critique of the different schemes of the category of grace    122
    c) Philosophical critique of the categories of grace and the supernatural    127

SECTION III:
Category of faith, factual and doctrinal schemes    134
    a) Descriptive phenomenology of the Judaeo-Christian religion    134
    b) The Jesus-fact assumed by the hierogenic consciousness of the early Christian community    149

c) The four means of expression of hierogenic consciousness 156
d) Projective mentality and truth of Christianity 165

*Epilogue*: Human Autonomy and Finitude 175

*Bibliography* 179

# INTRODUCTION

He must therefore plunge himself into the life of a godless world, without attempting to gloss over its ungodliness with a veneer of religion or trying to transfigure it. He must live a "worldly" life and so participate in the suffering of God. He may live a worldly life as one emancipated from all false religions and obligations. To be a Christian does not mean to be religious in a particular way, to cultivate some particular form of asceticism, but to be a man. It is not some religious act which makes a Christian what he is, but the participation in the suffering of God in the life of the world . . . it is only by living completely in this world that one learns to believe.[1]

This study intends to reduce Henry Duméry's Philosophy of Christianity to its general outlines. We were forced to take this approach because of the extensiveness of the topic and because of our wish to become acquainted with the different problems of contemporary philosophy of religion. Duméry's Philosophy of Christianity forms a good introduction to the study of contemporary philosophy of religion. His writings cover the main Christian doctrines and provide the reader with a continual confrontation of these doctrines with contemporary thought. Duméry is a Catholic thinker who has a deep awareness of the discrepancies between the world of the Christian discourse and the world of modern philosophy. Confronted with the objection that the Christian way of life is somehow unfaithful to the human dimension of our existence, he attempts a reconciliation between the autonomy of philosophy and the heteronomy of Christianity. Hence the title of this study: *Religion and Human Autonomy*.

This concern not to betray the human dimension of our existence belongs to what is most valuable and appealing in his Philosophy of Christianity. The creativity of the spirit and man's consequent experience of the absence of God form the main theme of contemporary religious

---

[1] Dietrich Bonhoeffer, *Letters and Papers from Prison* (New York: Macmillan, 1962), pp. 222-223-226.

thought. Exaltation because of man's creative power and desperation because of his frightful loneliness present us with the tragic greatness of modern man. The old system of symbols binding man to God, to his fellowmen, and to nature is evaporating. "There is a goal, but no way; what we call a way is hesitation." [2] A new synthesis of the finite and the infinite, of the relative and the absolute, of the human and the divine must be established. Such synthesis cannot be easily found. It is a most delicate balance of immanence and transcendence. Over-immanentization as well as non-immanentization of God are dangerous; both lead to the alienation of God from human experience. In the over-immanentization of God, God becomes a self-image of man. The "killing" of God becomes necessary in order that the God of transcendence may be resurrected. On the other hand, when God is but equivocally related to the immanent world of man, the existence of God becomes irrelevant.

How can this new synthesis of finite and infinite be realized? Duméry is right in maintaining that no authentic synthesis can be brought about as long as the human dimension is not given its full weight. Since such synthesis envisions somehow a complete coincidence of the human and the divine, the firm determination never to leave the human prematurely and to accept courageously that we live in an age of divine silence seems to be the only sound attitude. Christianity teaches that the Absolute must be reached through the relative. The whole problem, therefore, lies in determining what the meaning of the word THROUGH is. We paid special attention to this point so that, in a way, this book is nothing but an attempt to determine the meaning Duméry gives to this one word and to examine if his interpretation of this word is correct. As this study proceeded, we began to realize more and more both how necessary it is never to leave the human and also how, strangely enough, Duméry himself was not faithful to his own proposition. The human which he proposes is basically some kind of infinite. Duméry's concept of man and his approach to the divine is too idealistic and too univocal. The finite must be consumed, not just passed through.

"The true way is along a rope that is not spanned high in the air, but just above the ground. It seems intended more to cause stumbling than to be walked along." [3]

The merit of Duméry's Philosophy of Christianity consists in its original and personal combination of different influences. The rapprochement

---

[2] F. Kafka, "Reflections on Sin, Suffering, Hope and the True Way," in *My Dearest Father. Stories and Other Writings,* p. 36.
[3] Kafka, *op. cit.,* p. 34.

between Sartre, Husserl and Blondel on the one hand and Plotinus on the other hand, the insight that somehow the ancients were greater than the modern thinkers, is a stroke of genius one cannot but admire. It proves that no philosophy, however old it may be, becomes outdated. The great philosophers of ancient times still have their say in the philosophical "Symposium" of mankind, the "Philosophia perennis." Duméry has a deep awareness of this "new-and-yet-so-old" characteristic of the great philosophical problems. He, therefore, deserves to be counted among the great philosophers of our times. One must admire his dialectical skill and the rigid consistency of his thought. Faced with such learning and keenness of mind, we cannot help but feel quite inadequate in interpreting his philosophy. The dangers of misinterpretation are great. Nevertheless, we will face these dangers hoping that even a deficient exposition will throw some light on the religious problem of our times.

We should mention the ecclesiastical reprobation which weighs on the work of Henry Duméry. (Condemnation by the Holy Office of Duméry's major works, on June 4, 1958. Cf. *L'Osservatore Romano,* June 21, 1958, and *Acta Apostolicae Sedis,* Vol. 51, 1959, p. 432.) This negative reaction of the Magisterium has to be kept in mind, not because it would have a philosophical bearing, but because Duméry himself wants to respect the teaching of the Church. It is only because Duméry's Philosophy of Christianity intends to be faithful to the Catholic representation of the Christian faith that we mention the ecclesiastical reprobation.

Since only one work of Duméry has been translated into English (*Le problème de Dieu*), most of the quoted texts are our translations. Duméry's French is clear and distinct. On the contrary, Blondel's style is heavy and very often obscure, mainly due to the fact that he dictated most of his later works. The one English translation of his work was used (*Letter on Apologetics*). The other texts are our own translations. Most of the quoted texts of Sartre and Husserl exist in English. Finally, since Duméry follows Jean Trouillard's interpretation of Plotinus, very few original texts of Plotinus appear in his works.

We feel obliged to express our most sincere gratitude to the many who, with their encouraging aid made the writing of this work possible. We owe a great debt of gratitude to Dr. Louis Dupré, of Georgetown University, Washington, D. C., without whose guidance and encouragement this study would not have been made. Last, but not least, we acknowledge our indebtedness to Mrs. Ellen Tabb for helping with the style and format of this work.

CHAPTER I

# FREEDOM AND RELIGION

The God who is with us is the God who forsakes us. The God who makes us live in this world without using Him as a working hypothesis is the God for whom we are ever standing.... Man's religiosity makes him look in his distress to the power of God in this world; he uses God as Deus ex machina. The bible, however, directs him to the powerlessness and suffering of God....[1]

## SECTION I
### POSING THE PROBLEM

The foregoing quotation summarizes very aptly the contemporary religious problem and the attempt towards the revision and reinterpretation of the Christian faith in terms of today's experience in life. It is the old question of superstition and libertinism versus adoration, which always was and always will be the central difficulty of the religious attitude. It is superstitious to put one's hope in mere external formalities, but it is temerarious to discard the religious tradition as such. Pascal saw this clearly when he wrote:

There are few true Christians. There are those who believe because of superstition; there are those who do not believe because of libertinism; very few are in between.[2]

Superstition and libertinism are the two extremes which have to be avoided if one is to establish an authentic religious attitude.

It is by continually confronting these two extremes of superstition and libertinism that Henry Duméry tries to disengage the authentic religious attitude. Existentialism, in providing a thoroughgoing critique of theism, enables him to come to a clearer insight into the superstitious religious

---

[1] Dietrich Bonhoeffer, *Letters and Papers from Prison* (New York: Macmillan, 1962), pp. 219-220.
[2] Blaise Pascal, *Pensées* (Paris: Editions Garnier, 1957), num. 256.

attitude. Conversely, by criticizing the existentialist position on God and human freedom, Duméry reinterprets the main theses of atheistic existentialism so that they can be reconciled with and even lead to a theistic position.

In a short article entitled, "Vers un cinquième âge de la pensée," [3] Duméry makes the remark that the specific characteristic of existentialism is not that it is a philosophy of the tragic or a philosophical atheism but a philosophy in which human freedom is carried to the absolute. The thesis of a radical and creative freedom placed in the heart of man is the core of contemporary existentialism. Man's freedom consists in creativity, in the constitution of the orders of ideas and values. "Man is free because he creates the true and the good in all its forms." [4] At first sight such a statement seems absurd. Is it not contradictory to say that man creates his own ideas and values, since it is clear that one cannot affirm and deny as one likes? Creative freedom here means to be free *of*. Free of what? Of that which is extrinsic. This is the pivotal point: that man is the sole creator of the universe of truth and value, means that there exists no eternal and external realm of the real and the ideal, pre-existing man's thought and destined to be ratified or chosen by man.

> The human mind does not have to adhere to an ideal "order" of which it cannot be the source. It poses this order, it creates this ideal.[5]

This absolute freedom, according to Sartre and his disciples, necessarily results in the denial and refusal of God. Human freedom means the death of God, because it cannot stand reality prior to itself without being reduced to the state of an object. If God exists, then man is nothingness.

> Silence is God. Absence is God. God is the loneliness of man. There was no one but myself; I alone decided the Evil; and I alone invented the Good.... If God exists, man is nothing; if man exists ... .[6]

There is no alternative, either God or man, but not both. It is the great challenge of our times, Duméry maintains, to reconcile the thesis of radical human freedom with theism, and to prove that human creativity of ideas and values does not lead to atheism. Only in an essentially active contact with the absolute is man responsible for his universe of truth and value. The auto-creation of man and his universe, instead of being possible only

---

[3] Henry Duméry, *La tentation de faire du bien* (Paris: Editions du Seuil, 1956), pp. 150-153.
[4] *Ibid.*, p. 151.
[5] *Ibid.*, p. 152.
[6] Jean-Paul Sartre, *The Devil and the Good Lord*, trans. Kitty Black (New York: Random House, Inc., 1962), p. 141.

through the refusal of God, is impossible without God. In other words, the creation of the self by the self does not exclude the Creator but implies Him.

It is already clear that, according to Duméry, there can be no authentic theism unless it succeeds in proving that the thesis of radical human creativity, in one way or another, is at the very core of the religious experience. Only when this condition is fulfilled can one expect to present a theism which would be acceptable to a large number of unbelievers. "The theist assertion will be absurd to atheistic humanity as long as the admission of human creativity is not fully consented to by the believer." [7] Humanism and human creativity are synonymous and only when we are able to show that human creativity implies the presence of an Absolute, and vice-versa, can we talk about Christian humanism. As long as God is to be thought of, in one way or another, as that which limits human freedom as such, or as that which endangers the human subjectivity, so long will the idea of God be unacceptable. This implies that the heteronomy of the believer will have to be conceived in such a way that it leaves room for an authentic autonomy. God, therefore, is to be conceived, as rigorously as possible, as that which is at the source of man's autonomy. The laws of God are concurrently the laws of man's most fundamental freedom. "God is not man's rival, but the power of his strength; the source of his energy; the best guarantee of his autonomy." [8] Faith in God, consequently, is that which stimulates human creativity rather than that which stifles research and invention. But this likewise means that only faith ceaselessly searching is authentic, a faith which is not an escape from human responsibility.

Faith without repose; this is how one should understand faith; the true faith which searches for God; a hopeful and loving interrogation; an ever open quest of heart, soul and mind. It is clear, indeed, that if faith were saturating consciousness, if it were immobilizing it or fixing it, exempting it from all initiative or effort, it would be a monstrous alibi for courage and liberty.[9]

Nevertheless, faith as openness, as interrogation, is also fundamentally dependent, a dependence, however, which one can afford only in the most

---

[7] Duméry, op. cit., p. 20.
[8] Duméry, op. cit., p. 21.
[9] Duméry, Foi et interrogation (Paris: Téqui, 1953), p. xii. Beautiful text. For Duméry, faith is restless interrogation. "C'est là qu'un certain doute, inhérent à la foi, comme l'a vu Alain, lui garde vigueur et authenticité. Bien entendu, le doute dont-il s'agit est le refus courageux de se reposer sur des appuis empiriques, quels qu'ils soient, au lieu de continuer à les dépasser pour les valoriser. Ce doute, il vaudrait mieux, pour éviter toute équivoque, l'appeler interrogation. On définirait alors la foi comme ce qui ne doit permettre aucune lassitude dans l'interrogation." Duméry, Philosophie de la religion (Paris: Presses Universitaires de France, 1958), II, note 2.

authentic independence. There can be no authentic questioning nor receiving without a dependence in communication with the Absolute.

Only when faith can be perceived as a dialectic of the most fundamental dependence and independence can there be a place for real human creativity. One could say that the entire work of Duméry is an attempt to come to a deeper understanding of the human dialectic of dependence and independence. The more authentic human independence is, the more authentic also becomes man's dependence. Human existence is located in a difficult and equivocal interval between dependence and independence. It is one of the most fundamental paradoxes of our existence that there can be no independence without dependence, nor dependence without independence. This dialectic of dependence and independence reaches its deepest point in religion where man is faced at one and the same time with a most fundamental dependence and a possibility of a most radical independence. How complete dependence can at the same time be complete independence is the mystery of a God who creates free human beings, not robots.

"The paradox of action is to conquer its autonomy under a law of heteronomy." [10] In order to achieve this kind of thinking one has to pursue the *via media* of a certain creative faithfulness. On one side there is a danger of traditionalism where faithfulness becomes laziness and cowardice; on the other side, there is the danger of modernism where creativity becomes rashness and arbitrariness. In the subsequent pages, we shall attempt to explain how Duméry adopts the Sartrian critique on theism in its full strength, yet at the same time how he indicates that the Sartrian position on freedom excludes only the inauthentic God and includes faith in the authentic God. Sartre's philosophy invites the Christian believer to reconsider some of his positions: (1) to take the creation of the self by the self more seriously in accepting the theory that man is the creator of truth and value, and (2) to rediscover that the Plotinian and Dionysian tradition of the ineffability of God, which excludes all determinations on the level of the Absolute, is the only road to the discovery of an authentic God. Duméry shows, contrary to Sartre's thinking, how radical human freedom in time has to be based upon an eternal dimension in man in which he discovers his constitutional relation with the Absolute.[11]

Upon reflection one is amazed at the extent to which Duméry's thinking derives from a thoroughgoing reflection upon Sartre's philosophical

[10] Duméry, *La tentation de faire du bien,* p. 247.
[11] Duméry, *Foi et interrogation,* p. 111.

atheism. The article, "La question Sartre," [12] especially reveals Duméry's fundamental concern to graft a theism on a philosophy of radical human freedom in the existentialist sense. He uses the Sartrian critique of theism as a background in order to come to a better insight into the question: What constitutes an authentic theism which respects human freedom?

"It is less important to prove Sartre wrong – any polemic is a weakness – than to question ourselves about the accusation he raises against faith." [13] In the following section, we will try to summarize Sartre's fundamental position on freedom and God as Duméry sees it. The Sartrian theses of absolute freedom and consequent rejection of God have a very important positive meaning for our author. In the third section, we will observe Duméry in his critique of Sartre. This critique of Sartre will introduce the fundamental features of Duméry's concept of the relation, God-man (what we will call his Religious Philosophy, cf. Chapter III), and of his descriptive critique of religion in virtue of this theandric relation (what we will call his Philosophy of Religion, cf. Chapter IV).

SECTION II

DUMÉRY'S APPRAISAL OF SARTRE'S POSITION ON GOD AND FREEDOM

Descartes, according to Duméry, is the real starting point of Sartre. The famous Sartrian expression, by which he characterizes all existentialist thinking, "l'existence précède l'essence," [14] is actually a definition of the Cartesian God. Sartre found in the Cartesian God the realization of a radical contingent freedom not subjected to a pre-existing order of ideas and values. God is the creator of the essences, of the eternal truths which have their foundations in His Divine Will. This pure self-founded freedom of God, however, is for Sartre a perfect description of human freedom. If man is to be free, he must be responsible for whatever his intelligible universe contains. Man is first a project and *nothing* can exist previous to this project. Therefore, man is a being about which no definition can be formulated, which means that man is nothingness first and that his definition comes later. "Man first of all exists, encounters himself, surges up in the world, and defines himself afterwards." [15] The intuition of

[12] *Ibid.*, pp. 73-123.
[13] *Ibid.*, p. xiii.
[14] Sartre, *L'Existentialisme est un humanisme* (Paris: Editions Nagel, 1964), p. 17. (French text.)
[15] *Idem* in English translation of Walter Kaufman, *Existentialism from Dostoevsky to Sartre* (Ohio: The Word Publishing Company, 1964), p. 294.

complete freedom destroys with one stroke all the old bastions in which freedom was imprisoned. All laws, principles, order and determinism have to follow the explosion of freedom in the heart of man. They are creations of freedom.

Freedom thus cannot be founded but upon itself and consequently we should not be surprised that it is to be considered as a void, as nothingness. Nothingness is but the obverse side of the absolute. Freedom as nothingness, resting upon itself, has continually to risk itself in escaping and reconstructing the ideal as well as the real world. Man, for this reason, is task: he always remains to be made. God, conceived as the locus of pre-existing eternal ideas according to which the Divine Artisan [16] creates everything, means the end of such radical human freedom. Sartre compares the God-creator of the universe to the making of a paper knife by an artisan, by which he first conceives the idea of the object and then makes it according to this idea. Then individual man would realize a certain concept which already exists in the Divine Mind, which would mean that the essence precedes the existence. Only if God is dead can man be free. Once God is eliminated, the world of ideas and values, whether they exist in Him or in things, collapses and the whole world of ideas and things has its meaning only through an intelligible reference to man.

The positing of an absolute freedom with its consequent refusal of God does not do away with the pre-existing world of things. The world of things, however, is reduced to a mere resistance, yet a resistance which is a necessary condition for freedom to realize itself. Just as the air is simultaneously that which carries and resists the bird in flight, so also reality is both that which opposes and creates freedom.

Consequently the *resistance* which freedom reveals in the existent, far from being a danger to freedom, results only in enabling it to arise as freedom. There can be a free for-itself only as engaged in a *resisting* world.[17]

The spirit is negativity: the power to say no to nature and in doing so to create and affirm itself. This kind of reasoning is rather strange if one is accustomed to contemplate the notion of freedom as something positive, as something already there. But here again we encounter the particular nature of the existentialist notion of freedom. What is meant is not so much freedom as capacity to choose, but as capacity to affirm itself in contesting everything else. Freedom has to conquer itself in the encounter

---

[16] Sartre, *L'Existentialisme est un humanisme*, pp. 17-19.
[17] Sartre, *Being and Nothingness*, trans. Hazel E. Barnes (New York: Philosophical Library, 1956), p.483. (Italics mine.)

with the in-itself, its absoluteness and limitation are interdependent. Indeed, man is that being which fails to overcome the resistance of the in-itself, and in this very failure lies his possibility to exist. If it is true that freedom can never surmount the resistance of the in-itself, nor be completely absorbed by it, then indeed one must say that human life is a useless passion.

It is clear now that this freedom which *is* finitude would be destroyed if it were related to and founded upon an absolute order of ideas and values, since this would imply on the part of man an abdication of his prerogatives and a refusal to take up the burden of freedom. To live this actual finite freedom is the only way for man to be authentic, and all belief in an Absolute has to be regarded as an escape. Man is neither a supra-human being nor an infra-human being. "I want to be a man among men. Only that? I know; it is the most difficult of all things." [18] God devours the substance of man, heaven makes the earth unreal, saints and devils are only limit-ideas of man. "God does not exist... I have delivered us. No more Heaven, no more Hell; nothing but earth." [19]

Man must be fully responsible. Human existence is characterized insofar as it assumes itself as task which has to be taken up in a continual interaction of freedom and necessity; of being set apart from and yet being part of the world; of independence and dependence. It is the solicitude to be faithful to this fundamental paradox of man which leads Sartre to the denial of God. God is discarded to safeguard that which is most essential to man, namely freedom as historicity, freedom which creates itself in continual struggle with necessity; truth which creates itself in continual struggle with facticity.

It is clear then that Sartre's atheism is not just an easy solution; it is not indulgence in pride and search for unrestraint. He refuses the Absolute only in the name of a better absolute.[20] It is not the proclamation of absolute freedom as license, but the return to a notion of freedom conceived as duty to liberate itself in constant confrontation with that which is at the same time resistance and source of freedom. If existence really precedes essence, then man is responsible for what he is.[21]

Existentialism is strongly opposed to a certain type of secular moralism which seeks to suppress God at the least possible expense. On the contrary, the existentialist finds it extremely embarrassing that God does not exist, for

---

[18] Sartre, *The Devil and the Good Lord,* p. 145.
[19] *Ibid.,* p. 142.
[20] Duméry, *Foi et interrogation,* p. 29.
[21] Sartre, *L'Existentialisme est un humanisme,* p. 35.

there disappears with him all possibility of finding values in an intelligible world.[22]

The refusal of God, therefore, is at least as difficult as the acceptance of God, because human freedom understood as responsibility now faces a task which it has to fulfill on its own. Thus the first requirement of existentialism is to put man in full possession of his freedom and to establish the responsibility for his own existence completely on himself.[23]

Duméry agrees completely with the Sartrian notion of freedom as radical responsibility, but he maintains that this concept of freedom contains nothing irreconcilable with the notion of faith. His critique of inauthentic religion as superstition is based on a concept of freedom which cannot accept any pre-existing realm of truth and value. There is a way of believing in truth and value which kills the spirit. Indeed, one often wonders whether the believer really believes in truth and freedom. The whole question is to know whether the truth of my faith can be anterior and exterior to my own free engagement. The answer must be no, since then no additional achievement would be necessary.

A God who would be the arsenal of eternal truths, who would have made all the good and the true, would not have left anything for us to do, except evil which is the opposite of being.[24]

To believe in truth, therefore, is to believe that one has to make the truth, that one is fully responsible accordingly, and that it is in uncertainty and risk that the light of truth has to be won.[25]

Believers continually face the danger of alienating their freedom in the alibi of a "faith-resignation." It is only when one believes in a valid human freedom that authentic faith becomes possible. Only the conviction that freedom of conscience is inalienable can lead to true faith.[26] Without this faithfulness to radical responsibility, the absolute affirmation which is the act of faith runs the danger of resorting to either a fanatical dogmatism or a moralism of resignation. The affirmation of God is very often nothing but the idolization of human existence in one of its two fundamental aspects, either as freedom and project or as facticity and situation.

---

[22] *Idem* in English translation of Walter Kaufman's *Existentialism from Dostoevsky to Sartre*, p. 294. We find the same concern present in Nietzsche when he writes: "Wenn wir nicht aus dem Tode Gottes eine grossartige Entsagung und einen fortwahrenden Sieg über uns machen, so haben wir den Verlust zu tragen." *Wille zur Macht*, III, p. 174.

[23] Sartre, *L'Existentialisme est un humanisme*, p. 24.

[24] Duméry, *Foi et interrogation*, p. 33.

[25] *Ibid.*, p. 34. It is in the same context of thought that Sartre writes in his play, *Le diable et le bon Dieu*: "Pourquoi faire le mal? Parce que le bien est déjà fait. Qui l'a fait? Dieu le Père. Moi j'invente." (Paris: Gallimard, 1951), p. 77.

[26] Duméry, *La tentation de faire du bien*, p. 63.

The notions of tolerance and freedom of conscience have a rather sad history in the context of the religious tradition. Yet it is the essence of the Christian faith to expose free consciences to the mystery of God, and therefore to offend freedom means to offend faith itself.[27] The propagation of faith by force is the very destruction of faith. The force Duméry is talking about is of course not a physical nor even a moral force, but a certain understanding of religious truth which wounds freedom. No concept of tolerance is possible in a system where truth is apprehended as a "thing" which can be owned by a privileged group and which consequently would have the right to impose itself upon the masses: then one considers any fault against the institution which has the truth as a crime against mankind and oneself. This intolerance on the level of action is based upon an intolerance on the level of thinking, and all our effort has to go toward changing this false concept of religious truth by the acceptance of a radical freedom of conscience. The objectivism of religious knowledge has to be destroyed by a philosophy based upon the initiative and the personal responsibility of man.[28]

A Christian philosophy, centered on liberty of conscience, must be established. People imagine that ideas and values pre-exist in God and that it is man's task to ratify them.[29]

Such a concept of human activity leads to a caricature of truth and freedom, because nothing, positively, is left to the initiative of man. It is the idea of God as the sum of our knowledge, as the encyclopedia of our sciences, as the canvas of our freedom. Once God is understood in such a way, then faith is merely having divine thought at our disposal. We have the unexpected chance to think what God thinks and to govern all things according to His design.[30] This tyranny, this usurpation of the Divine standpoint, is the result of confounding the experience of the sacred itself with a trend of thought which reifies the religious ideas in order to subject conscience and freedom to a temporal authority with absolute power.

Such a reification of religious truth not only results in a fanatical idolization of freedom as will to power, but also in a fatalistic idolization of the human situation. Fatalism is but the reverse of fanaticism. When one uses God as the author of all determinations and essences, then human activity becomes impotent and has to accept in resignation the human

[27] *Ibid.*, p. 37.
[28] *Ibid.*, p. 47.
[29] *Ibid.*, p. 54.
[30] *Ibid.*, p. 55.

situation. Instead of seeing that freedom creates necessity by positing objective universal essences, necessity is substantialized to the point where it crushes creative spontaneity. With God's plans in one's pocket, one has the right to compel others, but at the same time one must accept that this means the end of one's own initiative. Obedience turns into slavery and action into passivity.

We cannot understand all this unless we are continually aware of the Sartrian background of Duméry's notion of freedom as finitude, a freedom which creates itself and its mediating necessity. Freedom must be its own law.[31] Nothing can be imposed. Everything stands *at the service* of freedom. Religious expressions should be viewed also as obligatory mediations: mediation, because freedom cannot create itself but in contact with objectivity; obligatory, because freedom must move on and can never rest upon its achievements. The God-object who freezes human creativity, or the God-axiom who allows us to tyrannize the others, is the result of a deficient insight into what freedom really means.

Sartre not only excludes a God creator (because His act of creation would reduce man to pure facticity), but he also rejects what Duméry calls an "Absolute of dialogue." [32] He finds another chance to deny the existence of God where he treats of human subjectivity. Man is subjectivity, self-realizing freedom, and free project of his world. But the presence of another subjectivity destroys my subjectivity because I am part of his objectified world: he is "the one who looks at me" and in his hateful look ("l'enfer c'est l'autre") I experience myself as being object-for-the-other, as being somebody and not as having-to-be. The look of the other therefore means the death of my subjectivity as being-able-to-be.

If there is an Other, whatever or whoever he may be, whatever may be his relations with me, and without his acting upon me in any way except by the pure upsurge of his being – then I have an outside, I have a nature. My

---

[31] *Ibid.*, p. 58.
[32] Duméry, *Foi et interrogation*, p. 119. Duméry himself coined this expression. It indicates the simplistic and erroneous concept of a God-partner with whom man deals according to the laws of human inter-subjectivity. Time and again, Duméry denounces this concept of the theandric relation. "Quant à cette religion du dialogue si décriée, si méprisée, il ne serait pas mauvais de prendre conscience que, pour l'homme religieux, elle est subordonnée à la transcendence et imposée par elle. On sait que les mystiques la dépassent dans le sens du mystère et s'y réengagent aussitôt pour exprimer ce mystère. D'elle-même, au niveau le plus radical, l'intention religieuse ne forme pas couple. L'Absolu n'est pas Autre; il est Simple. Il n'est le Tout-Autre que si nous comprenons que la perspective d'altérité vient de nous, de notre finitude. Il n'est pas un vis-à-vis; il est immédiat et caché. Il n'est pas un interlocuteur, un partenaire, avec lequel on discute d'égal à égal; il est l'interpellant ou l'interpellateur, celui dont l'appel retentit dans la réponse parce qu'il l'a créée." Duméry, *La foi n'est pas un cri* (Tournaix-Paris: Casterman, 1957), p. 168.

original fall is the existence of the Other. Shame – like pride – is the apprehension of myself as a nature although that very nature escapes me and is unknowable as such.[33]

One can understand now how the thought of God, the Other par excellence, is unacceptable because it would make all human subjectivity impossible. "God," Sartre writes, "is the quintessence of the Other." [34] The all-perceiving look of God would murder freedom and subjectivity. In the case of the other, I could recapture myself by also "looking" at him and thus reducing him to objectivity, but now no salvation is possible since no one can "look" at God. God is the being Who looks at everyone, without ever being looked at Himself. To accept God, therefore, would mean accepting oneself as a thing.

> The position of God is accompanied by a reification of my object-ness. Or better yet, I posit my being-an-object-for God as more real than my for-itself; I exist alienated and I cause myself to learn from outside what I must be. This is the origin of fear before God.[35]

God as the Other, the Absolute of dialogue, cannot be accepted in virtue of man's inalienable freedom. Duméry finds in this critique of Sartre again a valuable element which he will not accept as such, but which he will integrate in his mystical understanding of religion where in final analysis all representations of God have to be discarded. One such representation is a God of dialogue.[36]

Duméry not only accepts the Sartrian notion of freedom, but he also goes along, to a great extent, with Sartre's consequent critique of the *idea* of God. Sartre rejects the existence of God not only on the grounds of its incompatibility with human freedom, but also on account of the contradictory nature of the notion of God itself. Sartre's way of reasoning here

---

[33] Sartre, *Being and Nothingness*, p. 263.
[34] Sartre, *Situations*, I, p. 237.
[35] Sartre, *Being and Nothingness*, p. 290.
[36] It is interesting to notice that Paul Tillich thinks along the same lines. He maintains that the God of theological theism (what Duméry calls the "God of dialogue") has to be replaced by the "God above God." The God of theological theism is *a* being, not being itself. He is supposed to be beyond the ontological elements and categories, but every statement subjects him to them. "As such he is bound to the subject-object structure of reality, he is an object for us subjects. At the same time we are objects for him as subject. And this is decisive for the necessity of transcending theological theism. For God as a subject makes me into an object which is nothing more than an object. He deprives me of my subjectivity because he is all-powerful and all-knowing. I revolt and try to make him into an object, but the revolt fails and becomes desperate. God appears as the invincible tyrant, the being in contrast with whom all other beings are without freedom and subjectivity.... This is the God Nietzsche said had to be killed because nobody can tolerate being made into a mere object of absolute knowledge and absolute control. This is the deepest root of atheism." Paul Tillich, *The Courage to Be* (New Haven-London: Yale University Press, 1963), p. 185.

is determined by his concept of man. Human existence consists in the oppositional unity of facticity (in-itself) and subjectivity (for-itself). The existence of an in-itself-for-itself is a contradiction, because this would mean the falling together of pure positivity and pure negativity, the identity of being-oneself-sufficient and not-being-oneself-sufficient. This, Sartre maintains, is exactly what is meant by the idea of God. God is an in-itself, He is a being which is what it is as far as He is the foundation of the world.[37] At the same time, God ("ens causa sui") is a for-itself as far as He is self-consciousness and the necessary foundation of Himself.[38] In-itself and for-itself, being diametrically opposed, when brought together, neutralize and destroy each other, by either dissolving objectivity into empty subjectivity or condensing subjectivity into dead objectivity. Insight without content or night without light, God in both cases is inconceivable.[39]

Duméry discovers in this critique a precious truth. It teaches the impossibility of a God conceived as a monolithic being, which is the conception of God as a final explanatory principle of the realm of being (God-object) or of the realm of consciousness (God-axiom). The absorption of the for-itself by the in-itself leads to a massive objectivity, a totally indifferentiated infinity, while the absorption of the in-itself by the for-itself leads to an empty subjectivity, a totally abstract infinity. In both cases God would be swallowed by a complete unconsciousness, from below as a brute nature, from above as an empty axiom.[40]

The error in this natural theology is that God is simply considered as a prolongation of the finite order, either as nature or as consciousness, a scandalous anthropomorphism which destroys all real transcendence. It is what Bonhoeffer (cfr. quotation at the beginning of this chapter) called a God who on the level of theory is used as a working hypothesis and on the level of praxis as "deus ex machina." At the same time, such a concept of God indicates that one has a static concept of human consciousness in its relation to reality, a consciousness which is satisfied with a concept of truth as imitation of already existing absolute truth in God, and a concept of freedom as ratification of divine eternal norms.

They think that this link (of the mind with the absolute) is an adherence of the human subject to things included in the divine essence. Herein lies the difficulty. The imagination would err less on this problem if one would re-

---

[37] Sartre, *L'Etre et le Néant* (Paris: Gallimard, 1943), p. 133.
[38] *Ibid.*, p. 134.
[39] Duméry, *Foi et interrogation*, p. 21.
[40] *Ibid.*, p. 93.

member that the essence is "a meaning," "a norm," not a thing or object in itself.[41]

It is then the merit of Sartre to force us to overcome a natural theology of the infinite object, or even of a solitary subject.[42] An Absolute which is completely objectified or subjectified is a contradiction. This objection of Sartre, as well as the objections against a God creator and a God of dialogue, can only be liquidated by bringing the discussion to a higher level where God is shown as completely beyond human comprehension and where all these ways of conceiving God are creations of the human spirit. Only the concept of a transordinal [43] God will refute Sartre's objections.

After having shown how Duméry agrees with Sartre's concept of freedom and his critique of a God-object or God-axiom which destroys man's freedom in the act of creation and communication, we shall proceed with Duméry in his attempt to prove that Sartre's notion of freedom can and must be reconciled with an authentic concept of God.

SECTION III
DUMÉRY'S CRITIQUE OF SARTRE'S
POSITION ON GOD AND FREEDOM

In the previous section, we saw how Duméry discovers a precious truth in Sartre's triple critique of the idea of God: the critique of a God creator, the critique of a God of dialogue and the critique of the idea of God. Credit must be accorded to Sartre, this theologian without God,[44] for elevating the discussion to another plane. Indeed, Duméry believes that the Sartrian dialectic in itself cannot be refuted. Only by pushing this dialectic to its ultimate consequence can we do away with its atheistic characteristics. Sartre's atheism, according to Duméry, will then be nothing more than a wholesome critique of religious man's inauthentic concepts of his relation with the Absolute. Whereas Sartre attacks any belief in God as a "chosism" destructive of freedom, Duméry speaks of superstition, thereby implying that there is a theism which does not destroy freedom but liberates it.

We have seen how Sartre summarizes in the principle "the existence precedes the essence" the fundamental existential position. Existence itself

---

[41] Duméry, *La tentation de faire du bien,* p. 57.
[42] Duméry, *Foi et interrogation,* p. 93.
[43] Transordinal; i.e., God is beyond all essential determination, beyond all order of ideas and values.
[44] Duméry, *Foi et interrogation,* p. 120.

is irreducible to anything else, and all essences are reducible to the self-founding free subject. Man is the creator of the whole realm of determinations, the realm of ideas and values. This is what the existentialists call the thesis of axiogenesis. Duméry now maintains that the atheistic axiogenesis is not seriously enough concerned about the meaningfulness of freedom. Freedom, as Sartre conceives it, is a contradiction which leads to despair. Man is free, not despite his limitations but because of them. Freedom creates itself in a continuous struggle with facticity, but freedom uses this facticity without ever scoring a decisive victory. Freedom, therefore, resembles an empty flight into a future without a past. Its power to choose is coexistent with its power to refuse, the moment the value is conquered, freedom has to reject it in order to maintain its integrity. But does this not question the very possibility of freedom itself?

A dialectical play of endless positing and refusing makes no sense because it jeopardizes the very dynamism which is at the source of this dialectic. If nothing can ever satisfy freedom's urge for liberation in and through its projects, why then does freedom always need a datum? Does this infinite yearning not imply that one cannot enclose freedom in a rigorously finite world? Does this not also mean that we must transcend a merely human and moral universe towards a religious one? No one has ever shown more clearly than Sartre that a moralism imprisoned in a mere human world is a dead-end street. Sartre's philosophy is a:

> ... moralism emanating from a negative freedom, but also fanaticism of exertion, clenching of ideas one refuses but requests again and again – all this is an attitude of courage: a demanding, obstinate, stubborn courage. But all this is only an illusory freedom, a cultivation of a set-back, a display, repeated escape, a measure of delayed salvation.[45]

Essentially freedom is less interested in escaping all objectivation by continually negating all incarnate ideas and values than in making and keeping them alive. Otherwise there would be neither past nor future. Therefore one must accept a freedom which is a source of permanent actualization that makes past, present and future one. There can be no complete dispersion, otherwise there would be no consciousness of dispersion. There can be no infinite willing without the presence of the Infinite.[46] Time exists by the power of eternity.

> Time spreads itself out with a vivid recapitulation – *not* by mechanical recall but by unceasing re-establishment in a central focus which is called eternity.[47]

---

[45] Duméry, *Philosophie de la religion,* I, p. 287.
[46] We could apply the saying of Blondel to Sartre's notion of absolute freedom: "To will infinitely without willing the Infinite," which is indeed an absurdity.
[47] Duméry, *Foi et interrogation,* p. 107.

Freedom, Sartre maintains, rises from nothing since every anterior state would destroy it. Therefore, the essence is derived and assimilated by what is past. Recurrently, freedom has to make an absolute beginning by rejecting the essences it has created. How can this be done without a transformation of the past itself? Without a radical recapture of the past, consciousness would be a bottomless receptacle which constantly loses its content.[48] This radical recapitulation which is required by the nature of freedom itself can only be realized at a point which resumes the previous moments and makes them living and permanent. This focal point is eternity in time. Man is absolute freedom which reveals itself in the exigency to overcome all determination. That freedom must overcome all limitations, that it must reveal itself as exigency of complete undetermination, is a sign of the presence of an absolute stimulation on the side of freedom. Man carries in himself an absolute freedom which reveals the presence of God in man.

Sartre is coherent when he says that man fails to be God, for his absoluteness and limitation are interdependent. But he is no longer correct when he believes that the awareness of it does not require a basis in the Absolute of pure spontaneity which transcends all finiteness and all limit.[49]

Indeed, man fails to be God, and his very existence lies in this failure. But this failure is only a *condition* of his freedom and not a *cause*. Sartre, however, does not want to accept this because he cannot see how God could be cause of and at the heart of man's freedom without destroying it. God either reduces freedom to mere ratification of a divine order of ideas which is the destruction of freedom or limits man's initiative to a mere invention of evil. At this point, Duméry introduces the notion of a transordinal God, a God who is to be sought in the direction of the infinite power of freedom rather than in the direction of substantialized truths and values. Those who, like Sartre, put God and man in competition for the creation of values, think of a God-object, place of the eternal Truth and subsisting Good.[50] But nothing prevents us from conceiving the human axiogenesis as the manner in which God creates man. Man's creativity, then, becomes co-creation of the spirit united with God, and mans' supreme dependence becomes the very source of his supreme independence. In this view, freedom has nothing to fear from dependence since it is the source of its real autonomy.[51]

As a result, one escapes the dilemma of either reducing freedom to a

[48] *Ibid.*, p. 89.
[49] *Ibid.*
[50] *Ibid.*, p. 101.
[51] *Ibid.*, p. 23.

mere ratification of a pre-existing order or condemning man to create only evil. The means to eliminate the concept of a human universe in which all laws are externally imposed without likewise doing away with all norms, is to conceive a universe in which man creates the intelligible realm in union with the Absolute.[52] The norms are provided by the spirit's intrinsic and constitutional relation with the Absolute. This relation with the Absolute is more demanding than any extrinsic norm since unfaithfulness to God would also mean destruction of oneself.[53] Everything depends on interiorizing the subjection to a norm by considering God as the *creating force* rather than as the *pre-existing order*. It is here that Duméry turns to the Plotinian tradition in which the ideas are not in God and in which God must be thought of as radical spontaneity richer than any representation. Consequently in this tradition thought and being belong to and are created by the order of finite spirits. Human creativity can be reconciled with a God conceived as the Plotinian One. Henology takes the conclusive force away from Sartre's arguments.[54]

Both man's independence and dependence gain by this view because his dependence upon God is the creation of his own independence. Freedom itself, man's creation of ideas and values, requires an energy which transcends all determinations and which, therefore, cannot be identified with man. Hence, man assumes the prerogative of the Absolute without being the Absolute. Far from enslaving man, the relation to God is his only chance for complete liberation. God leads us to ourselves by what is not ourselves and in and through us He leads us away from Him back to Him.

But how can the *Other* be at the source of *my* freedom? Once we say that God is at the source of all being, can the mode of His presence change the fact that He remains the alienating Other? Here we have to remember that God, being transcendent is also immanent, so much so that He is the principle of my interiority. The argument of Sartre against the idea of a God who watches us and hereby reduces us to mere objects does not hold because God is not really the Other. There are not two subjects, there is not I and the Other, the human ego and the divine Thou.

[52] *Ibid.,* p. 104.
[53] Duméry, *Philosophie de la religion,* I, p. 54.
[54] "Sartre et Polin placent à la racine de la liberté, soit le Néant, soit le refus du donné. Aucune de ces deux notions ne s'éclaire elle-même; elles sont admises comme des postulats. On se donne la liberté avec mille privilèges en particulier celui de la négativité efficace. Mais le fait de cette productivité absolue ne soulève aucune curiosité. On en profite, et ne cherche pas à l'élucider. Il est vrai qu'on identifie à tout coup théisme et objectivisme. On se ferme ainsi la voie vers Dieu. A notre sens, *l'hénologie la rouvre et disloque l'humanisme athée.* Grâce à elle, en effet, la créativité humaine se trouve réintroduite de plein droit en contexte théiste." *Ibid.,* p. 71.

These are only reducible psycho-sociological schemes.[55] When man is conceived as the creator of all determinations and God as completely above all determinations, then they cannot really be opposed to each other as two individualities. The ordinal and the transordinal do not belong on the same plane, and, consequently, they cannot contradict each other. They are perfectly compatible if we do not look upon them as equal.[56] God sustains man's immanence in the same set by which He transcends him. He therefore cannot be another nor an alter-ego. When language, cult and reflection express the religious experience in terms of a dialogue between God and man, we must realize that these expressions, although indispensable, must be surpassed. We will see later the sense in which Duméry maintains that a God of dialogue can be acceptable. But the terminus of the religious ascent is a transessential God, the God of the non-dialogueing mystics, the God of concrete, living spirituality.[57]

Sartre's third objection against the *idea* of God also loses its strength against a transordinal Absolute. An Absolute, indeed, which is completely objective or completely subjective is a contradiction. The objection, Duméry maintains, can be disposed of on a higher level where reason suggests that perfect subjectivity can only exist in a threefold relation at the heart of a unity so as to balance the respective rights of subjectivity and objectivity.[58] Yet, Duméry, in a later work,[59] doubts whether one could use the doctrine of the Trinity in a philosophical discussion. Furthermore, the reference to the dogma of the Trinity is unnecessary in refuting Sartre. The concept of a transordinal One which by its very nature is beyond all determination, and consequently beyond all concept of a determining principle, escapes Sartre's objection which is based upon the subject-object opposition.

We see, then, how Duméry, after a serious reflection upon Sartre's objections, feels confident that they can be adopted in a philosophical theism, provided that it places God beyond the intelligible world. He accepts the Sartrian thesis of axiogenesis and admits that all Sartre's objections to theism are valid, but only in the hypothesis of a God-object. But God must be reached beyond objectivism and beyond determination. He concludes that Sartre, instead of closing the way to theism, is actually opening the way to a most authentic affirmation of God. By putting so much stress on freedom's exigency for indetermination, Sartre prepares

[55] *Ibid.*, p. 167.
[56] *Ibid.*
[57] *Ibid.*, p. 67.
[58] Duméry, *Foi et interrogation*, pp. 94-95.
[59] Duméry, *Philosophie de la religion*, I, p. 69, note 1.

the road which can lead to absolute freedom of indetermination – which is God. The God whom Sartre rejects is not the real God and, consequently, his arguments are sterile. The God who dies never existed.

When atheism and the rejection of objectivism coincide, it is a sign that the God who dies is an Absolute-Object, the same one that we previously called the "God-Object." Therefore, is the atheist who misses his goal any more than an abortive atheist? [60]

The irony of it all is that Sartre seems to be more of a believer than he wants to admit. By stressing the point that no authentic faith can be realized unless one accepts radical human freedom as source of all determinations, Sartre, willing or not, is brought to some sort of faith. Only the conviction that freedom of conscience is inalienable can lead to true faith. This implies the paradox of a sincere unbelief, and apparent incredulity which is belief in unbelief.[61]

This seems to be a rather strange turn of thought, but not too surprising when we realize how close Duméry's notion of faith approaches the Sartrian notion of freedom. He sees the nature of man's spirit as a need for the transdeterminational God. In a certain traditional way of thinking, faith is understood as acceptance of a certain number of inviolable truths which defies all critique of science and philosophy. Duméry changes this orientation by stating that authentic faith is rather that which questions everything. Faith is essentially a mysterious ignorance, a "docta ignorantia," which stimulates man's search for insight. It is the state of grace of the human intellect.[62]

Faith is not what is questionable in the name of knowledge or techniques; it is that which questions all knowledge and all techniques, and which prevents them from rising to the absolute and from expecting daily miracles or unchallengeable certainty.[63]

In his search for a middle position between superstitious objectivation of religion on the level of expression and determination, and the libertine refusal of any transcendent dimension in human existence, Duméry at once agrees and disagrees with Sartre. Man is freedom, autoposition and creator of the whole realm of determinations, but he is all this by virtue of his union with the source of all power to be free. There is no real antinomy between free thinking and free faith: they are connected in man's dissatisfaction with whatever is partial and incomplete. When God

---

[60] Duméry, *Foi et interrogation*, p. 123.
[61] Duméry, *La tentation de faire du bien*, p. 63.
[62] *Ibid.*, p. 83.
[63] *Ibid.*, p. 82.

is apprehended as undetermined force, as pure energy and perfect spontaneity, faith in God becomes the supreme liberation.

The function of the Divine Word is not to say for us what we ourselves cannot say. It must remain ineffable; the one that cannot be said and who for this very reason makes us speak indefinitely.[64]

Authentic faith liberates man in a deeper sense than Sartre's freedom, because it recognizes an absolute force of indetermination present in the heart of freedom. When man has recognized this presence, there will be no end to his energy to build and rebuild his universe of determinations. The idea of God is the great lover of human emancipation, because it regards all achievements as failures, all objects as insufficient and all orders as finite.[65]

In this sense, the very nature of faith implies a certain unbelief. This paradox accounts for the fact that we could speak about a faith inherent in Sartre's atheistic position. Faith is the attitude by which we take the finite order most seriously without taking it too seriously. Faith contains a certain irony because it knows itself completely inadequate before the infinite; it strives toward a God through expressions and representations which are unable to grasp Him. It contains a moment of ignorance which can be called unbelief as far as it defies all expression.[66]

At the end of this first chapter, we see how Duméry is involved in a profound dialogue with Sartre's atheistic existentialism. He will reinterpret the "fait primitif" of existentialism, the notion of the intentionality of existence understood as oppositional unity of subjectivity and facticity. Man is that being realizing himself by self-expression, he liberates himself by creating and assuming necessity. The same idea is expressed in Duméry's fundamental theory of the Act-Law: man is at once spontaneity and determination: freedom creating itself through necessity. Man is essentially linked to this world of determinations which he creates and to which he is at the same time subjected. Duméry and Sartre differ in the interpretation of man's absolute power to refuse all determinations. Does freedom's absolute power of contestation imply the presence of an Absolute in man? Duméry answers yes, despite the fact that human freedom cannot exist without its limiting law of expression and exteriority.

The fact that Duméry accepts Sartre's notion of freedom as power of supreme contestation and that in this power he discovers the Absolute, accounts for his positive evaluation of Sartre's atheism. God is not present

---

[64] *Ibid.*, p. 21.
[65] *Ibid.*, p. 81.
[66] *Ibid.*, p. 82.

in this world in the way objects are. He has to reveal Himself to man as the source of his creativity. For that reason, man cannot discover God, God himself has to reveal His reality. Otherwise man either equates God with the things of His creation, and this is idolatry; or he allows his belief in God to remain abstract and verbal. It is clear that the experience of the sacred is absent in many people of our time and that in this case a sincere unbelief is preferable to a verbal acceptance of God. Simone Weil expresses this idea very beautifully when she writes:

The state of non-belief, then, is what St. John of the Cross called a "night." Belief is verbal and does not penetrate into the soul. In our time, if the incredulous loves God, and if he is like the child who does not know that somewhere there is bread, but cries out for it, this incredulity can be equivalent to the dark night of St. John of the Cross.[67]

Duméry envisages bringing Sartre's atheistic existentialism to its fulfillment by naming, without really labeling as such, the ultimate reality at the source of man's absolute freedom, by making the Plotinian One the source of the subject's power to create the order of ideas and values; and by maintaining a most rigorous transcendence of the One and suppressing all danger of alienation by an alter ego. Duméry intends to go even further.

Sartre's conviction of man's utter incapacity to achieve his freedom might provide a good basis for the construction of a Christian metaphysics. Indeed if one indicates that the fundamental design of man is to be absolute freedom, but that left to himself man is unable to realize this design, then one might consider the Christian dogma of redeeming grace as a possible answer. One has to expose simultaneously the greatness and smallness of man before one can consider a possible elevation of man to that which seems to be necessary (belonging to man) and impossible (not belonging to man). The paradox of an absolute human freedom which nevertheless is utterly impotent might be a foreshadowing of man's call to participation in the Godhead. Sartre's philosophy expresses in a pathetic way the enormous distance between man's aspirations and his incapacity to realize them.

It is the paradox of the human mind, whose task it is to create what is necessary, that he cannot raise himself up to the level of being – like those fortune-tellers who predict the future for others but not for themselves. This is why, deep in the human being and in nature, I see sadness and boredom. It is not that man does not think of himself as a being. On the contrary, he is unflinching in this regard. Consequently, there emerge Good and Evil,

[67] Simone Weil, *Attente de Dieu* (Paris: La Colombe, 1950), p. 211.

ideas of man working on man. Useless ideas. The idea of determinism which curiously tries to synthesize existence and being is also useless. *We are free as much as you want but impotent* ... for the rest: the will to power, action, life are only vain ideologies. There is no will to power anywhere. *Everything is too weak: all things tend to die.*[68]

But if man discovers that everything is too weak, does that not mean that there is a force working in him which is more powerful than man and whatever he makes? The failure *to work out* a design does not do away with the power *to conceive* such design.

Nothing really *is* – everything is incapable of achieving its existence. This is a very valuable insight. It must enable us to understand that, indeed, only a supernatural gift can make life meaningful and possible. Sartre's philosophy then becomes a philosophy which manifests the ontological insufficiency of everything, its defects and its need of being accomplished, its "desiderium naturale sed inefficax" (Blondel). It calls for the "hypothetical necessity of the supernatural" (Blondel, see next chapter). Here again, just as in the case of Sartre's objection against the idea of God, we have to go to the Christian teachings in order to give him an answer.

---

[68] Text of Sartre quoted by Simone de Beauvoir in *Mémoires d'une jeune fille rangée* (Paris: Gallimard, 1958), pp. 486-487. This text is one of Sartre's earliest expressions of his fundamental philosophical intuition. It was written while, as a student at the Sorbonne, he took part in an "Enquête auprès des étudiants d'aujourd'hui" directed by "Les nouvelles Littéraires."

CHAPTER II

# SEARCH FOR A METHOD TO BE USED IN THE PHILOSOPHICAL STUDY OF RELIGION

Whether the philosopher is aware of it or not, the notions he connects hold together by means of the living Cogito, and the latter, instead of being pure form, is an act which expresses itself at different levels. Consequently, philosophy remains the restoration, or the methodical recovery, of an act that transcends its multiple expressions. Philosophy mediatizes this act, it depends on it, it returns on it; it is able neither to supplant it nor to immerse it in an objective series.[1]

SECTION I

METHOD OF EXPLICATION AND
METHOD OF CONFRONTATION

## a. Stating the Problem

In the previous chapter, we saw how Duméry readily accepts the existentialist thesis of axiogenesis: the freedom of the Cogito constituting the orders of ideas and values. This thesis, according to Sartre and his disciples, necessarily leads to the refusal of God. God, they maintain, has only been invented to give foundation to the laws. But man himself is the source of all laws. If then one adheres to the acceptance of God, one is obliged to degrade human freedom, to take away from man the privilege of the constitution. Duméry does not contest the thesis of axiogenesis, but thinks it necessary to integrate the truth of God into the truth of the constituting Ego and vice versa. Thus Sartre thinks theism untenable, for exactly the same reason that Duméry thinks it necessary. Sartre says: Man is free, therefore God does not exist; Duméry answers: Man is free, therefore God exists. Freedom can only construct and constitute by going to the fountainhead of a divine energy, it can only create the orders and determinations by relying upon a trans-determination in act. "The mind

---

[1] Duméry, *The Problem of God*, trans. Courtney (Evanston, Ill.: Northwestern University Press, 1964), p. 30.

creates the intelligible in an essentially active contact with the One, its source." [2] Only a transordinal One, because He cannot be added to our universe, leaves us room to develop our orders in full autonomy. The basic principle of Duméry's theism can thus be formulated as follows: *That which is condition of authentic freedom is at the same time criterion for an authentic Absolute.*

The condition of radical human freedom is constitutive exigency to surpass all determinations. The whole realm of human expressions has to be subjected to the jurisdiction of reason. "L'existence précède l'essence," man creates the value and truth of everything, the order of the world depends upon the free decree of man and man depends upon himself only. Duméry's Absolute is to be seen in the context of this radical human freedom. He has to be able to show how faith itself is not contrary to, but lies in the very direction of, free thought. "There is no real antinomy between free thought and free faith. They converge in the same feeling of refusal towards everything partial, incomplete and unstable." [3] But how can belief in an Absolute be maintained in such a way that freedom as absolute indetermination is not curtailed in one way or another? How can the gratuitousness of freedom be respected in accepting an Absolute as the foundation of this gratuitousness? The axiogenic power of freedom is not the power to affirm and deny arbitrarily, but the power to liberate freedom from external influence. Can the ideas of the Absolute be freed from all extrinsicism and still remain a reality with which a relation can be established? [4]

L. Malevez, in the introduction to his work on Duméry's book, *Le problème de Dieu en philosophie de la religion. Examen critique de la catégorie d'Absolu et du schème de transcendance,* notes that the title and subtitle of Duméry's work do not indicate adequately the subject of the work:

They [title and subtitle] mislead one into thinking that the critical analysis includes only the concept of God. In fact, it also includes the affirmation of God and tends to pronounce a value-judgment on the belief in God's existence.[5]

This remark indicates the crucial point of Duméry's philosophy of religion. Where exactly does the phenomenological description become a

---

[2] Duméry, *La tentation de faire du bien,* p. 153.
[3] *Ibid.,* p. 81.
[4] Cf. the Thomistic doctrine of the one-sided relation between God and His creature.
[5] L. Malevez, *Transcendance de Dieu et création des valeurs. L'absolu et l'homme dans la philosophie de Henry Duméry* (Paris-Louvain: Desclée-De Brouwer, 1954), p. 9.

philosophical critique? One cannot understand the scope of Duméry's work without having studied thoroughly the method of the author in his treatment of religion. To stake out what belongs to the field of conceptual and imaginative critique and what belongs to the field of affirmation; to find out how Duméry affirms the transcendent reality while attempting to remain on the level of a critique of the expressions, are major points of Duméry's thought which we must attempt to clarify. In remaining faithful to the existentialist doctrine that all the determinisms of thought must be conceived as creations of the free determining subject, he faces the problem of how the trans-conscious reality of the Absolute can be reached. How talk about the religious reality without destroying its transcendence in the objectivation of concepts and without reducing the religious concepts to empty ideas unrelated to reality.

Our author, seeking an adequate method for the study of religion, is trying to solve this problem of rational thought facing the super-rational reality of religion. Reason cannot touch the religious reality in itself; the reality of religion can only be attained in the religious praxis.

He [the philosopher of religion] knows very well that the Ineffable of religion cannot be grasped by one who does not live religiously. In this domain, practice only unveils the secrets of practice. It is not the Ineffable which has to be attained by or through others when one ignores it himself. The attempts made with this purpose would result in failure. The only thing the philosopher can encompass is what he can understand, namely, the meaning, signification and intentionality.[6]

There are two things which may not be confused: on the one hand there is the superior principle which immanent expression may not dissolve and which remains inaccessible to him who does not participate in it directly; and on the other hand there is the universe of signs, symbols and phenomena whose significations can be understood by any human being.

In the realm of expression, even if the illumination comes from above, the religious man possesses no other means of reasoning, signifying or expressing except that which is at the disposal of every individual.[7]

Duméry thinks it possible to express the reality of religion meaningfully without destroying its transcendent term.

What exactly does Duméry mean by this method of bringing and keeping the philosophical critique of religion merely on the level of the expressions? How does this allow him to pass through the horns of the

---

[6] Duméry, *Critique et religion* (Paris: Sedes, 1957), p. 17.
[7] *Ibid.*

dilemma of either affirming the Absolute in objective expressions, endangering by this his Transcendence, or affirming the Absolute through intentional expressions hazarding the affirmation itself? In either case, there would be no Absolute. By saying too much one destroys the Absolute. By not saying enough one makes the existence of the Absolute irrelevant – too far off. Duméry has these two pitfalls constantly in mind and tries to find "how one can remain a believer after a critique of religion and a philosopher after an eventual affirmation of faith." [8] He first deals with those who cannot remain believers after their critique of religion because they use *the method of explication*. Then there are those who endanger the autonomy of philosophy by using *the method of confrontation*. The former err by saying too much, the latter by not saying enough.

### b. *The Method of Explication*

The method of explication [9] is based upon the naturalist prejudice in which one tries to reduce the reality of religion to the objective level, forgetting that spiritual activity cannot be decomposed in merely objective elements. "It is impossible for the subject to objectify itself entirely. He cannot forget that he is subjectivity at the source of this movement of objectivation." [10] Naturalism for Duméry has a triple meaning: first, the opposition to the supernatural which he calls immanentism; secondly, the tendency to absorb everything in the chain of empirical phenomena which is causalism; thirdly, the tendency to reduce everything to one principle of explication which is monism. We will mainly treat the immanentist tendency, since causalism and monism are nothing but realizations of the immanentist principle in the context of the two possible elaborations of idealism: empirical idealism or rational idealism depending on the priority given to sensation or to reason.

The major weakness of the method of explication lies in its immanentism. Duméry defines immanentism as: "the state of mind according to which any reality never exceeds what man, conforming with Nature and

---

[8] *Ibid.*, p. 22.
[9] The words "expliquer," "explication," "explicative" have a pejorative connotation in the context of phenomenological existentialism. To "explain" is a procedure which can be used in the study of natural phenomena but which is completely inadequate for the study of human behavior. One cannot "explain" human behavior, one can only "understand" it. To understand thus is to respect the subjectivity in oneself and others. Whereas to explain would mean to deny what makes man human, namely: the capacity to direct oneself in directing the world and to make oneself in making -- in a word freedom. (*Ibid.*, pp. 17-18.)
[10] *Ibid.*, p. 17.
[11] *Ibid.*, p. 47.

his own nature, can do or explain." [11] Immanentism in relation to the study of religion maintains that the religious datum is a human datum, of the same nature as all human data. Christianity, far from being based upon a revelation of an Absolute, is a creation on the human level, a human attempt to answer questions which man asks himself.[12] Immanentism therefore is characterized by: "a will determined never to leave humanism; man is, according to this doctrine, the criterion and the measure of everything." [13]

But by defending a strictly human ideal, does immanentism not preserve what is most precious in man, namely his autonomy of reason: "Philosophy should proceed under the exclusive sign of reason," [14] and all attempts to escape reason would be a treason of reason. Does the autonomy of reason necessarily entail that religion as such must stay "within the limits of reason alone"? [15] No, religion as an ensemble of intelligible structures falls under the jurisdiction of reason, but this does not mean that the Transcendent, if religion lives on such a presence, has to be objectified. What the philosopher perceives of religion is its expressive body and the Transcendent by definition escapes all determination. When a philosopher, however, tries to objectify the spirit's exigency of the Absolute, he confuses thought-in-actu with its products. Spiritual activity exists only in expressing itself, but it does not coincide with its expressions. A spontaneity which resists all objectivation and which, therefore, is irreducible, always remains. This cannot be "explained."

Spiritual activity allows objectivation. It is *that by which there is objectivation,* but the spirit itself escapes objectivation . . . it is through the spirit that we are conscious but it is not itself an object of knowledge.[16]

The same holds for freedom, which is the dynamism of thought. Freedom creates values, but does not stiffen in these objective values. Freedom has to objectify itself in an alien object, but even in this very process, it is

---

[12] Cf. Sartre in *Le Diable et le bon Dieu*: "When God is silent, man can force Him to say anything he wants." (P. 116.) See also *L'Existentialisme est un humanisme,* where Sartre shows how the signs we receive from God are actually signs we give to ourselves, prayer is nothing but self-suggestion. It is interesting to see how Duméry approaches this problem. "To converse with God is not to talk to Him as to an interlocutor who answers in the same language. Rather, being in the presence of Him who is unable to speak any human language (He is transcendent) *one converses with oneself,* in order to express, on the psychological level, the mysterious and ineffable relation which links the mind to God." *Philosophie de la religion,* II, p. 259.

[13] Duméry, *Critique et religion,* p. 49.
[14] *Ibid.,* p. 50.
[15] Kant, *Die Religion innerhalb der Grenzen der blossen Vernunft.* 1793.
[16] Duméry, *Critique et religion,* pp. 52-53.

*freedom* objectifying and alienating itself. Freedom never is completely alienated.

Therefore, whether it concerns spiritual activity or freedom, it is impossible to place on a par the principle of construction and the constituted objects – although one cannot separate them either.[17]

This elicits the question of how to reach the spiritual act and freedom without reducing them to their expressions. The simple answer is that spiritual activity and freedom can only be touched in the experience of living activity. The function of philosophy, therefore, is not to dissolve living spirituality in concepts but to show how it is irreducible to its expressions.

The philosopher's role is to make each man cognizant that he is a free and responsible subject whose duty it is to behave as such in all circumstances.[18]

Religious behavior must be treated in the same way. The relation of man to God, which defines the religious attitude, cannot be grasped in a process of conceptual objectivation. Likewise, the free and spiritual act, which is at its basis, resists all attempts of systematization. The God which prayer, cult and sacrifice imply can only be transcendent. Therefore, one cannot deny nor affirm the object of faith because it does not appear in the course of the religious expressions. One has no right to question that for which one is not looking. The philosopher, in making a rational critique of religion, should only be concerned about religion as the believer sees it and omit the question of whether or not the transcendent reality underlying the religious discourse exists at all. He should know that all spiritual activity transcends its ways of expression and that the first thing that concerns him is to have a faithful description of religion as it appears in the living faith of the believer. The justification of the phenomenon as such does not belong to the phenomenal level: it remains trans-phenomenal.[19] One must not deny the sacred because it cannot be reduced to any form of objectivity.

One should not deny the existence of freedom under pretext that it refuses reduction to an object. Nor should one deny the existence of the sacred, the divine, because it cannot be found outside of the religious experience.[20]

Thus the philosopher has every right to subject religion as a whole to the interlocutory questioning of reason. But the danger is that the critique

[17] *Ibid.*, pp. 53-54.
[18] *Ibid.*, p. 55.
[19] "De fenomenaliteit van het fenomeen is zelf nooit een fenomenaal gegeven." Dondeyne.
[20] Duméry, *Critique et religion*, p. 61.

which is affected by the immanentist prejudice will not overcome objectivism and subjectivism. After admitting that only the spirit and not the world (empiricist positivism) supports the significations, one must also avoid spiritual positivism. The fact that freedom cannot be captured in any reflective analysis may mean that freedom itself takes its origin in an infinite principle.

> Freedom always keeps an unemployed reserve which gives it the possibility to undo after having done, to continue doing indefinitely. But this perpetual excess of vitality may be due to a principle of infinite fecundity.[21]

The spiritual act and the act of faith cannot be inserted in an ensemble of determinations. Therefore, if they exist, they must be found not in the bare fact, nor in the significations, but at the heart of consciousness.

The immanentist tendency in the philosophical study of religion goes back to an immanentist concept of subjectivity and consequently fails to respect the specific nature of the act of faith. One needs to have a correct insight into the nature of consciousness before one comes to a correct understanding of the religious activity in which the subject engages. Immanentist philosophy tends to conceive the life of consciousness as mere spiritual interiority closed upon itself. Consequently it advocates a notion of being which is form, determination rather than act. It confounds the abstract, the disincarnated with the spiritual and the real.[22] Objectivity and determinations are ways only to the exterior. The subject, therefore, can never be trapped. Only in the living act can the subject be touched. "Living spirituality can only be penetrated in the measure that it is lived directly." [23] There is no interiority outside of its expressions, yet it cannot be identified with its expressions. On the one hand, it is wrong to talk about an "interior life." "The real spiritual life, even in the religious order, never breaks the tie which links it to the world, due to the duty of witness and charity, of prayer and devotion, which it should never neglect." [24] On the other hand, subjectivity always transcends its expressions: "The inherence of sound in material signs, of meaning in visible conduct, reveals profound subjectivity as a source which exceeds its expressions, even when these are inseparable from the former." [25] Subjectivity then is a paradox of immanence and transcendence, it exists

---

[21] *Ibid.*, p. 65.
[22] "La méthode explicative n'est peut-être, après tout, que cette illusion de la réductibilité du vécu au représentatif, du concret au réflexif, de l'expérience réelle à la 'Thématisation' notionnelle." *Ibid.*, p. 76.
[23] *Ibid.*, p. 54.
[24] *Ibid.*, p. 54, note 2.
[25] *Ibid.*, p. 54.

and realizes itself in and through the expressions, it is "the dominant unity of its own manifestations." [26]

The different methods of explication reduce the religious datum to a mere philosophical one. They bring clarity, but they have the great disadvantage of changing the data to a level which is not intrinsically religious. They have a tendency to rationalize, to conceptualize and to reduce the religious truths to immanent ideal significations. There is no room left for a transcendent theology of Gods' sovereign initiative in the history of salvation. Their philosophy of religion is very often a mere rational transcription of the dogmas. Such, for example, can be seen in the philosophies of religion of Kant, Hegel and Alain. Instead of seeking these notions on the level of the believer for whom they have a meaning, because they form a rule for life in the face of the mystery of God, these philosophers immediately extract the mere conceptual elements of these notions.[27] In doing so, they forget that a dogmatic definition is inseparable from the religious life. The principal fault therefore of the method of explication is that it leaves no room for the specific nature of religion.

*c. The Method of Confrontation*

The method of confrontation, contrary to the former method, respects the religious object. It is applied mainly by believers who are anxious not to violate the religious mystery and therefore proclaim the heterogeneity of the two orders of religion and philosophy. Yet, although it is dualistic, the method of confrontation does not necessarily separate faith and reason in two completely independent disciplines. It tries to unify the heterogeneity of both in the heart of both disciplines. The medieval philosophers have used this method in forming the Christian philosophies. We will review the method in the philosophies of St. Bonaventure and St. Thomas. The basic problem here is whether philosophy is able to establish an autonomous approach to religion, especially in relation to the "philosophia ancilla theologiae" theory.

St. Bonaventure maintains that reason has been profoundly hurt by original sin and that only faith can restore the integrity of reason. The

---

[26] *Ibid.* Cf. also the concept of consciousness in phenomenology and existentialism. Consciousness is "Welterfahrendes Leben" (Husserl), is "in-und-bei-der-Welt-sein" (Heidegger), is "être-au-monde-à-travers-un-corps" (Merleau-Ponty).

[27] "Ainsi, ce que nous avons à reprocher à la méthode explicative, c'est bien de se 'représenter' la religion, de s'en donner un ersatz notionnel, après l'avoir arrachée à son contexte vécu, à la complexité de la conscience concrète. Au lieu de l'étudier à l'intérieur de l'expérience religieuse, elle l'en abstrait, elle l'en sépare, elle l'étale sur un plan qui n'est pas le sien; bref, elle l'isole et elle la vide, elle la tue sans le savoir." *Ibid.*, p. 78.

philosopher must first make the act of faith, after which his reason will function normally on its own.[28] Faith cures reason and makes correct immanent reasoning possible. St. Thomas, however, restores for the first time the idea of an autonomous philosophy, competent to explore its own domain. He distinguishes rigorously between truths of faith and truths of reason, philosophy and theology. Theology judges everything according to the data of revelation and from the formal standpoint of faith, whereas philosophy judges things in themselves and from the formal standpoint of natural reason.[29] The opposition is even so great that it is impossible to believe and to know the same thing.[30]

Whereas St. Bonaventure proclaims the necessary coexistence of faith and philosophical activity in order to cure reason and to guarantee an authentic rationality, St. Thomas maintains that reason, if it stays in its order, can on its own accord attain the truth belonging to this order. Yet, St. Thomas also philosophizes in reference to faith, not because reason needs faith to reinstate itself, but because of the unity of truth. Revealed truth and natural truth, having the same source – God, cannot be opposed to each other. God cannot reveal anything contrary to reason, which is also His work, and consequently reason cannot oppose faith. So for both, St. Bonaventure and St. Thomas, there can be no conflict between faith and reason.

St. Bonaventure had removed the danger from the outset, since the act of faith opens and guarantees the rationality of philosophy. But St. Thomas is just as prompt to establish a reign of harmony and concord through the argument of the (de jure) agreement of these two truths.[31]

Both systems thus use the method of confrontation, that is, their philosophical exposition is a continuous confrontation with the exigencies of faith. "There is, therefore, constant reference to faith; in virtue of the philosophical method in Bonaventure; in virtue of the unity of truth in St. Thomas Aquinas." [32] The medieval intellectual becomes philosopher because of his theology. His purpose is to make the rational level accord with the level of faith. His aim is to "rebuild philosophy, so that its agreement with theology appears as the necessary consequence of the requirements of reason itself and not as the accidental result of a simple desire

---

[28] Cf. E. Gilson, *La philosophie de St. Bonaventure* (2d ed.), pp. 76-100.
[29] *Contra Gentiles*, II, 4: "... etiam et alia circa creaturas et philosophus et fidelis considerat.... Si qua vero circa creaturas communiter a philosopho et fideli considerantur, per alia et alia principia traduntur."
[30] *Quaest. disp. de Veritate*, q. XIV, a. 9, ad Resp. et ad sixtum.
[31] Duméry, *Critique et religion*, p. 85.
[32] *Ibid.*, p. 86.

of reconciliation." [33] This accord is the result of purely rational procedures, yet it is based on the postulate of the truth of faith which prevents reason from losing sight of divine exemplarism (St. Bonaventure) and from dividing truth against itself (St. Thomas). "Faith indicates to the philosopher the direction to take, the way to follow. Otherwise he might, in betraying Divine revelation, mislead human reason at the same time." [34] To the rationalists, this approach to truth is insincere. One feigns doubt and acts as if one discovered rational certainties by means of natural reason alone. Yet there always is revealed truth to fall back upon if reason fails to attain its truth. Alain therefore compares the Catholic thinker to the acrobat who performs gymnastic feats above a net.[35] Bertrand Russell passes a severe judgment on St. Thomas' philosophy for the same reason.

The appeal to reason is, in a sense, insincere, since the conclusion to be reached is fixed in advance.... There is little of the true philosophic spirit in Aquinas. He does not, like the Platonic Socrates, set out to follow wherever the argument may lead. He is not engaged in an inquiry, the result of which it is impossible to know in advance. Before he begins to philosophize, he already knows the truth; it is declared in the Catholic faith. If he can find apparently rational arguments for some parts of the faith, so much the better; if he cannot, he need only fall back on revelation. The finding of arguments for a conclusion given in advance is not philosophy, but special pleading. I cannot, therefore, feel that he deserves to be put on a level with the best philosophers either of Greece or of modern times.[36]

But the Christian philosopher answers that faith serves only as an extrinsic guide. Reason may be led by faith, but it remains reason as long as it has the sole power of evidence in its field.

The medieval philosopher wanted to establish a harmony between reason and faith. He distinguished clearly in order to unify better. Here, as in the case of the immanentist modern philosophers, a certain method of transference was applied. But it could not be a simple transcription of the religious notions into metaphysical notions since their main concern was to respect the specific nature of religion. What happened then is a process of alternative verification, so as to make sure that reason posits its own truth in accord with faith. On the one hand, we then have a philosophy constructed by reason according to the exigencies of faith: i.e.

---

[33] E. Gilson, *Le Thomisme* (4th ed.; Paris: Vrin, 1942), p. 39.
[34] Duméry, *Critique et religion*, p. 86.
[35] *Ibid.*, p. 87.
[36] Bertrand Russell, *A History of Western Philosophy* (New York: Simon and Schuster, 1945), pp. 462-463.

faith has its rational implications which can be given an accounting by reason. On the other hand, we have a theology conceived as a superior metaphysics because it uses the same logical procedures and ontological correlations as philosophy. "Metaphysics, although purely rational in its demonstrations, is an expression of faith's requirements; while theology, although supernatural in its animating principle, is a hyper-metaphysics or a metaphysics of the second degree." [37] So philosophy is really the "ancilla theologiae" because the philosophical phase consists in faith projecting itself on the level of reason so that reason may project itself on the level of faith: which is the theological phase. "Fides quaerens fidem, media rationis," that is the motto of the Christian doctors.[38]

Due to the development of the scientific and historical critique upon the sources of Christianity and the consequent emergence of atheistic rationalism, the medieval theological and philosophical perspective is no longer satisfactory. Faith apparently already exists in an expression, a language, a culture, all of which have to be subjected to a rational critique. Theology, in using philosophical tools, does not raise them to the level of revelation, which means that they, too, must be subjected to a rational critique. Therefore philosophy claims its rights to criticize the expressions of spontaneous as well as reasoned faith. Reason wants to judge the guide itself. Therefore, it has to find a method to penetrate as philosopher into the heart of faith. Religion has to be subjected to reason's jurisdiction instead of being used as term of reference. To the "fides quaerens fidem, media ratione" we have to add "intellectus quaerens intellectum, media fide (objectiva vel phenomenali)." [39]

Both the method of explication and the method of confrontation have to be discarded as methods in the philosophical study of religion. The first method is inadequate because it replaces living religion by its notional equivalent on the basis of the illusion that the spiritual activity of the believer in his commerce with the Absolute is contained in the series of the religious phenomena. The second fails to respect fully the autonomy of reason. It merely confronts the philosophical problems with the religious data, but it does not study in a critical fashion the structures of the religious data themselves. Philosophy is not merely an invention which springs from its contact with religion, it should also criticize religion itself. It does not suffice to be led extrinsically by faith. Reason wants to judge

---

[37] Duméry, *Critique et religion*, p. 97.
[38] *Ibid.*
[39] *Ibid.*, p. 38.

its guide. The medieval doctors did not feel this need. Theology, as the science of faith, was sufficient for them.

The first method does not allow us to remain believers after the philosophical critique of religion. The second method does not give sufficient room for the exertion of a radical autonomous reason. But at the same time both teach us something valuable which must be kept in mind in the search for an adequate method for the study of religion. The method of explication teaches us that the jurisdiction of reason is universal, whereas the method of confrontation reveals to us that there is something specific and irreducible in religion. How does one combine the positive assets of these methods without including their negative sides? Duméry seems to think that an answer to this question can be found in the philosophy of Maurice Blondel. Although the answer is not present in the form of a completely elaborated and applied method, at least it provides the fundamental standpoint which allows the philosopher to remain philosopher in treating religion and to remain believer while criticizing religion.

We believe that Duméry found his fundamental standpoint for the study of religion in the philosophy of Blondel, which standpoint, however, he enriched with the phenomenological method of Husserl. But the fundamental insight seems to come from Blondel's Christian philosophy. Indeed Duméry's first writing was devoted to Blondel's philosophy of action, *La philosophie de l'action. Essai sur l'intellectualisme blondelien.* – The title is interesting. It indicates Duméry's concern for the intellectual nature of the philosophy of action.

SECTION II
BLONDEL'S METHOD OF IMMANENCE AND
THE PHILOSOPHICAL STUDY OF RELIGION

*a. Introducing the Framework of the Blondelian Thought*

The problem we are mainly concerned with is to find a way of thinking by which we can respect fully the rights of faith and reason. We saw how Duméry is torn between the demands of the axiogenic reason of humanistic atheism and the demands of the act of faith in an Absolute. How can one be at the same time an autonomous philosopher and a faithful believer? He finds in Blondel's Christian philosophy "the double example of an independent thought and a lucid conviction." [40] Moreover, Blondel found himself somewhat in the same situation as Duméry, facing in his

---

[40] Duméry, *La tentation de faire du bien,* p. 11.

day a non-Christian autonomous philosophy. The source of his famous doctoral thesis, *L'Action. Essai d'une critique de la vie et d'une science de la pratique* (1893), lay also in his concern for the indifference of his masters and co-disciples in regard to the Christian faith. He, therefore, wanted to re-think the relation of faith and reason in order to satisfy the exigencies of modern thought. Duméry, in his study, "La question Sartre" (in *Foi et interrogation*), also forced himself to come to a bold and honest confrontation with humanistic atheism. He endeavors to achieve an understanding of religion which would be reconcilable with the demands of today's philosophy. After submitting himself to Sartre's radical critique of Christianity, he turns to Blondel and finds there an example of someone who in all honesty and courage tried to reconcile his philosophical insights with his religious convictions. The example of Blondel is thus precious to Duméry. The attempt of Duméry will be to work out a philosophy of religion which Blondel might have written if he had had the time and confidence of the Church. Duméry indicates, however, that "in order to follow the intuition of Blondel to its ultimate, perhaps one would have to go beyond its expression." [41]

Blondel thus asked himself the question how philosophy, which is primarily concerned with man and his destiny, could be disinterested in the problems of religion, which are par excellence centered on the spiritual ends of man. How could philosophy pretend to construct itself completely without seriously taking into consideration the answers given by religion? On the other hand, however, one must keep in mind that the destiny of man, as revealed by religion, is supernatural. It cannot be deduced from a simple analysis of human nature. How then could philosophy instruct us about this destiny if its means are by definition purely rational and natural? Would one not have to conclude from this that philosophy cannot be self-sufficient, that it never will be able to answer the fundamental demands of man? This has often been asserted by Christian philosophers. Thus Blondel maintained that it is the task of philosophy itself to manifest clearly, not accidentally but essentially, the insufficiency of philosophy and indicate how this insufficiency itself can help us to define the nature of philosophy. The necessity to leave the rational "scandalizes reason" [42] and can only be accepted when it can be proved that philosophy is obliged simultaneously to state the problem of human destiny and to admit its incapacity to adequately solve it. If such

---

[41] Duméry, *Critique et religion*, p. 99.
[42] Maurice Blondel, *Letter on Apologetics,* trans. Alexander Dru and Illtyd Trethowan (London: Harvill Press, 1964), p. 153.
[43] Blondel, *L'Action* (Paris: Presses Universitaires de France, 1950), p. 42.

can be done, then it is clear that man, in following a light which does not come from nature, still obeys his own reason and his own most profound needs.

The problem of religion becomes then, in the strict sense of the word, a rational problem, which could be formulated in the following way: the aspirations of the human soul point necessarily and of themselves to a fulfillment other than the rational one. It is clear that the necessity of the supernatural does not follow from a simple analysis of human nature, since the supernatural is by definition that which transcends reason. No a priori method can, therefore, prove the necessity of such a supernatural consummation of the natural. The only possible approach will consist in an analysis which does not apply itself to nature as pure essence, but to man in his concrete historical existence. Indeed, if there is in man a need and aspiration of which his nature cannot give an adequate explication, "concrete reflections" should be able to tell this. A concrete reflection, according to Blondel, consists essentially in an analysis of human action, including all the different types of human behavior, metaphysics, ethics, science, and technology. Action, Blondel writes, contains "the whole field of human knowledge; action unifies sense experience, as well as scientific knowledge and philosophical speculation." [43]
Blondel proclaims thus that philosophy must study the spontaneous life of the human subject, its relations with others, with the universe and with God.[44] How does one study action? Does it not escape the ideal world of philosophy? Must philosophy not satisfy itself with the universe of ideas? No, because for Blondel philosophy is a universal critique of the whole of human behavior. In contemporary terminology, philosophy is the reflected thematisation of the unreflected. A distinction is to be made between the prospective knowledge of action and the retrospective knowledge of philosophy. Retrospective knowledge is reflection "sensu stricto." It is reflection in the second power, which turns to spontaneous knowledge (first reflection) in order to analyze it. "It is the purpose of philosophy to put into practice a thought of this kind. It is the reflective analysis of all that is lived; that is to say of all that is thought, wanted and realized by each one in the praxis." [45] The philosophy of Blondel is characterized by the thesis that philosophy and life, abstract reflection and concrete action must be clearly distinguished. He has a deep awareness of the distance there is between thought and life. Time and again one must re-

---

[44] "It is in action that we will have to transport the center of philosophy, because the center of life is also there." *Ibid.*, xxiii.
[45] Duméry, *La tentation de faire du bien,* p. 169.

member this fundamental distinction between the reflective and the effective in order to grasp the meaning of Blondel's "dialectic of action." Action is precisely the synthesis of these two. "In it, and only in it, all the lines which had been divergent or confused come together as in a geometrical figure...." [46] The smallest human act contains everything that analysis distinguishes: ideas, tendencies, decisions, everything. It is the role of the free option to bring the two levels together in an act completely penetrated by reflection, which is wisdom. Philosophy becomes the rule of action; one thinks in order to act. According to Blondel, "to be is to will and to love." [47]

Being is love; therefore, one does not know if one does not love. That is why charity is the means of perfect knowledge; it puts in us what is in others ... what necessarily imposes itself upon knowledge is only the appearance. Each of us keeps, deep inside, the intimate truth of his singular being.... Charity alone, placing itself in the heart of all, lives above appearances, communicates itself to the very depths of substances and completely solves the problem of knowledge and being.[48]

This primacy of the act must not be understood as a defense of arbitrary action. Action, for Blondel, means the entire dynamism of the incarnated spirit.

... by this word [action] we must understand the concrete activity of living thought which expresses to ourselves both ourselves and everything else, although we shall never become "adequate" to the least of our ideas; and also the initiative by which our instincts, our desires and our intentions are expressed in everything else, although our constantly renewed efforts to attain to ourselves never makes us "adequate" to ourselves.[49]

Therefore, the philosophy of action promises to be at the same time a philosophy of freedom and reflection. To liberate and to realize one's own law is one and the same thing because the norm is but the expression of a faithfulness to oneself which action carries in itself.

Blondel then shows how it is impossible not to act, or in acting not to

---

[46] Blondel, *Letter on Apologetics*, p. 185. "... everything consists in equating the reflective motion with the spontaneous motion of my will. This relation of equality or discordance is determined in action. Therefore, it is very important to study action; it comprises in itself a world which is its original work and which must contain the complete explanation of its history – all its destiny." Blondel, *L'Action*, p. xxiv.
[47] *Ibid.*, p. xxiii.
[48] *Ibid.*, pp. 443-444. We recognize here the Augustinian character of Blondel's philosophy. E. Gilson in his study on Augustine writes: "The proper task of the philosopher is not so much to make known as to impart the desire to know, but, to excite love, one does not demonstrate ('démontre'), one shows ('montre'), and that is what St. Augustine never fails to do."
[49] Blondel, *Letter on Apologetics*, p. 181.

carry the responsibility for one's acts. Suicide and dilettantism are both contradictory because the very act of suicide indicates that one wants more than life which is the opposite of nothingness, and in dilettantism there is a hidden will to live which no fantasy can satisfy. The only real solution lies in taking life seriously and in making a choice of values. Man, himself, in his activity then strives to provide the useful, the beautiful, the true and the good. But nothing can satisfy. Art promises more than it can give; it gives the absolute, but in symbols. Ethics also is insufficient in that it gives only the form of the good, not the good in itself. Even religion can deviate and become superstitious in that it makes the absolute serve man instead of man serving the Absolute. Can human action find a satisfying object? Blondel points towards an ultimate solution but on condition that action does not look for this solution on the rational level. Man must turn to God, hoping that God will give himself to man. God is pure freedom without determination and He could thus give man the means to escape his own determinations. This calls for a divine gift, it calls for "the necessary hypothesis of the supernatural." This can only be reached progressively in the dialectic of an integral spiritual life which is thought and action.

One wishes that everything be clear to the mind and that there be a unique center of perspective. There is none, this center is everywhere. But what one cannot see clearly, one can do completely: the true commentary is the practice.[50]

Again we see how everything revolves around the fundamental distinction between the reflective and effective level. On the one hand, one verifies that the subject remains dissatisfied even with the best human realizations. In each one of them man is prisoner of his determinations: there is always "a surplus of aspirations," "an excess of exigency and hope," left. On the other hand, Blondel knows that Western civilization carries a religious message which proclaims that the supernatural is effectively given to man. The philosopher has the duty then to investigate whether or not this religious message answers the problem of human action. Blondel goes beyond natural theism and postulates the necessity of the supernatural. The big question, however, is how one can proceed here as philosopher?

*b. The Problem of the Supernatural and the Method of Immanence*

The principal text dealing with this problem is the *Lettre sur les exigences de la pensée contemporaine en matière d'Apologétique et sur la méthode*

[50] Blondel, *L'Action*, p. 411.

*de la philosophie dans l'étude du problème religieux*,[51] which Duméry submits to a thorough investigation in his *Blondel et la religion. Essai critique sur la "Lettre" de 1896*. We will follow Duméry's interpretation of Blondel's "Lettre." Duméry maintains he found his method to subject religion to a philosophical critique partially applied in the first writings of Blondel (the writings of Blondel before 1900). Blondel, therefore, is the founder of the philosophy of positive religion. "We are inclined to think that Blondel has really founded the philosophy of positive religion or at least that he established it on a solid basis." [52] As soon as philosophy is defined as a methodical reflection on all significations constituted by spontaneous thought, a philosophy of positive religion becomes possible because one is able then to subject the whole religious universe to the philosophical critique without compromising either the rigor of philosophy or the transcendence of religion. This is in short what Blondel's method of immanence will lead to.

Blondel as philosopher facing the problem of religion asks himself the question, "how the philosophical problem should be put if religion is not to be simply a philosophy and philosophy is not to be absorbed in any way by religion." [53] Rather than weaken the opposition between faith and reason one must show this opposition in its full strength. Modern thought has discovered that the notion of immanence is the very condition of philosophy: the idea that no truth nor precept can be accepted unless they are, in one way or another, autonomous and autochthonous, the conviction "that nothing can enter into a man's mind which does not come out of him and correspond in some way to a need for development. . . ." [54] But this is exactly the opposite of what the Christian notion of supernatural means. The supernatural is completely gratuitous. There is nothing in man which implies that this reality should be given, because what we get from ourselves is nothing compared with what we receive.

Even if (to suppose the impossible) we were to recover by some effort of human genius the whole letter and content of revealed teaching, we should have nothing, absolutely nothing, of the Christian spirit, because it does not come from us.[55]

---

[51] This is the famous "Lettre" written during his stay at the University of Lille as "Maître de conférences à la Faculté des Lettres" in 1895, two years after the publication of *L'Action*. We use the English translation by Alexander Dru and Illtyd Trethowan – *Letter on Apologetics*.

[52] Duméry, *Blondel et la religion* (Paris: Presses Universitaires de France, 1954), p. 4.

[53] Blondel, *Letter on Apologetics*, p. 151.

[54] *Ibid.*, p. 152.

[55] *Ibid.*, p. 153.

Only when one is honest and courageous enough to express the scandal (for the immanence of reason) of the supernatural in its entirety, can one expect to respect the religious datum and to find a point where autonomous reason can attain it. The scandal of the supernatural consists in the death of reason. The doctrine of the supernatural teaches that man cannot save himself. It also maintains, however, that man can miss his final salvation by refusing the gift of grace. Man cannot save himself, yet he can be lost through his own fault. That which is by definition completely gratuitous is at the same time necessary. How can this be proven from a rigorously rational standpoint?

Blondel answers this objection in his exposition of "the method of immanence." By following the principle of immanence, which has become the heart of philosophy in modern times, philosophy reveals its most fundamental insufficiency. Increasingly, modern philosophy has realized its limits and in this limitation we find the point where philosophy can come to grips with the supernatural. What is the role of thought in human life? Reflection projects in an ideal order a series of notions and norms which form the intelligible structure of action. This ideal order is a determinism, a chain of necessary and universal ideas which give meaning to living action. The realization of these ideas does not belong to the level of thought. In themselves the ideas and norms are conditions of living action, therefore they remain merely *possible* as long as freedom has not realized them. As far as they form a logical whole, the ideas are *necessary* because they form an indispensable link in the chain of thought. It is this determinism of thought which makes it possible for philosophy to establish itself as science.

To say that the method of immanence, like all methods of a scientific character, shows us nothing more nor less than the "necessary" is not to use the word in an ontological sense as if it were a question of absolute existence or of truths whose contraries would imply contradiction; it is merely to observe that our thoughts are inevitably organized in a close-knit system, and it is this determinism, underlying as it does even the use of our freedom, which makes it possible to constitute philosophy as a science.[56]

Thought serves action, and philosophy then is a reflective systematization of spontaneous reflection which precedes action. Philosophy, therefore, continues the primary function of thought. In itself it has only possible intellectual truths, and it needs the realizing act of freedom to turn the possible into the real. Because for Blondel "to be real" means "to act," he can maintain that "down to the last detail of the last imperceptible

---

[56] *Ibid.*, p. 161.

phenomenon, mediative action makes the truth and being of all that is." [57]

Philosophy's work, then, is to criticize all the phenomena of our interior life by confronting them, by studying their relations, by developing an integral determinism ("déterminisme intégral") of the conditions of action which is thought.

In thinking, we suspend the reality of the objects and the means of salvation; we study, for example, the ideas of God "not just as God, but in so far as it is our necessary and effective thought of God. . . ." [58] Thus philosophy has absolute autonomy on the level of the intelligible conditions of action. But it must recognize its most fundamental incompleteness. Philosophy never can substitute its rational universe for the universe of reality. In the very exaltation of autonomous reason lies its principle of limitation. It can establish a completely autonomous universe of intelligibility (subjective knowledge, i.e., knowledge of phenomena), yet it needs the intervention of the realizing option to reach reality (objective knowledge, i.e., knowledge of being). By defining philosophy as the constitution of a "complete phenomenalism of thought and action," philosophy extends its field to the whole of human expressions, yet in another sense it is reduced to methodical and systematic reflections.

Philosophy, just like spontaneous thought, stands at the service of freedom, and is itself willed by freedom. It is only a means "to acquire or lose the possession of reality." [59] Reality is not founded on the necessary forms of the phenomena, but in mediating action which allows the phenomena to be what they seem to be.[60] The true role of philosophy is thus to define the conditions of being and acting and to present them to freedom which realizes them in the optional act.

---

[57] Blondel, *L'Action,* p. 465. We can see here how Blondel's primacy of freedom comes very close to the axiology of contemporary philosophers, who also maintain that determinism and freedom, instead of opposing each other, need each other. They coexist on different levels, the first is product of the second. There is no order without a free subject; freedom is the source of determinism through which it realizes itself. One can see that the ultimate effort of man will be to subsume all of determinism in life through an utmost effort of freedom to use it in its own self-realization. "Nothing tyrannical in human destiny; nothing involuntary in being; nothing in the truly objective knowledge that does not come from the depth of thought: this is really the solution to the problem of action." *L'Action,* pp. xxiii-xxiv. Such thinking can easily lead, and to a certain extent does, for instance in the case of Sartre, to the denial of fate, of necessity on the factual level.

[58] Blondel, *Letter on Apologetics,* p. 157.

[59] Blondel, *L'Action,* p. 486.

[60] "La réalité des objets connus est donc fondée, non pas en une sorte de double sous-jacent, non pas dans la forme nécessaire de leur phénomène; elle est fondée dans ce qui nous impose une option inévitable; elle est réalisée dans l'action médiatrice qui leur donne d'être ce qu'ils paraissent. Leur existence est donc en eux, puisqu'ils sont tels qu'ils sont connus, et hors d'eux, puisqu'ils sont connus tels qu'ils sont." *Ibid.*

Thus, it seems, the chief and indeed the unique aim of philosophy is to assure the full liberty of the mind, to guarantee the autonomous life of thought, and to determine in complete independence the conditions which establish its sway.[61]

The first step to freedom is a theoretical one. The principle of immanence, rational activity, is the source of order and means for freedom to realize its ends. Philosophy then covers the whole field of human activity, but only to conceive a chain of necessary ideas at the service of action. It is this necessity [62] of thought to serve freedom which brings philosophy from the level of mere description to the level of judgement, from phenomenology to ontology. Action is the link between the order of the intelligible conditions and the order of effective reality. Philosophy describes in order to prescribe, it verifies in order to judge. It would not be correct, therefore, to accuse Blondel of phenomenalism, because the very principle of immanence reveals the necessity of transcendent freedom to come to objective knowledge. Subjective knowledge does not suffice. To "attain" reality, theoretical insight is not enough. Through the realizing option of freedom one has to move on and come to objective knowledge. Thus the strength of philosophy lies in its weakness. It can construct an autonomous system of necessary ideas, because where there is necessity there is no being. But since truth is equation of thought and reality, subjective knowledge proposes and imposes the option so as to arrive at knowledge of being (objective knowledge). The notion of immanence implies thus the notion of being. In describing the phenomena and finding out how they constitute a logical order, one must not forget that they are dependent upon reality, just as scientific determinism is dependent upon freedom.

The principle of immanence provides reason with a standpoint from which to view all of the human expressions, but only as long as reason remains faithful to the principle of immanence, the hypothetical necessity of a system of thought.

The fundamental principle on which philosophy depends as a specifically defined science is that even the complete knowledge of thought and of life does not supply or suffice for the activity of thinking or of living.[63]

This essential reserve, too obvious to mention, must become *the principle*

---

[61] Blondel, *Letter on Apologetics*, p. 152.
[62] Notice that this "necessity" characteristic of the phenomenal level (the ideal level) is to be distinguished from the "necessity" which belongs to the phenomenal level because of its *ideal* nature. The former "necessity" is *the necessity to act, to make a lived option*.
[63] *Ibid.,* p. 180.

*of doctrine*. Philosophy has as its function to determine thought and the postulates of action, without either providing the being of the notions it studies, or the fulfillment of the exigencies it studies. Actual thought and life are transcendent to the immanence of this integral determinism of philosophy, and it is on condition that reason recognizes the integrity of its immanent system of thought that it will discover its own insufficiency. The more complete and rigid the system of logically linked ideas will be, the more reason will recognize that its power does not lie in the recuperation of freedom and reality, but in its mediating role vis-à-vis of freedom.

Let us now return to the problem of the supernatural. It is clear, from what has been stated, that the immanent affirmation of the transcendent – be it freedom or the supernatural – does not touch the transcendent reality of these immanent affirmations. The whole field, therefore, of religious expressions is given to the critique of reason. As anywhere else, the distinction between subjective and objective knowledge allows the philosopher to study religion from the mere theoretical standpoint.

Formerly identical with objective faith, subjective faith is entirely at the mercy of rational criticism, while objective faith remains untouched.[64]

If, therefore, the study of the conditions of action forces us to include as a final condition the complete gratuitousness of the supernatural, then philosophy will include this notion as the final link in the conditional chain of thought.

If in the study of sensible reality and even of the lowest forms of existence, we find, in so far as we try to disengage some objective element, that our thought loses itself in an endless flight and continually goes beyond itself without ever being able to pin down this sensible or scientific or metaphysical phenomenology, it is perhaps because we can never touch being at any point without encountering at least implicitly the source and bond of all being, the universal Realizer. Neither sensation, nor science, nor philosophy terminate absolutely in themselves.[65]

Because action cannot complete itself on the natural level, Blondel adds one final link: the supernatural.

It is at this point that philosophy and theology meet. "For both faith and reason teach that the supernatural must be humanly inaccessible." [66] Blondel finds in the very principle of immanence the reason for philosophy's radical autonomy and concomitantly the reason for its most funda-

---

[64] *Ibid.*, p. 158.
[65] *Ibid.*, pp. 201-202.
[66] *Ibid.*, p. 160.

mental limitation. "It is when it is fully developed that it becomes most clearly incomplete." [67] It is important to see that the method of immanence not only means that philosophy *CAN* discuss religion without destroying its transcendence, but also that philosophy *MUST* discuss religion because the principle of immanence reveals man's most fundamental contingency. The required transition from subjective knowledge to objective knowledge is possible only by adding the hypothetical necessity of the supernatural to the chain of action's necessary conditions. This is what Blondel means when he writes: "We must now face the fact that the question of method which we have had to raise here as a particular problem is at bottom a quite general and essential question of philosophical doctrine." [68] This should not surprise us if we remember that in philosophy method and content are but the two sides of the same coin.

The principle of immanence, source of philosophy's most fundamental autonomy, is also source of philosophy's most fundamental heteronomy, in that it reveals the peculiar nature of human freedom. We have seen that the role of philosophy consists in building an antecedent (to the option) logical and necessary system which enables freedom to realize itself. Philosophy is nothing but the methodical and systematic organization of spontaneous thought at the service of realizing freedom. We cannot, therefore, understand the nature of philosophy's determinist system, of which the supernatural forms the final link, unless we relate this "necessity" to freedom. It is in its relation to freedom that the determinism of reason enables philosophy to be an autonomous science.

"... it is this determinism, underlying as it does even the use of our freedom, which makes it possible to constitute philosophy as a science." [69] The necessity of the supernatural, of a gratuitous gift which would fulfil man's most fundamental aspirations, results from the necessity of reason's system of determinism to be complete and to serve freedom. We can only understand the nature of this necessity by relating it to freedom, because in the last analysis everything rotates around freedom. The reflective judgment of reason is completely subordinated to the practical judgment of freedom.

This necessity is part of human freedom itself. The necessity of an order of conditions whose realization is to be obtained by free consciousness and not by reflective consciousness is "a scientific necessity," "a hypothetical necessity." [70] The reality and the realization, however, of that which is

[67] *Ibid.*, p. 159.
[68] *Ibid.*, p. 168.
[69] *Ibid.*, p. 168.
[70] *Ibid.*, pp. 163-164.

seen as necessary depends upon another element which remains outside of philosophy. Only the effective praxis of life clinches the matter through a lived relation with God.

What is necessary is that, in some form which cannot be defined to cover particular cases, the thoughts and actions of each one of us together make up a drama which cannot reach its conclusion unless the decisive question arises, sooner or later, in the consciousness. Each one of us, simply by using that light which enlightens every man coming into this world, and by the use of his own resources, finds himself called upon to pronounce upon the problem of his destiny. For, in order to make the simplest considered affirmation about the reality of the objects which make up our thoughts, in order to produce deliberately the most elementary of those acts which enter into the determinism of our wills, we must reach implicitly the point at which the option becomes possible between the solicitations of the hidden God and those of an egoism which is always evident enough.[71]

Man is confronted with a decisive question when freedom in its progress discovers its basic incapacity to fulfill its own destiny. The only recourse to be taken is to surrender and expect to receive from God what man cannot provide himself. Only then is the *reality* of God attained. The option no longer gives us the idea of God but the reality of God. After furnishing action with all the natural conditions for its expansion, there is still a demand for something else. But in the natural order there is nothing more, so that the only solution is a gratuitous addition which positive religion calls the supernatural. The supernatural, therefore, is required as supreme condition of action yet it cannot be provided by us. Freedom alone can decide whether this condition is realized or not. For reflection, it is a possible yet necessary condition of human action.

It is in this context that Blondel is finally able to assure the ontological reality of things, which up to now he only envisaged as simple phenomena. We could summarize the whole reasoning as follows: Our actions, when taken as phenomenal facts and subjected to the critique of reason, reveal at the same time that there is in the subject a need to become completely oneself and free, yet that the free subject is never able to come to complete self-identification. The "volonté voulante" and the "volonté voulue" never fall together, the "pensée pensante" always surpasses the "pensée pensée." [72] How, then, is meaning found in our actions?

[71] *Ibid.*, p. 162.
[72] The "volonté voulante" is what man essentially wills, whereas the "volonté voulue" is what man supposes himself to be willing. The "volonté voulante" is the primitive aspiration present in every man. This most fundamental movement never reaches its goal on the natural level. Throughout the course of the dialectic of action, the discrepancy between what we essentially will and what we think ourselves to be willing is always declaring itself. "Il est impossible de ne pas reconnaître l'insuffisance de tout

According to Blondel, this can only occur in the affirmation of God, who is perfect freedom and who, by our participation in Him, assures the unity of willing and that which is willed, of thinking and that which is thought. God has to give Himself gratuitously to man, in the gift of the supernatural, so that man may realize himself as spirit.

Absolutely impossible and absolutely necessary to man – that is, indeed, the notion of the supernatural: the action of man surpasses man. And the whole effort of his reason is to see that he cannot, and must not, stay on the mere natural level.[73]

These (God and the gift of the supernatural) are for reason only possible but necessary ideas. Only the option gives us the reality of God and the supernatural. Action then becomes meaningful, it can complete itself, it can be efficacious. There is no reality outside of action. Things become real only through the mediation of the spirit which can achieve itself. Here Blondel points to the Christian dogma of incarnation, to Christ as the universal link providing the mediative and creative power to actualize the aspirations of the "volonté voulante."

Maybe, it was necessary that, having become flesh himself, he made, by an altogether necessary and voluntary passion the *reality* of what is apparent determinism of nature and forced knowledge of the objective phenomenon; the *reality* of voluntary failures and of privative knowledge which is the result of it; the *reality* of religious action and of the sublime destiny reserved to man and completely consequent to man's own desires. It is He who is the measure of all things.[74]

---

l'ordre naturel et de ne point éprouver un besoin ultérieur; il est impossible de trouver en soi de quoi contenter ce besoin religieux. C'est nécessaire, c'est impraticable. Voilà, toutes brutes, les conclusions du déterminisme, de l'action humaine." *L'Action*, p. 319. The "volonté voulante," the "pensée pensante" require thus that we should perform the great action, the good option, which throws us open to divine action.
[73] *Ibid.*, p. 388.
[74] *Ibid.*, p. 461. (Italics mine.) There is a striking parallelism between Blondel's Christian ontogenesis and Teilhard de Chardin's Christian cosmogenesis. They both think along the same line, the former from a philosophical standpoint, the latter from a scientific standpoint. Claude Tresmontant, in his book, *Introduction à la métaphysique de Maurice Blondel* (Paris: Editions du Seuil, 1963), brings this out most convincingly. "Si la métaphysique de Blondel est construite selon un dynamisme qui ne s'achève que par en haut, dans un problème suprême, que Blondel a appelé le point capital de la métaphysique chrétienne, c'est que cette métaphysique de la création, soucieuse de suivre la création dans son devenir, dans sa genèse, dans sa constitution progressive, dans son dynamisme interne, qui ne s'achèvera que par en haut, dans une clef de voute qui n'est pas fourni d'en-bas, par des mains d'homme, mais qui est donnée d'en haut, par Dieu même. Notons déjà une analogie, une parentée profonde entre la vision du monde de Blondel et celle de Teilhard, qui écrivait: 'Contrairement aux apparences encore admises par le Physique, le Grand Stable n'est pas au-dessous dans l'infra-élémentaire, mais au-dessus, dans l'ultra-synthétique.' (*Le Phénomène humain*, p. 301.) 'Si les choses tiennent ce n'est qu'à force de complexité, par en haut.' (*Ibid.*) Teilhard est conduit à cette conclusion par les analyses de ce qui apparaît dans

The necessity of the supernatural is not *just logical,* because it is a necessity which is called for by freedom in its growth towards meaningful self-fulfillment. It is more than a deductive necessity because it is a necessity of human action. On the other hand, it is less than a necessity of fact since it is postulated on the ideal level of the conditions of action. This ambivalent necessity is characteristic of human action, of a being which must realize itself without being source of itself, of a freedom which must subsume that which is already there. It is a necessity which permits freedom to realize itself, and shows that there is no human freedom outside of a process of self-liberation.

> It [the necessity of the supernatural] cannot be necessitating or constraining, in the common meaning of the term, since it allows freedom to spring forth and to receive the benefit of this emergence of freedom.[75]

The need of a supernatural elevation reveals an element of unfreedom at the heart of human freedom. Freedom, of its own, is unable to realize the conditions required by the rigorous system of determinism to make action meaningful. The ideal system of the conditions of the possibility of action explicated by means of the principle of immanence is necessary yet impracticable. The *ideal* autonomy can only become *real* through the acceptance of and participation in the absolute freedom of God. But again this can only be envisaged by reason, not realized. Freedom as the faculty of the real needs the help of grace. ". . . the real and effective synthesis of nature with the supernatural comes about only through effective action, and by grace. . . ."[76]

It is important to see that the universal jurisdiction of reason is based upon its fundamental limitation: viz., that it cannot attain the transcendent reality which is at the source of the activity of the spirit.

If then we consider our own *action* in this way, we find that this immanent activity is always transcendent in regard to every equilibrium provisionally established by it and to all knowledge extracted from it, and we do philosophy the service of providing it with that matter and that form which alone, by adapting themselves to one another, constitute it in its own essence.[77]

---

la réalité cosmique, biologique et humaine, par une description fidèle de la cosmogénèse, de la biogénèse et de l'anthropogénèse, par une phénoménologie de l'évolution dans sons sens plénier, c'est à dire de la création en train de se faire, mais vue si l'on peut dire, du dehors, en savant, en physicien, en naturaliste. Tandis que Blondel parvient à un resultat convergent par une analyse ontologique." Pp. 31-32.

[75] Duméry, *Blondel et la religion,* p. 33.
[76] Blondel, *Letter on Apologetics,* p. 166.
[77] *Ibid.*

The object of philosophy, then, is to build an ideal and coherent system of all human activity, profane as well as religious, for the use of freedom. But philosophy, in virtue of the principle of immanence, not only *can* approach the religious problem, it also *must* tackle the problem of religion as soon as it discovers that effective and transcendent freedom cannot come to self-fulfillment. Freedom in its search for the natural goods, does not really seek these natural goods (what is willed never coincides with the primary drive of the willing act), and, therefore, God, who in His generosity gives man his pure freedom, has to be added as necessary hypothesis to the chain of the conditions of human action.

Blondel seems to imply that the necessity of the supernatural is written in the principle of immanence itself. "In its boldest effort to close the door to faith reason has gathered strength to open it." [78] Is what Blondel in the *Letter* calls "the method of immanence" fundamentally identical with the dialectic of *L'Action*? Is *L'Action,* the dialectic – seen more from the standpoint of the "volonté voulante" versus the "volonté voulue," and the *Letter* the same dialectic – seen more from the standpoint of the "pensée pensante" versus the "pensée pensée?" We think that something like this is the case.[79] The *Letter* presents the dialectic of action in terms of freedom and determinism. The incapacity of freedom to realize the conditions of action portrayed in the ideal system of thought, the incapacity to realize the *idea* of complete autonomy (disengaged in virtue of the principle of immanence) points to the fact that absolute autonomy may be possible only on the basis of a radical heterogony.[80]

... for when we study the close-knit system of our thoughts, it becomes apparent that the very notion of immanence is realized in our consciousness only by the effective presence of the notion of the transcendent. The idea of

---

[78] *Ibid.,* p. 207.
[79] Later on in our study, it becomes clear that it is here that Duméry gives his own interpretation of the "method of immanence." He disregards the necessity of equating "the term willed with the principle of the voluntary aspiration itself" (*L'Action,* p. 406), he sees in the determinism of action *only the intelligible structure of action.* Although there is a tendency in the *Letter* to define philosophy as an ideal system of thought *independent* of action, one should follow what is clearly Blondel's main idea as explained in *L'Action* (viz., the dialectic of action) in the interpretation of a smaller work (viz., *Lettre*) written only three years after *L'Action.*
[80] The determinism of the system of conditions of action does not only indicate the logical coherence of the conditions of action, but also the *necessity to act.* It is this last meaning of the determinism of action which Duméry fails to take into account. He loosens the ideal system of the conditions of action from the necessary options. This gives him free hand to treat religion as *merely* an ideal system. But if reality is so far off, does one not run the danger of substituting this ideal system for the reality of religion?

an absolute intellectual and moral autonomy is conceivable only on condition of our conceiving also, and necessarily, of a possible heteronomy.[81]

Blondel discovers in the rigorous division of a necessary and hypothetical order of reason and the free and real order of freedom, man's most fundamental contingency, and the nature of philosophy.[82]

The fundamental principle on which philosophy depends as a specifically defined science is that even the complete knowledge of thought and of life does not supply or suffice for the activity of thinking or of living.[83]

This signifies on the one hand that what is immanent in the philosophical act is still transcendent (it calls for realization), and on the other hand that the philosophizing act itself is part of a transcendent reality (freedom).[84] So instead of thinking that philosophy contains all reality or (which is the other extreme) that philosophy is just a mental construction, we give philosophy its real scope *by inserting its own dynamism in the total determinism which it studies.* The difficulty consists in conceiving the philosophical work as part of self-liberating freedom, and in the nature of its role lies its sufficiency and insufficiency. Philosophy is self-sufficient insofar as it builds an integral determinism of action and life, but not self-sufficient insofar as it never can provide the being of the notion it studies. Blondel's philosophy is built on the very simple truth ("ce truisme") that thought and life are not identical.

c. *How the Principle of Immanence Can Provide a Method for the Philosophical Study of Religion which Escapes the Pitfalls of Immanentism and Dualism*

Duméry writes: "Curiously enough, it is because philosophy, for Blondel, is of a critical nature, that he approaches the supernatural question." [85] Blondel can approach the religious problem because of his special concept of philosophy. He shows in the third part of his *Letter* how philosophy

---

[81] Blondel, *Letter on Apologetics,* p. 159.
[82] We discover here the Kantian structure of Blondel's universe, the distinction between the realm of theoretical reason and the realm of practical reason. But Blondel is more successful in filling the gap between the two, through his dialectic of action.
[83] Blondel, *Letter on Apologetics,* p. 180.
[84] The terms "realizing freedom" and "realizing option" have an idealistic connotation. Some texts in Blondel's *Lettre sur les exigences de la pensée contemporaine en matière d'Apologétique* allow such interpretation. Yet one should not interpret the *Lettre* independent from *L'Action*. The option is the link with subsisting reality. "Il ne s'agit pas, en voulant, de faire que la réalité subsiste en soi parce qu'un décret arbitraire l'aurait créé en nous; il s'agit, en voulant, de faire qu'elle soit en nous parce qu'elle est comme elle est en soi. *Cet acte de volonté* ne la fait pas dépendre de nous; il nous fait dépendre d'elle." *L'Action,* p. 440.
[85] Duméry, *La tentation de faire du bien,* p. 189.

discovered its real nature under the influence of the Christian idea of the supernatural. He also makes clear how both the danger of immanentism and dualism are overcome by bringing philosophy to its real self.

The roots of Western philosophy lie in the Greek concept of reason which always tends to envelop the whole order of thought and reality in order to immanentize all of reality by thought and to replace praxis by theory.

> Its implied postulate is the divinity of Reason – not only in the sense that God is Logos, but in the sense that our speculative knowledge contains the supreme virtue and of itself consummates in us the divine work.[86]

But in this manifest exaltation of reason was secretly implied a principle of limitation which became apparent under the influence of the Christian idea. Scholastic philosophy made the Greek concept of reason its ally, but the antagonism between the Greek concept of sufficiency and the Christian idea of insufficiency could not be concealed for long. Scholasticism had admitted an element which was completely foreign to the Greek mind and, therefore, the equilibrium of Scholasticism was essentially unstable. The Reformation discovered the enemy and refused to let autonomous reason touch the Christian principle, because being completely the antipodes of the Christian idea, it could do nothing but destroy the essence of Christianity. The result was a complete separation of faith and reason which lead to the establishment of a self-confident independent philosophy and an irrationalism of faith (Protestantism).

Left completely to itself, however, philosophy came to discover its limitations. Gradually it had to admit its fundamental illusion. Philosophy exposed its erroneous pretentions for a total and absolute hegemony by maintaining that there is an identity of life and knowledge. But then it also became clear that, even if there were a knowledge adequate to reality and identical with being, this knowledge was not able to equate the "volonté voulante" with the "volonté voulue." "It came to realize that the 'method of immanence' excludes a 'doctrine of immanence.'" [87] By the same token, philosophy escapes all danger of immanentism, of reducing reality to thought, and philosophy is given a universal jurisdiction over the whole field of human expressions. Even if philosophy must abstain from all effective solutions, it must not abstain from "any solution in regard to postulates." [88] It can study the most precise phenomena of the religious life by the same prerogative by which it studies, for instance,

[86] Blondel, *Letter on Apologetics,* pp. 172-173.
[87] *Ibid.,* p. 178.
[88] *Ibid.,* p. 182.

sense perception. Philosophy studies only that which is immanent to reason. "Philosophy ... consists not in the heteronomous application of reason to some material or to some object, *but in the autonomous application of reason to itself.*" [89]

This concept of philosophy, which allows us to approach the whole religious phenomenon, at the same time destroys the immanentist approach by its essential reserve of reality, and the dualistic approach by giving reason a real grip upon the religious phenomenon. Both the method of explication and the method of confrontation [90] erred by an objectivism of the concepts, by a realism of thought: scholasticism by trying to make an objective projection of reason on the level of faith (a pseudo-Christian philosophy), and immanentism by trying to make an objective projection of faith on the level of reason (a rationalistic pseudo-philosophy).

Do not believe that faith is a superior metaphysics from which reason imbibes through its own responsibility ... philosophy of religion does not consist in attempting rational transpositions of the revealed dogmas.[91]

Philosophy and religion can be united without destroying the immanence of reason or the transcendence of religion. It does so by discovering that our action remains transcendent to all knowledge extracted from it, and that this action does not find its completion on the natural level. Thus, it finds an immanent transcendence in reason. The concept which must be destroyed is not the Christian idea nor the philosophical idea, but the middle term which has been used to reconcile them, viz., the ancient concept of the divinity of reason, the ontological and intellectual realism of a thought which dominates everything and which is everything.

Thanks to this method of immanence, "it becomes possible to discuss questions which concern religion of the most positive kind without making this religion itself a matter of dispute, without pronouncing on what it offers or trespassing on its preserves." [92] All of reality, the natural as well as the supernatural, falls outside of the philosophical jurisdiction. For reason, they remain hypothetical necessities, the natural as far as action cannot complete itself, the supernatural as far as it is necessary for the completion of action. Philosophy studies the religious phenomenon with the same reserve as it studies any other kind of phenomena. The danger always lies in thinking that philosophy is the application of reason to an outside reality, forgetting the radical distinction of reflective and concrete

---

[89] *Ibid.*, p. 186. (Italics mine.)
[90] Cf. this Chapter, Section I, b and c.
[91] Duméry, *La tentation de faire du bien,* note 208.
[92] Blondel, *Letter on Apologetics,* p. 165.

order, a distinction on which philosophy is based. It might be deduced from Blondel's thought that the transcendent reality of any natural phenomenon is as much out of the grip of reason as the supernatural phenomenon. The fundamental distinction, for Blondel, does not lie so much in the distinction between the natural and supernatural as in the distinction between the reflective and the real. The natural real is as much a problem as the supernatural real, and the possibility of the former calls for the possibility of the latter.[93] Blondel's important dividing line is vertical, between the real and the ideal; for Scholasticism the important dividing line is horizontal, between the supernatural and the natural.

But Blondel, so Duméry maintains, has only *opened* the road to an integral critique of Christianity. He was not able to apply his method to religion and establish a philosophy of religion in "actu exercito." Allied to his desire to penetrate into the heart of religion, there still was a tendency to study religion with the method of confrontation. He applied the method of immanence only to the necessity of the supernatural to complete the human destiny.

*La Lettre* defines a method which it applies to the case of the supernatural but it postpones the application concerning the particulars of religious expression. It remains centered upon the preparation to the faith.[94]

Further on, in his philosophy of Christianity, he merely confronts the philosophical problems with the theological data. For instance, he confronts the philosophical enigma of God with the Christian mystery of the Trinity. In doing this, Duméry observes, Blondel himself was not faithful any more to the all-important distinction between the reflective and the real. He too hastily introduced the practical decision, the "option réalisatrice." He should have extended his study of the necessity of the supernatural to the study of the necessity of all the religious expressions in "concreto." Duméry thus intends to take more seriously Blondel's remark at the end of his *Lettre*:

Let us say then, contradicting Pascal's remark [95] in a spirit of peace and truth, that we are "happy to be able to speak, to be obliged to speak, to see so many constrained and eager to speak, about the very heart of religion." [96]

[93] There is a beautiful illustration of this trend of thinking in Hammerskjold's diary, *Markings*. "From this perspective, to believe in God is to believe in yourself as self-evident, as illogical, and as impossible to explain: if I can be, then God is." Dag Hammerskjold, *Markings*, trans. Leif Sjoberg and W. H. Auden (New York: Alfred A. Knopf, 1964), p. 127.
[94] Duméry, *Critique et religion*, p. 107.
[95] "The wretches who have obliged me to speak about the heart of religion..." Pascal, *Pensées*.
[96] Blondel, *Letter on Apologetics*, p. 208.

## SECTION III
### HUSSERL'S METHOD OF COMPREHENSION AND DUMÉRY'S METHOD OF DISCRIMINATION

*a. The Method of Husserl and the Service It Renders to the Phenomenology of Religion*

Philosophy is the science of the immanent. Husserl's phenomenological method, based on the same principle of immanence, will be used by Duméry as tool for his philosophy of religion. Husserl's remarkable invention of the transcendental analysis will be especially useful in the study of religion. Duméry will use the phenomenological method as the stock for what he calls his "method of discrimination." [97] It will bring in the notion of the transcendental Ego, which, as one might suspect, will be of tremendous importance for Duméry's understanding of the process of revelation, the most important religious phenomenon. The necessary mediation of the transcendental Ego, understood according to the Husserlian inspiration, will allow him to establish an integral critique of religion without touching the religious reality. In the end it will also permit him to remove the parenthesis of the phenomenological "épochè" by adding the so-called henological reduction to the transcendental reduction. Thus the Husserlian transcendental Ego is the backbone of his whole philosophy. "The discovery of the transcendental Ego conditions the soundness of philosophy." [98] Let us briefly examine the Husserlian method.

The first step in the Husserlian method is the *eidetic reduction*. This is the description of the object or the religious act freed from all blinding prejudices through the practice of the "épochè," which is the provisional parenthesizing of all rational and dogmatic judgment. In this way, the "épochè" by eliminating all empirical elements leads to the comprehension of the meaning, a comprehension which the phenomenologists

---

[97] The "Method of Discrimination" consists in discovering on what level of consciousness the different religious expressions originate. It allows the philosopher of religion to determine their respective value. "Au lieu de se borner à dresser un inventaire même détaillé, *la méthode de Discrimination* classe et hiérarchise d'après des critères normatifs. Elle sait que la conscience comporte plusieurs niveaux distincts et qu'il parcourt, degré de dignité qui est un degré d'efficacité médiatrice." Duméry, différenciée, c'est parce que le Cogito est un acte libre; pour se poser, il doit poser ce qui le conditionne, le monde de la perception et celui des valeurs. Le monde sensible, le monde idéal sont les étapes d'une dialectique de réalisation de soi et de tout; par là s'expliquent le dynamisme orienté de la conscience et le degré de dignité des plans qu'il parcourt, -degré de dignité qui est un degré d'efficacité médiatrice." Duméry, *Critique et religion,* p. 222.

[98] Duméry, *Philosophie de la religion,* I, p. 28.

call the intuitive grasp of the essence ("Wesensschau"), the *eidos*.[99] The eidetic reduction aims then to attain the facts of consciousness, not as empirical happenings but as essences which are characterized by necessity, universality and impersonality. "Religion, studied by the phenomenologist, will appear in its intelligible structure, not in its individual and contingent expressions." [100] But this intelligible structure is not abstract, it is "intended" and therefore at the same time ideal and concrete. The "Wesensschau" does not strive to penetrate the heart of things, but simply tries to circumscribe the possible frame in which a thing stands. The word "intuition" is thus somewhat misleading, because it implies something like a direct and complete grasp of the object. We must not forget that for Husserl intuition means intention and intentionality. Consciousness can only be intuitive by putting things at a distance and by "in-tending" them, reaching for them. It is in this sense that Duméry understands the "Wesensschau" and its way of avoiding the simplistic realism of empiricism as well as the psychologism of a closed Cogito. Knowledge lies neither in the object nor in the subject, but in the intentional relation.

How can one admit that the reduction is intuitive? It will be admitted, if it is understood, that the intuition with which we are concerned *is of a special type*. It does not see the *essence* as the eye sees an object in space, nor does it see it as the imagination contemplates images; much less as a mystic, by supernatural illumination, would see something of the next world. To see the *essence* is to see the meaning or the signification. But a meaning cannot be seen as an internal or external object. To see it can only be to comprehend it; and to understand it is to seize it while considering it as an originating datum or else as a creation of the giving intuition, which maintains itself eternally contemporaneous with its own data.[101]

To the eidetic reduction Husserl adds the *transcendental reduction* which aims at showing on the one hand the transcendental character of the Ego in its relation to the world, and on the other hand the world as mere intentional correlate of the Ego. The Cogito of the phenomenologists, in contradistinction to the Cogito of Kant, is concrete, incarnated, socialized and situated. The important result of this is that the object can only be intuited through a bodily behavior, a contingent language and a historical tradition. The first duty of a philosopher then is to understand that in man there are several levels of consciousness and correlatively several levels of reality. This is important for the understanding of the religious phenomenon.

[99] "Eidos" in Greek means the external aspect and consequently the form of a thing.
[100] Duméry, *Critique et religion,* p. 140.
[101] *Ibid.,* pp. 137-138.

If all knowledge, all knowing, far from being a seizure of a sovereign and separated intelligible structure, is a group of graduated structures where the intentionality seeks itself by expressing itself and progresses by integrating the forms which it surpasses, then, it is the whole man who cooperates in the genesis of truth. Compared to this scheme, religious knowledge is also enlightened. It employs the body in the rite, the imagination in the myth, long before using the abstract reflection in the dogma or precept.[102]

Through the discovery of the transcendental Ego one overcomes the natural attitude of the intramundane Ego which erroneously seeks to register exterior meanings existing in things. The subject understands that it is the giver of meaning; also, that meaningful reality (and this is the only reality we know) constitutes itself in the pure look of the spirit. Pure consciousness can thus be considered as retired from the world. It contains neither fact nor form,[103] yet as related to the world, as pure relational act, it is an intentional act continually tending toward the world.[104] It is then apparent that the constituting Ego is not the creating Ego of a triumphant idealism. The moment of constitution lies beyond the constituted meaningful reality and the constituted intramundane subject. *The formations of meaning are, therefore, not gratuitous, but, rather, the mediations by which the pure intentional relation constitutes itself and the world.* "The phenomenological reduction is the awareness of the subordination of the essences to the act which mediates itself through them, which expresses itself in them and reconquers itself upon them." [105] The transcendental Ego is pure relation to the world, not a relation which it undergoes, but a relation which it erects in order to affirm itself.

It is important, for the understanding of Duméry's philosophy of religion, to notice that the object-constituting function is thus a function of *expression,* that meanings are mediating expressions of a presence (for instance presence to the world in its sacred dimension). The function of expression has a mediating role. It is rooted in and fed by this experience of presence and also serves to deepen the experience of presence. This has a double effect. On the one hand it indicates the intentional, relative character of all objectifying expression. Conversely, the objectifying ex-

---

[102] *Ibid.,* pp. 148-149.

[103] *Ibid.,* p. 148.

[104] We can see how this understanding of consciousness is best defined by the notion of negativity, nothingness. Consciousness is a "look," "un regard sur le monde," which implies very well that the meaning is neither in the thing looked at nor in the one who looks. "Mais il n'est pas tellement facile de mener une description sans tomber victime, soit du positivisme, soit du psychologisme. Seule la réduction transcendentale, effectuée délibérément et constamment maintenue, peut éviter de prendre le concept pour un décalque de la chose, ou l'intuition pour une modification subjective." *Ibid.,* p. 150, n. 1.

[105] *Ibid.,* p. 147.

pression can be viewed as a first form of reflection upon the experience of presence. This spontaneous reflection belongs to the essence of the intentionality itself. It is a prephilosophical (what Blondel called "pensée prospective"), a prereflective consciousness (la pensée directe): "There is a word immanent in life even before that word is elevated to the level of the philosophical discourse." [106]

At this junction, we approach the third moment of the Husserlian method; namely, the study of the *constitution*. The eidetic reduction brought us to the discovery of the object as cogitatum, of the Ego as the *place* of the cogitata. The phenomenological reduction [107] in its turn made the Ego discover itself as the *source* of the meaning. Now, we must define the intentionality which constitutes the object as its correlate. This is done by examining the relation between that which is implicitly aimed at ("visé") and that which is explicitly intentioned, the relation between the experience of a presence and the function of expression. In this, the object, or in the case of the religious phenomenon, the religious representations, is constituted.

To constitute the religious object, if one adheres to the Husserlian method, consists in following in its entirety the course by which religious man reaches for the Absolute (or the Divine) – through this or that means of expression. One sees that the religious intentionality departs from the intimacy of the spiritual subject, crosses the psychological Ego, the body, the world, the society, to rejoin the Absolute Himself, in virtue of revealing objects and gestures which have a mystical or sacred efficaciousness.[108]

This leads to the distinction of different elements inherent in the constitution of the religious object (or representation). There is first of all the subject as hierogenic source, then the different levels of the natural Ego (the "Erlebnisse" or the noeses), the objective sphere of the religious significations (the noemas), and finally the God-object.

The analysis of the different elements which determine the constitution of the religious representations completes the comprehension which the phenomenological proceeding wanted to reach. There is no judgment of value as yet. The épochè neither affirms nor nullifies the supernatural character of the religious object. Only living freedom has the right to undo the "épochè" and to make an option on the meaning of being.

For Blondel, the subject is not only transcendental, it also is relation to the Transcendent. The phenomenological reduction is absorbed by a more funda-

---

[106] Duméry, *The Problem of God*, p. 13.
[107] Duméry uses the term "phenomenological reduction" for what is usually called the transcendental reduction. *Critique et religion*, p. 141.
[108] *Ibid.*, p. 151.

mental one. We personally believe that an ultimate reduction (the henological reduction) is necessary in order to confirm the phenomenological reduction completely.[109]

But a reflective and critical study of religion, which Duméry has in mind, cannot stop here. Yet, one may not think that the phenomenological comprehension installs us in God or in the transcendental Ego from where we can deduce religion in its form and content.

It is at the heart of the *situated* religious subject, that we have to locate the spiritual initiative in its contact with the divine and the variety of the detailed intentions which lead to different lived patterns of behavior. *Nevertheless,* as soon as the Absolute is in question, one must, no doubt, go beyond the instructions of Husserl and determine as Scheler does whether or not the effort to reach him effectively is valid and under which conditions.[110]

Duméry intends thus to leave the brackets of the phenomenological "époche" in order to evaluate the different religious objects as conditions of the religious ascent. Here we will see how Duméry makes use of Blondel's ontology based upon an active participation in the Absolute.

## b. *Objections against Husserl's Phenomenological Method*

Duméry has some objections against the phenomenological method. Husserl achieves a deep insight into the immanent nature of thought by reducing the whole world of objects as noematic correlate of the transcendental Ego. He, therefore, has more or less lost sight of the problem of thought's relation to reality (unless one believes that transcendental idealism gives a satisfactory answer to this problem). This results in the inability of phenomenology to establish itself as ontology, remaining as it does on the level of mere immanent description. The Blondelian insight, that philosophy is thought immanent in action itself, and that for the possibility of this action a participation with the Absolute is necessary, brings philosophy to ontology by a retroactive influence of God discovered at the end of the phenomenological description of action. On the other hand, Blondel did not have a theory of the auto-constitution of the subject and did not sufficiently stress the creativity of the spirit. This, however, was implied in the principle of immanence on which he founded philosophy as science. Husserl has a more rigorous explication of the principle of immanence. Yet he did not see, as Blondel did, the implication of a possible heteronomy in the very principle of autonomy. He did not under-

---

[109] *Ibid.,* p. 143.
[110] *Ibid.,* p. 151.

stand that realizing freedom may be possible only through a liberating participation in the Absolute.

The main objection then against Husserl will be in the lack of metaphysical range of his philosophical insights. Duméry will remedy this with the Blondelian integration of the reflective into the effective through the mediation of the theistic affirmation. But Duméry intends also to complete the phenomenological description as such by adding to the eidetic reduction a genetic phenomenology.[111]

In order to know how Christian consciousness exercises its religious intentionality, it is not enough to disengage its abstract and static structure. We must also regain possession of its total intentionality in the multiple expressions which religious intentionality has given itself throughout the ages. Phenomenology itself requires, for the genesis of meaning, the safeguarding of the historical dimension. If one adheres only to a static comprehension of the religious expressions, one runs the danger of ending up with a super-temporal and super-spatial constellation of universal and necessary ideas – the very thing phenomenology is trying to avoid.

> The essences never subsist in a separate state, in a factitious a-temporality which is only a caricature of living eternity. The religious essences and values form no exception to this rule. On the contrary, they are characterized by a very deep incarnation in time and space. The experience of religious men is always structured by a positive teaching, which one calls revelation, dogma, or precept.[112]

It must be kept in mind, however, that the religious experience is intentional like all other experiences. Therefore, the genetic comprehension will not be an empirico-historical explanation, nor a psychological analysis of the origin of meaning.

Duméry's correction of the first step of the phenomenological method is of capital importance for his understanding of the religious phenomenon. It remedies a tendency to dispose of religion's positive historical context, a tendency which will constantly be the temptation of any philosophical approach to religion. On the other hand, by seeing the religious phenomenon as an *intentional event,* we escape the slavery of brute facts laying the foundation of religious meanings. Faith in Christ, therefore,

---

[111] The intentional analysis excels in disengaging intelligible structures, but it disregards the historical and genetic dimension of the significations. The genesis Duméry is talking about here should not be understood in any empirical way. "Elle (la génèse) se situe au niveau phénoménologique; en ce sens, elle peut être dite transcendentale. . . . La génèse, au sens phénoménologique, c'est donc la façon dont l'intention constituante et vécue utilise le rapport au monde pour lui faire porter telle ou telle signification." *Ibid.,* p. 166.
[112] *Ibid.,* pp. 167-168.

will not be a mere passive appropriating of his manner of existing. Rather, it will be the active recapture of his attitude through the giving intuition of the religious experience. We will also encounter here the paradox of a meaning which is made by us and given to us.

> Faith in Christ, enlightened by its radical origin, not by its empirical genesis, is a certain relation to the world and history which adopts a spiritual outlook until then never edited in its contingent expressions. On the other hand, faith in Christ is also undeducible from all raw fact. It is also as incommensurable to any accident, to all factuality, as any signification can be.[113]

It is insufficient to describe the religious representations. We must also look for the history of their origin, for their radical transcendental origin. It is imperative that we pierce through to the spontaneity of the living intentional consciousness. Here we find the working intentionality which shapes the world prior to any reflective recapture. We will subsequently understand how Duméry describes and analyzes this projective mechanism of the religious consciousness which the Ego excites in order to create the representations by which it posits itself, its world, and reaches out for God.

The absence of the genetic standpoint in the phenomenological description forms the first objection. The second objection, namely, the absence of the theistic affirmation, confronts us with a difficult point. How do we have to understand the nature of the creativity of the original giving intuition, which is the last norm of authenticity? The meanings are concomitantly *given* and *created* so that we could name the "giving intuition" a "giving given-ness." The intuitive evidence cannot be based upon the objective affirmations nor on the apodicticity of the Cogito. The only escape would be to convert the Ego into a producing subject, to make the transcendental intentionality productive and creative. Otherwise, it is impossible to found the universality and necessity of the essences. Many cannot accept this because they do not see how a subject can create objects which appear necessarily and eternally as given. This paradox of a "giving given-ness" is, according to Duméry, the fundamental insight of Husserl.

> For the subject, to create is to posit the essences whose objectivity has to be recognized as irreducible to the subject's own dispositions. In this sense, the spiritual act creates, not any replica of itself that it can master or improve, but intangible, universal and necessary laws. According to us, the most original and valuable invention of Husserl resides in this: there is a creation of essences compatible with the intentional structures of the Ego.[114]

[113] *Ibid.*, pp. 168-169.
[114] *Ibid.*, p. 163.

The only means of escape is to grant creativity to the intentionality and see that the paradox of a "giving given-ness" implies and supposes an Act which does not have to be intentional in order to be active. One must accept that God cannot fulfill the role of intuitive producer of objects, yet that He is necessary to make the intentionality meaningful; i.e., to assure the link with reality. The subject creates itself by creating the essences which it intends but since neither consciousness nor the world can found the meaning-fulness of this *activity,* one has to think of God as the one who makes this activity of the spirit possible.[115] The intentional Ego itself, insofar as it must create objects in order to affirm itself, has something reducible, since the reduction is only complete when a radical oneness is discovered. The transcendental Ego reveals a certain duality at the heart of its giving intuition. It is this duality which makes our author decide to add the *henological reduction* to the transcendental reduction. He quotes for this view an important text of Husserl:

> The transcendental "Absolute" which we have laid bare through the reductions is in truth not ultimate; it is something which in a certain profound and wholly unique sense constitutes itself, and has its primeval source in what is ultimately and truly absolute.[116]

The difficulty in grasping this intrinsic relation of the spirit with the Absolute lies in the fact that only in the act itself, in the living intentionality, one can reach the Absolute. "The point of contact between the mind and the Absolute is not reflective, but is the source of reflection and thought." [117] It is the point where theoria and praxis converge, where the reduction becomes ascesis and conversion, and where the reflective analysis transforms itself into effective freedom. At this point, we return to Blondel.

Through the discovery of the transcendental Ego, the whole world of meaning has been reduced to the immanence of thought. In this, philosophy as rigorous science has been established. Phenomenology as science does not provide us with ontological judgments because the transition to being is not the work of reflective consciousness but of the concrete subject. If the world as correlate of consciousness must possess reality, if through the mediation of essences reality is to be reached, the Ego must

---

[115] Just like Blondel, Duméry establishes an ontology through the retroactive influence of God who is discovered at the end of the phenomenological description of reality. Philosophy has then necessarily a phenomenological stage before it reaches the ontological stage.
[116] Edmund Husserl, *Ideas. General Introduction to Pure Phenomenology* (New York: Collier Books, 1962), p. 216.
[117] Duméry, *Critique et religion,* p. 200.

exceed the collection of categories, it must be a creative dynamism. The pivotal problem, according to Duméry, is to find the link between *the realizing dynamism of freedom* and *the transcendental formalism of the Cogito*. How does one make the transition to reality? Two conditions are required. First the conditions of intelligibility must be transformed into conditions of realization. It is necessary to view the essences as mediations for the ontological realization of the subject and its world. Secondly, the Ego must be discovered as creator in its intrinsic relation to the Absolute.

As has been expounded, Blondel similarly elevated philosophy from the level of mere immanent description to the realm of judgment. The necessity of thought to serve freedom and the impossibility of freedom's self-realization point toward the hypothetical necessity of a gratuitous participation in the absolute freedom of the Absolute. This localizes the act of faith at the source of the possibility of spiritual activity. The question then arises whether ontology is at all possible without the act of faith, without the gratuitous realization of human freedom by the Absolute. We are inclined to think that Duméry pursues the same course. "There is no authentic ontology unless the dynamism of the subject sustains formal thought and God is recognized as principle of the auto-constitution itself." [118] But the spirit in its relation to the Absolute can never be touched by speculative thought. The mystery of the spirit is as untouchable as the mystery of God, because they are one and the same mystery.

> Whether it is question of the mystery of God, of the mystery of the spirit, of freedom, of love or of any lived attitude, theoretical reflection never gives their speculative equivalents. The reality of God will never be retained in a determination nor will the "apex mentis." They can only remain super-conscious, such as the Plotinian ecstasy.[119]

The spiritual act is super-conscious because it generates consciousness. This generation requires the presence of an Absolute at the heart of freedom to give realizing freedom that which it cannot give to itself. We have to presuppose the act of faith for the possibility of the spiritual act. This comes very close to Bonaventure's thesis that faith is necessary for the healing of reason. However, Duméry and Blondel differ from Bonaventure insofar as they maintain that faith falls under the jurisdiction of philosophy, only as condition – *necessary condition for the realization of freedom*. Faith is a necessary condition for the realization of man; religion is the school of freedom.

---

[118] *Ibid.*, p. 172.
[119] *Ibid.*, p. 200.

Religion is the discovery of the excess which one must add to any thought, to any action, so that they may remain valuable. It is the discovery of an increase of exigency that no object, no definite good, can satisfy.... It is Maurice Blondel's merit to have shown that not only is man not content with natural goods, but that it is impossible for him to be satisfied by them. The reason is that man still meets an element of determination in the best things and in his most perfect inventions. Now, the mind contests any determination; it aspires to Undetermination, it tends towards pure freedom.[120]

Blondel found in the principle of immanence a means to establish a rigorously autonomous philosophy to which the whole field of human expressions is given (not only man's profane behavior but also his religious behavior). He also discovered a way to show the hypothetical necessity of the gratuitous gift of grace liberating freedom in its attempt to realize itself. Likewise, Duméry found in the creative intentionality a way to bridge the gap between consciousness and the world of objects. He does so by reducing everything to the transcendental consciousness and thus making a universal science of meaning possible. At the same time, the fact that the intentionality cannot completely bridge the gap between object and subject leads to the acceptance of an Absolute. The Absolute supports this duality which otherwise would collapse. The principle of immanence, the intentional spirit, reveals then both a privilege and an infirmity. Man creates his world of meaning but he has to do this by putting the things in front of him (ob-jicere); by creating the division of the "Ego cogito cogitatum." This scission can only subsist thanks to the existence of an absolute unity. In this sense, it is correct to say "Surgit intentio, Deus est." [121]

### c. Duméry's Method of Discrimination: Reflective and Critical Analysis

The core of Duméry's theory of knowledge lies in his peculiar understanding of meaning as the mediations by which the pure intentional relation constitutes itself and the world. Man in order to realize himself, to liberate himself, has to create an objective world. He has to bind himself to a system of laws; he has to divide himself in order to reintegrate himself.

The human subject, the finite spirit, cannot subsist without projecting itself; nor think without expressing itself; nor posit itself in existence without originating a mediating world of essences.[122]

[120] Duméry, *Philosophy de la religion*, II, p. 287.
[121] Duméry, *Critique et religion*, p. 175.
[122] *Ibid.*, p. 194.

We recognize in this the Husserlian thesis of the intentionality which sees every meaning as a correlation of object and subject, and the Blondelian thesis that the universe of expression is at the service of the realizing dynamism of freedom. God, who by definition transcends the distinction of essence and existence, escapes this division of object and subject. He, therefore, cannot enter the correlation object-subject; He cannot be reached in the order of knowledge. But God is present at the source of man's being and it is this inexpressible presence which man tries to describe indirectly in an infinite series of objectivations. We have to keep this indirectness constantly in mind so as not to confuse the order of knowledge and the order of life and action. The order of knowledge is mediating and is at the service of the order of action. God is reached for directly in the order of action, but indirectly in the order of knowledge through the representations of Himself. God is more present in the mechanism of representations in "actu exercito" than in the representations proper. On the other hand, man cannot reach for God except by projecting this super objective-subjective presence on the objective-subjective level. So man has to posit and to deny the mediations he uses. The fact that there is always an inadequacy between what man does and what he wants to do, this surplus of exigence is the surest sign of the presence of the Absolute at the heart of consciousness. "Aliquid superest, ergo Deus est." [123]

On account of this *mediation* on the objective level of man's ascent to God, religion as a whole falls under the jurisdiction of the philosophical critique. Religion is the need for the Absolute lived as a tension toward God who is also represented to consciousness under the form of ideas and images taken from objects which reveal God. This necessary detour of objectivation aligns religion with a process of revelation.

> Everything happens as though the subject, in the impossibility to take God himself as an immediate object of knowledge, can only attain Him indirectly, by aiming at certain objects as revealing the Infinite. This surprising paradox accounts for the essence of the religious phenomenon. At the same time, one must maintain that man on the lived level (unreflected or prereflected) reaches for God without any intermediary, but, on the cognitive level (reflected) aims at Him through signs: *per speculum et in aenigmate*.[124]

The purpose of the philosophical critique then is to see whether the representations created by the religious intentionality are coherent among themselves and whether they express faithfully the religious intention. Because the structures of consciousness have value only insofar as they

[123] *Ibid.*, p. 197.
[124] *Ibid.*, p. 202.

manifest the intentionality of which they are the expression, the philosophical critique cannot restrict itself to mere description and has to judge their validity.

The difficult task is to further clarify, if possible, the point where thought restrains itself from touching the Absolute, and the consequences of this for the value of knowledge. If we understand this rightly, then we would say that, according to Duméry, conceptual knowledge has *in itself* no relation to reality. We recognize here the Blondelian thesis that the reflective and ontological level are interdependent yet not confusable. It does not belong to reflection to actualize the aspirations of the spirit. Reflective knowledge has only expressional value and is not an entering into being. The reflective level does not reach God for the same reason, because the conceptual content of our representations are finite creations. When we say that God is good, then we predicate a human goodness of God. But where does this affirmation get its truth? The solution is that *the concepts are true*; i.e., have a relation with reality, *not out of themselves, but because of the dynamism of the human spirit in its search for the Absolute.*

"The mind is, in its depth, exigency of the Absolute." [125] The contents of our concepts are absorbed in this dynamism of the spirit and are transcended and projected toward God. The knowledge of God is thus a projective act by which we, through concepts, tend beyond concepts in virtue of this infinite impulse of the spirit.

It is now clear why Duméry can take the whole universe of the religious discourse and submit it to a thorough critique without endangering the transcendence of the Absolute. His *epistemological instrumentalism* allows him to do this. By a rigorous division of the reflective and the effective order, one has no problem with the transcendence of the Absolute since our concepts have *of themselves* no value of reality. Thus one is reducing the scope of philosophy to the immanent ideal level and widening it most extensively so as to include the entire human universe of representation. The question, however, arises whether in the reduction of the Christian universe of representation to a mystical dynamism (the spirit as exigency of the Absolute wants in final analysis to overcome all expression), one does not destroy religious language by overemphasizing the animating dynamism and underestimating the concepts and images which express it. Indeed the whole problem is to know whether Duméry is correct in placing the apophatic [126] drive of the spirit at the source of

---

[125] *Ibid.*, p. 202.
[126] From the Greek apophasis: denial, refusal. The spirit wanting to joint the Abso-

everything. The ontological imperative (what Blondel calls the necessity to act) he maintains is written in the heart of reflection. But this ontogenic movement seems to result only in mediations continuously to be overcome. Never do we reach reality. We cannot help thinking of Sartre's freedom with its ever-failing attempt to reach itself.

The philosophy of religion will now assume the role of describing and comprehending the religious discourse as a coherent system of ideas and images. It will, on the other hand, determine the ontogenic or realizing value of the representations at the service of freedom, in its process of liberation. "Consciousness is an exigency of self-liberation by means of reflection or action." [127] Accordingly, everything must be judged proportionate to this exigency. The different stages of liberation of the self then become degrees of being and truth. This is the meaning of the varied grades of intentionality which create different noetical levels and which are brought to realization by effective freedom. The diversity of expressive levels introduces the distinction of the variegated steps of consciousness. These levels are hierarchised and are thus different in degree of dignity. This provides us with a criterion of discrimination (hence: method of discrimination). It establishes a scale of values which will enable us to analyze human behavior, to differentiate the function of the levels of consciousness which it encloses when they are effectively lived.

Which are the different stages of consciousness through which man passes? Duméry conceives the human reality as determined by two limits. The inferior one he calls matter, the superior one he calls God. Human reality is in contact with these two limits, both on the level of sensitive life with the inferior limit, and on the ideal level with the superior limit. He immediately solves the difficult problem of the relation between the ideal and the sensible by introducing an intermediate level, namely, the rational. We will not discuss Duméry's anthropology here (cf. Chapter III), we insert this only to explain his distinction between category and scheme which he uses in a technical sense. It refers religion to the scale of noetical levels – to "discriminate" various levels of expression. In order to differentiate the religious structures in relation to the levels of consciousness, it suffices to distinguish between religious structures which express the intelligible conceptually (categories), and those which link imaginatively understanding and sense perception (schemes). Category joins the intelligible and the rational:

---

lute who is "Nihil per excellentiam" (Scotus Erigena), in the end, therefore, refuses all objective expression.
[127] Duméry, *Critique et religion,* p. 206.

From the intelligible reality, it draws the idea which is an a priori of comprehension and evaluation. From the rational, it draws the concept as determination. Those two are interdependent. We do not know any intelligible reality without rational determination, nor an idea without concept. The link of the two in actual consciousness is precisely what we mean by category.[128]

The scheme joins the rational and the sensible.

Mediating link between the rational and the sensible, the scheme draws from the rational the element which structures the images. From the sensible, it draws that which connects things themselves to the concepts; that is to say, that which gives the concepts an objective meaning.[129]

A category is the Cogito present in its determined intention. The scheme is the Cogito present in its concrete perceptions. Since there are no intentions without perceptions and no subjectivity without incarnation, there will be no categories without schemes and vice versa. We will not judge these theoretical distinctions before we have seen their consequences in the critical study of the schemes and categories of Christianity. We will be in a position to judge their value after observing our author apply the threefold reduction: viz., eidetical, transcendental and henological reduction to the universe of the religious discourse.

---

[128] *Ibid.*, pp. 211-212.
[129] *Ibid.*, pp. 212-213.

CHAPTER III

# DUMÉRY'S RELIGIOUS PHILOSOPHY. THE SPIRIT AS CONSTITUTIVE EXIGENCY OF THE ABSOLUTE

There is a spirit in the soul, untouched by time and flesh, flowing from the Spirit, remaining in the Spirit, itself wholly spiritual. In this principle is God, ever verdant, ever flowering in all the joy and glory of his actual Self. Sometimes I have called this principle the Tabernacle of the Soul, sometimes a spiritual Light, anon I say it is a Spark. But now I say that it is more exalted over this and that than the heavens are exalted above the earth. So now I name it in a nobler fashion. It is free of all names and void of all forms. It is one and simple, as God is one and simple, and no one can in any wise behold it.[1]
But how then am I to love God? You must love Him as if He were a non-God, a non-Spirit, a non-Person, a non-Substance; love Him simply as the One, the pure and absolute Unity in which is no trace of duality. And into this One we must let ourselves fall continually from being into non-being. God helps us to do this.[2]

## SECTION I
### TRANSITION FROM METHOD TO DOCTRINE

Duméry dislikes the expression "religious philosophy" because it more or less implies that one can talk about religion outside the framework of a concrete given religion. He prefers, therefore, to call his philosophy a philosophy of religion in the sense of a rational critique of positive religion, namely Catholicism.[3] The fact, however, that he can attempt a critical and judicial description of the whole body of the religious discourse implies, as we have already noticed, a certain particular understanding of human subjectivity, namely, as freedom which realizes itself in and through mediating expressions. Duméry nowhere gives a systematic expo-

---

[1] Meister Eckhart, quoted by Aldous Huxley, *The Perennial Philosophy* (Cleveland: The World Publishing Company, 1962), pp. 16-17.
[2] Dag Hammerskjold, *Markings*, p. 110.
[3] Duméry, *Critique et religion,* p. 8.

sition of his philosophy, but he affirms several times that his philosophy of religion presupposes a philosophy of the subject. "All philosophy of religion presupposes a philosophy of the subject. One must expound unreservedly the philosophy one embraces so as not to deceive anybody – either the reader or oneself." [4] Since Duméry discovers a constitutive presence of the Absolute in the heart of the spirit as exigency of complete undetermination ("the spirit and the Absolute are never disunited"),[5] his philosophy of religion is based upon a certain understanding of this relation between the spirit and the Absolute. At the same time, this makes his philosophy of religion possible and explains the nature of his view of the religious representations of Catholicism. "As for a critique of religion, all depends upon the ideas one has about God and the spirit." [6] Therefore, a study of the notion of the subject *and* the Absolute must precede the study of the positivity of religion, since they constitute the two terms of the theandric relation on which religion is based. It is this conception of the theandric relation which founds the spirit, the exposition of what is irreducible in consciousness and which forms the philosophical basis of Duméry's interpretation of Christianity, which we call his religious philosophy. Man IS exigency of the Absolute (object of religious philosophy) which he projects on things and in history (object of philosophy of religion) in order to join the ground of his being.[7] To understand the nature of these projections and to be able to reduce them to their origin, we must first disclose the nature of that which is irreducible and to which everything else can be reduced. Revelation is the expression of the presence of God in the spirit. The nature of this revelation depends upon the nature of this presence.

Before anthropology, phenomenology, axiology ... can serve to elaborate in detail a philosophy of religion, the apophatic reduction must have displayed the only irreducible element of conscience, namely, the theandric relation which constitutes the foundation of the spirit.[8]

---

[4] *Ibid.*, p. 201.
[5] Duméry, *Philosophie de la religion*, I, p. 5.
[6] *Ibid.*, p. 90.
[7] The object of religious philosophy is the *affirmation* of God present in the spirit's exigency of the Absolute. In this sense, one could say that religious philosophy answers the traditional question: "An Deus sit?" The object of philosophy of religion is the *critical analysis* of the categories and schemes used by the spirit in its ascent to the Absolute. Philosophy of religion comes thus close to the traditional critique of the attributes, the answer to the question: "Quid sit Deus?"
[8] Duméry, *Critique et religion*, p. 228.

It is the particular conception of this theandric relation, of the spirit in its ascent to the Absolute, which allows Duméry to give a universal critique of religious expressions. He adopts the Blondelian insight that what man wants, whether he acknowledges it or not, is the substitution of his will by the divine will. Hence the nature of things in the last analysis, must be a series of *means* which one has to will in order to accomplish one's destiny. Duméry in discussing the range of the philosophical jurisdiction also sees the line of demarcation not so much between faith and reason, between nature and supernature, as between the exigency for the Absolute and its functions of expression. Philosophy as the second reflection [9] does not autonomously treat of reality as such. It stands at the service of living spirituality (first reflection), it has a *mediating* role in building a determinism of coherent ideas which is the series of conditions which the will imposes upon itself in order to realize itself. But as we have previously seen, Duméry makes this mediating character of the idea and of philosophy, which is the science of immanent ideas, more radical. He does so by giving, under the influence of Husserl's discovery of the creativity of the transcendental Cogito, more creativity to the thought immanent in action. "Blondel's position as opposed to Husserl's would be totally valid and complete, if the theory of the auto-constitution of the subject were part of his philosophy." [10] But what in a Husserlian context is only condition of insight becomes in a Blondelian context condition of realization, and is taken up in the dialectic of action seeking self-fulfillment. It is here then that the "volonté voulante" of Blondel and the transcendental Ego of Husserl unite in Plotinus' second hypostasis.[11] Conversely, Blondels' "option" and Husserl's "reduction" are identified with the "conversio" of Plotinus. The spirit becomes the sole mediator between God and things: God creates the spirit and the spirit creates things.

In this manner, Duméry is also able to disengage creativity and atheism, because the creation of the self by the self coincides with the creation of the spirit by God. It suffices to conceive a creative link between the spirit and the intelligible system in which subject and object are contemporary in order to defend the thesis of auto-creation, without having to deny the existence of God. God, in order to create the ideas, created spirits which create the ideas. But this also means that God, in order to become intel-

---

[9] The *first* reflection is thought accompanying living action. Philosophy is the *second* reflection because it is "thématisation" of the reflection present in living action.

[10] Duméry, *Critique et religion,* p. 172.

[11] This will be clarified in Section II, b, of this chapter: "Plotinian Translation and Completion of Husserl's Reductions," pp. 77-82.

ligible, had to create spirits which create significations by turning themselves to Him. Man does not find his ideas and values in God. They are his own creation. But this creation is possible only through the impulse of the mysterious presence of God in man. The reduction or conversion is at the same time a procession. "The divine fecundity is the ascending creation of the spirit through itself; it is the finite's access to the Infinite." [12]

We saw in chapter two how the Blondelian distinction between the prospective knowledge of spontaneous action and the retrospective knowledge of reflection allowed Duméry to find a method with which to subject the whole body of religious expressions to the critique of reason without endangering the transcendence of the religious experience. There is no danger that religious theism will be dissolved and absorbed by reflection if one understands the nature of philosophy as second reflection (living spirituality being the first reflection). Philosophy is only a reflective critique applied to life and can never replace life itself. It is a presumption of life which can never be identified with life. Philosophy then is "the word of life; it is not life itself." [13] This, however, does not mean that concrete human life has no moment of insight and is completely irrational. Human life is self-consciousness – it is thought in action. There is a theoretical moment in action, because man acts according to a certain theory. But this thought, this reflection of action, does not know itself as thought and reflection. It is a reflection which is prereflective. In order to become reflective, in the proper sense of the word, it has to return upon itself. It has to perceive itself in itself, and has to change its attention from the concrete and immediate to the abstract and mediate. These two orders, the speculative one and the concrete one, may never be confounded on penalty of reducing life to thought and vice versa. "Lived experience, whatever it is, is always 'transcendent' to the reflective plane. In this respect religious reality is in the same position as all other 'lived experience.'" [14] So to the extent that one nowhere confounds the reflective level and the level of life, there can be no infringement upon the transcendence of the religious experience. The immediate religious discourse of the living subject and the reflective religious discourse of the philosopher have the same material object. Their difference lies in the modality of the judgment: the latter defines the conditions under which the religious expressions are valid; the former makes the choice and the

[12] Duméry, *The Problem of God*, p. 17.
[13] *Ibid.*, p. 5.
[14] *Ibid.*, p. 11.

concrete engagement. The living subject *affirms* whereas the philosopher seeks for the *affirmable*.

But what is meant by saying that life as such, be it profane or religious, always transcends the order of reflection? Is it not the aim of thought to bring insight into life, to come to grips with reality, to relate itself to life? Duméry certainly does not mean that thought has no relation whatsoever with reality. But he has a special understanding of the relation between thought and reality which allows him to give a universal jurisdiction to reflection without endangering the transcendence of the religious experience. Everywhere in his works he repeats that the spirit *expresses* itself, *incarnates* itself, *realizes* itself, *projects* itself, *manifests* itself. These very terms imply that the real self and its relation to reality is never caught in the objectifying function of thought. These expressions, projections and manifestations which proceed from the spirit, and which therefore form a completely immanent world, enable him, as a philosopher, to envisage a method to treat the whole universe of religious discourse. Only if the subject is creator of his own ideas, only if the ideas are completely immanent in the subject, only if reflective thought as such does not reach transcendent reality, can philosophy be given a universal jurisdiction over all expressions of the religious praxis. If rational thinking is completely captive in an immanent human world, one can understand that, since the religious discourse is also spoken of in this immanent rational language, natural reason has a right of speaking in matters of religion.

Faith is undoubtedly a singular perspective on God, a unique intention. But when it formulates itself, its categories and schemes are taken from a logico-rational context upon which the philosopher has the right to bring a judgment. This is why, even if religious tradition has its own manner of posing God, the philosopher does not exceed his authority by demanding to verify this approach.[15]

Does this mean that we must let the mystics talk about God and that on the rational level we are faced with a complete agnosticism? No. It only says that the living religious intentionality always escapes the closed immanent system of reflective thought and that the inner movement of conversion, by which the living subject tries to join the Absolute, can never be caught by objective reflection. The philosopher has the task of determining the a priori conditions which are required so that the subject can recognize the Absolute in its existence and mystery without falling short of the exigencies of his rational nature. The spiritual act in its ascent to the Absolute can never be inserted in an objective series of ideas.

[15] *Ibid.*, p. 10.

The meaning of the philosophical system, therefore, is to determine the conditions of realization of this spiritual act, not to build an explaining system which would allow consciousness to disappear in the contemplation of its elements. These elements are but the expressions of the act, not the act itself. The act itself is irreducible and is by essence unobjectifiable.

Whether the philosopher is aware of it or not, the notions he connects hold together by means of the living Cogito, and the latter, instead of being a pure form, is an act which expresses itself at different levels. Consequently, philosophy remains the restoration, or the methodical recovery, of an act that transcends its multiple expressions. Philosophy mediatizes this act; it depends on it, it returns to it; it is able neither to supplant it nor to immerse it in an objective series. This is why the philosopher is justified in working for the unification of consciousness, but not for its suppression as act.[16]

We see, then, that the methodological distinction between the prospective and retrospective order which founds Duméry's philosophy of religion, is based upon a special interpretation of the order of reflective thought. It is completely subordinated to the living subject. It is of an instrumental and derived nature and refers to a higher level of spirituality which stands at its origin and utilizes it. On the one hand, Duméry shows that the Absolute is beyond all determination, is transordinal and, on the other hand, that the order of reflective thought is derived. This logically leads to the acceptance of an intermediate and creative level of spirituality: the hidden dynamic source of reflective thought and of the projections expressing consciousness' ascent to the Absolute. This is the heart of Duméry's thought – the point from which his whole philosophy of religion is suspended, namely, the doctrine of the Act-Law, intermediate order between the transordinal One and psycho-empirical consciousness. It is this doctrine of the Act-Law which allows him to establish a universal critique of religion without endangering its transcendental dimension.

Through the mediation of the transcendental Ego or Act-Law, Duméry is able to escape a double objectivism of philosophy which is his main enemy. Objectivism for our author is this "natural" attitude by which one thinks of reaching preexisting objects-in-themselves in things or in God. This attitude destroys human freedom by enslaving it to external data. Freedom, to be creative, cannot be mere ratification of an anterior datum, nor can there be a thing-in-itself which dictates its formula or which imposes its choice. The initiative of the spirit has to remain complete. The *objectivism of an exterior datum* is overcome by

[16] *Ibid.*, p. 30.

accepting the creativity of the transcendental Ego which through the giving intuition objectifies the world; i.e., gives itself an object. The Ego Cogito as pure relational act never reaches a pure object nor a pure idea, they are always the object of an intention. Also the *objectivism of a superior datum,* which imposes itself from above through the acceptance of our ideas and values from the will of God, is overcome; since God is completely beyond all determination, the determinations and orders have to be written on the account of the transcendental consciousness. By bringing the spirit and its constitutional relation with the Absolute to a meta-empirical level which can never be the object of thought but which is that by which there is thought and object, Duméry is able to reconcile theism with existentialism's thesis of the axiogenesis. At the same time a philosophy of religion is possible as rational critique of the mediating expressions which the spiritual act posits in positing itself, through the theurgic presence of the Absolute. The Absolute and the spiritual act belong to a different order and are completely beyond the level of the objectified reality of rational and sensible knowledge. These belong to the natural, intramundane Ego of the constituted psycho-empirical consciousness.

In Section II of this chapter we will treat of the higher level of consciousness where the spirit reveals itself as essential relation with the Absolute. Section III will then describe how this higher consciousness is related to the lower consciousness and to the world.

## SECTION II
## THE IRREDUCIBLE RELATION OF THE SPIRIT WITH GOD

### a. *The God of Living Religion*

Duméry commences his exposition of natural theology by refuting the traditional distinction between the God of the philosophers and the God of the believers. This is completely in accordance with his method which wants to stay as close as possible to the living religious experience. Living spirituality is always first, philosophy is second. This obvious truth, which is taken into account conscientiously, has very important and far-reaching consequences in his attempt to disengage an authentic Absolute. Philosophy, here more than anywhere else, comes after the living experience. When we begin to think about God, the living God is already there, present in the religious life of the Christian West. Western philosophy owes a great deal to Christianity, and it is strange that the more faith and reason refrained from interfering with each other the more vehement became the conflict which finally gave origin to the antithesis of the God of philosophy and the God of revelation. This, Duméry maintains, is due to an incorrect understanding of the distinction between philosophy and religion.

First of all, the philosopher should remember

> that his discipline is only a reflective technique applied to lived experience. He does not supplant the concrete subject, the thinking and acting man. Only the latter is really engaged and brings value into play. Only he does a free act; only he effectively conforms the means at his disposal to the end he pursues.[17]

But if such is the situation, then "the God of the philosophers" can easily be an illusion, since the role of philosophy is not to make ideas, to build a system all its own, but to criticize living spirituality and determine according to what conditions it has value. The affirmation of God must be left to the free and spontaneous consciousness. To philosophy is delegated the role to say how this affirmation is coherent and binding or meaningless and empty. So there is really no place for a God of the philosophers unless one forgets that the idea of God takes origin not in the mind of the reflecting philosopher, but in the heart of the living subject.

Nor is there a God of religion on whom reflection would have no grip. Here the believer is incorrect in thinking that the absoluteness of the object of affirmation is conveyed to the logico-rational tools used for this affirmation. He likes to think that the God he adores idolizes the logical instruments and places them beyond discussion. He erroneously believes that the means of expressing faith transcend the human realm and belong to the divine realm. This can easily lead to an idolatrous attitude by which a particular idea is substituted for the living God and God is forced to serve human ideals and convictions. No idea is more useful to tyrants than the idea of God in order to make the timid and scrupulous respect the order imposed upon them by the whims of authority in order to steal the freedom of man. "Corruptio optimi pessima"; that which can bring man to his highest self-realization, can also lead to his deepest downfall. When God keeps silence, and in a certain sense He always does, one can make Him say anything. (Cf. Sartre.)

This false distinction between a God of philosophy and a God of tradition leads to a misconceived division of the tasks of philosophy and of faith. In this trend of thought to which Duméry is diametrically opposed, philosophy has to prove the existence of God, whereas His nature and

[17] *Ibid.*, p. 5.

intimate being can only be seen through faith. This procedure is valid if one accepts the medieval division of truths of faith and truths of reason and if one concedes that autonomous reason must subject itself to the demands of dogma. Furthermore, it is inconceivable to think that one can affirm the existence of God without saying anything about His nature. Therefore, we have to look for a standpoint which gives all of the religious affirmation at once to reason and to faith. This position can only be found if one understands that the dividing line here does not run between an intelligibility open to reason and another open to the eyes of faith, but between the order of the reflective and the order of the effective. ". . . the line of demarcation passes, not between faith and reason, but rather between *living spirituality and critical reflection.*" [18] Faith stands completely on the side of the concrete living subject who affirms God in his existence and in his mystery. The same reality is completely given to reason but from the viewpoint of critical reflection. St. Bonaventure is thus right in maintaining that in the case of transcendent reality, one has to believe and know at the same time. But he should have maintained this for all of living reality since reflection as such is everywhere unable to perform the realizing option without the intervention of freedom. Does this mean that one has to abolish the distinction between reason and faith? No, but one has to realize that the only valid distinction can be found in abolishing the idea that faith and reason lie in the same path, that faith has to take over where reason abdicates. Faith is on the side of the free choosing subject, whereas reason is on the side of the "époche"-making attitude of critical reflection. The real proof (in the strongest sense of the term) of the existence of God does not belong then to the reflective order.

In fact, philosophy's task is less to prove God than to establish the subject in the rational and moral dispositions through which the notion of the Absolute will prove itself. Or, if philosophy is able to construct the proof of God, it is because God is, from the beginning, immanent to reason and to all the powers of the concrete subject. Criticism only transposes and makes rigorous a norm that *remains implicit but is really operative in all consciousness.*[19]

One cannot thus study the idea of the Absolute without referring continually to the living religious spirituality and without keeping in mind that the real God can never enter any reflective order of explanation. God, therefore, can never be reached as the term of an analytical regression because the effect always remains of the same nature as the cause. If God is an

[18] *Ibid.*, p. 22.
[19] *Ibid.*, p. 24.

explaining principle, He is no God at all, because then He would be immanent to the order He explains.

Now, between an explanatory series and the Absolute, there is the infinite distance from the reflective to the concrete, an impassable distance for any other initiative than that of the acting subject. God remains on the side of life, while objectivist thought would like to place Him on the side of determinations.[20]

The spiritual act, when it reaches out for God, escapes all attempts of reduction and instead of making God into a link of the chain of determinations we see that He is that by which the determinations hold. God cannot be found in the line of essences but only in the line of the determining act which refers to a principle of transdetermination, not of determination, a principle of autoposition not of explanation.

It is here that Duméry departs from the traditional way of thinking on this subject. Without completely disregarding the traditional approach, he points to the dynamism of the spirit in its ascent to the Absolute as that by which the a posteriori arguments have proving value. It has been forgotten too often that what one usually calls "démonstration" is nothing but the projection, under the form of an objective dialectic, of the spirit's actual need of the Absolute, and that this objective reasoning has consequently no proving value of its own. The demonstration ignores several of its operations. It does not justify the consciousness of the finite from whence it starts; nor the coming to the stage of the Infinite where it arrives; nor the necessity to stop there the regression; nor the value of the causality between such heterogeneous terms. The force of the demonstration lies in a previous unreflected affirmation which is not brought to the level of reflection. It is this previous affirmation which Duméry will try to bring to the reflective level by attempting to give an argument which is nothing but the reflective translation of the religious experience in its affirmation of God. It is for this reason that he uses the term "reduction" instead of "demonstration," because his ways of showing and pointing towards the existence of God is but bringing "to light the source of religious conversion and the dynamism that carries the spirit to the threshold of mystical experience." [21] Whereas the objectivistic demonstration followed the series of determinations, the reduction (which is the technical name for the religious conversion) will describe the spiritual act in its need of unity. The reduction does not prove, but "shows" the presence of a transdeterminational force which is not ours at the heart of human freedom. It is this

[20] *Ibid.*, p. 53.
[21] *Ibid.*, p. 63.

presence which never really enters the reflective order of argumentation and yet is the foundation of the argument. The point where the spirit coincides with the Absolute is irreducible and, therefore, we have to say that nobody can effectively reach for the Absolute unless by the Absolute itself. God can never be found at the end of our action unless He is first the efficacious norm of our action. The question about the existence of God presupposes the anteriority of the solution. The intention implies the presence and the essence implies the existence. This is the truth of the ontological argument. The only failure of those who proposed the ontological argument was that they gave no explicit proof that God cannot be enclosed in an objective series of determinations. If they had done this they would have shown convincingly that it is in the power to contest all finiteness, all determination, that the Absolute is implied as pure spontaneity and not in the determinations themselves. This hidden irreducible affirmation of the spirit in exigency of the Absolute in "actu exercito" is what forms the core of the reduction. ". . . the mind has an intrinsic relation to God, a living relation" [22] and consequently ". . . to know God is to know oneself as spirit." [23]

Duméry will thus attempt a technical recapture of the religious attitudes of the concrete subject by means of the phenomenological reduction which he extends by adding a fourth reduction. The reduction is nothing but the spirit's exigency of unity and is, therefore, the best way to respect living spirituality. The reduction, which is the technical name for religious conversion,[24] tries to overcome the different orders by its exigence of

[22] *Ibid.*, p. 101.
[23] *Ibid.*, p. 104. Duméry does not, thereby, reject completely the a posteriori arguments of St. Thomas, for instance, in favor of the a priori arguments. By placing them in a spiritual climate, St. Thomas also implies that the proving value lies deeper in a previous affirmation, which in the medieval world was universally accepted. Gabriel Marcel points towards something similar when, confronted by the fact that these a posteriori arguments are not accepted anymore, while, great minds always considered them valuable, he writes: "N'y a-t-il pas lieu de présumer bien plutôt qu'ils mettaient dans leur argument quelque chose d'essentiel qui n'arrivait pas à passer complètement dans les formules et qu'il s'agirait pour nous d'expliciter au prix d'un effort dont il n'est même pas certain que nous soyons tout à fait capables?" He then pursues the same direction as Duméry by saying that *what* must be shown is simultaneously the force *by which* it can be shown. "On aboutit donc à ce paradoxe que la preuve n'est efficace d'une façon générale que là où à la rigueur on pouvait se passer d'elle: et au contraire, elle apparaîtra presque certainement comme un jeu verbal ou une pétition de principe à celui auquel elle est précisément destinée et qu'il s'agit de convaincre. Disons encore que non seulement la preuve ne peut pas se substituer à la croyance, mais qu'en un sens profond elle la suppose." Gabriel Marcel. *Du refus à l'invocation*, pp. 226-236.
[24] The rapprochement of the Plotinian conversion and the Husserlian reduction is based upon Jean Trouillard's gnoseological interpretation of Plotinus' emanation theory. According to Trouillard, the procession is only cosmogenic in appearance. The coming into existence of the universe is identical with the emergence of thinking. This

unity. It does this, not by founding the superior order upon the inferior, but by discovering the transcendence of the superior order and changing and reversing the perspective – the "natural" attitude about which Husserl talks. To make the final reduction, a great spiritual effort is necessary, and it can only be done by those who "realize" the final reduction in their lives.

One must be ready to challenge all that one has, all that one is, all being, in order to discover the single incontestable that depends only upon itself and whose only foundation is its spontaneity: the Absolute, the One, God. This attitude is so daring that at this point it threatens all objective security. It severely upsets established habits that hesitate to adopt it or even to consider it correct. Of course it is impossible to make it known to those who do not "realize" it themselves; that would be the same as showing colors to a blind man.[25]

The lived reduction of the religious ascent is, as Hammerskjöld says, "A continual allowing oneself to fall into non-being." It is a courageous acceptance of the fact that our representations are in final analysis completely incapable of grasping the reality of God and that hence we have to abandon them. "Perhaps the meaning of faith is to testify that one must transcend all science to approach a state of nescience – a recognition of the mystery." [26] That which reveals the presence of God is not the truth of things as term of an illumination or participation, but the nothingness of things. The strongest manifestation of God lies in His absence. To reduce is to seize the finite, the multiple, the relative as such. The reduction, therefore, is intrinsically apophatic because it reveals that all objective relation with the Absolute is our work.

## b. *Plotinian Translation and Completion of Husserl's Reductions*

One cannot see the relevance of using the reduction in natural theology, unless one keeps in mind that reduction for Duméry means the technical translation of the concrete religious ascent to the Absolute. Through charity, the religious man frees himself of all partiality and overcomes all

---

indeed comes very close to the Husserlian constitution. On the other hand, Ricoeur stresses the ascetical and religious characteristic of the Husserlian reductions. "L'opération principale – ou réduction – est une *conversion* du sujet lui-même qui s'affranchit de la limitation de l'attitude naturelle. Le sujet qui se cachait à lui-même comme partie du monde se découvre comme fondement du monde.... La question de Husserl, selon E. Fink, c'est la question de l'origine du monde; c'est, si l'on veut, la question impliquée dans les mythes, les religions, les théologies, les ontologies." Edmund Husserl, *Idées directrices pour une phénoménologie*, translation and introduction by Paul Ricœur (Paris: Gallimard, 1950), Introduction, pp. xxv-xxvi.

[25] Duméry, *The Problem of God*, p. 57.
[26] Duméry, *La tentation de faire du bien*, p. 28.

limitations and determinations in order to unite himself with his source, which is the pure freedom of God. This religious strife towards the Absolute is thus a real contestation of all being and having, and is therefore a reduction in act. "Charity does *practically* what reduction verifies *critically*." [27] It is at this point that Duméry borrows from Plotinus in saying that the reduction is the expression not merely of the spirit's formal need of unity, but also of its effective need of unification. The spirit is essentially exigency of unity, a dynamism which reveals itself in the formal need of unity of thought. Plotinus' philosophy here plays the same role as Blondel's in that it provides an ontological basis for the phenomenological reductions. But unlike Blondel, Plotinus is able to give an ontological basis for phenomenology in its idealistic form. For Plotinus, the conversion (reduction) discovers itself as a real procession which takes origin in a transdeterminational source whose presence is revealed in the power of contestation of freedom. But one must remember that the Plotinian procession, and this is exactly the point where Plotinus and Husserl converge, is only cosmogenic in appearance. The conversion, according to Jean Trouillard, master of Duméry, is the elaboration of a theory of knowledge which explains the birth of the world at the moment one seizes the birth of thought. The difference, however, between Husserl and Plotinus is that Plotinus sees the productive constitution of the transcendental Ego as an act by which the spirit posits and realizes itself. Furthermore, and this is another difference, this auto-position of the self is made possible ultimately through the presence of the Absolute One in the transcendental Ego.

It is this presence which must be revealed by showing that there is a power of supreme contestation of all multiplicity in man. This power, nevertheless, is not his, since man is not supreme unity even at the peak of unity which is the transcendental consciousness. "... everything happens as if the spirit were the One, but the One minus what the spirit itself is, namely, subject-object." [28] Thus the very possibility of making a rigorous reduction is what proves the existence of an Absolute. "God founds his proof in us." [29] Duméry will then seek to free the exigency of unity of all determinations which leads to the One. In order to question this procedure, one would have to prove that this need of unity of the spirit is not real. But this would be contrary to the most fundamental characteristic of the spirit. "... to think, to act, is always to unify. It is

[27] Duméry, *The Problem of God*, p. 62.
[28] *Ibid.*, p. 58.
[29] *Ibid.*

only a matter of knowing how far, by right, the unifying impulse goes." [30] Let us now see how, according to Duméry, the affirmation of God in his pure unity terminates legitimately the exigency of unification of the spiritual act; also, how a power of infinite contestation is present in man without being identifiable with man.

The spirit as exigency of unity first of all reduces, that is, unifies the mere particular facts to general essences by dropping all reference to the individual and particular. The *eidetic reduction* eliminates all elements of fact in order to consider only the objective essences. By the first reduction phenomenology tries to grasp the facts of consciousness not as empirical events which are external or internal, but as essences which are characterized by necessity and universality. But we have to go further. The spirit in its search for underlying unity discovers that the multiplicity of essences and eidetic regions are significations which refer to a subject of which they are the intentions. They appear as the intentional correlate of the Ego. In the *transcendental reduction,* then, phenomena are freed from all transphenomenal elements, thus leaving us with what is "absolutely given." What remains is on the one hand consciousness as pure point of reference of the intentionality, and on the other hand the object which has no existence other than its intentional given-ness to the subject. The movement of reduction has here reached pure consciousness for which the world does not appear any more as something there and the self over against it as a certain part of it, but consciousness as pure, non-substantial, intentional relation. The transcendental reduction disengages a subject which is at the source of both the objects and the psycho-empirical subject. It discovers that the meaning of the world can only be understood by seeing that the meaning is given by this higher consciousness, which is essentially a "look" upon the world. This reduction in moving away from the world of the natural attitude is at the same time a moving towards that which is really real, namely, transcendental consciousness. The phenomenological reduction is thus more than a mere withdrawal from the world in order to discover the relation man-world. It is also the discovery of the spirit on a higher level of consciousness. This pure relation to the world is not something which is undergone, but is an act of this higher consciousness. It is necessary again, therefore, to penetrate more deeply to the discovery of this transcendental consciousness as constituting freedom: the *constitutive reduction.* Transcendental consciousness has to be creative, has to be an intuition which gives itself its objects; otherwise the search of an absolute indubitable which is the aim of the reduction cannot come to an end. The pure Ego does not discover itself only as a locus of intentions, but it seizes itself immediately as productive. "When presented with the products of thought, reduction immediately interprets thought as productive. . . ." [31] Husserl himself was hesitant on this point, although he suggested that there are three hierarchical concepts of intentionality: the intentionality of psychological receptivity (which corresponds to the eidetic reduction), the intentionality of the correlation noema-noesis (with the transcendental reduction), and the productive and creative constitution. Duméry immediately sees transcendental consciousness as creative and therefore brings the constitutive and transcendental intentionality together in his notion of the intelligible, where the Act-Law operates. "The phenomenological reduction is the realization of the subordination of the essences to the act which mediatizes itself by them, expresses itself in them and reconquers itself through them." [32]

The movement of reduction has brought us, so far, to the discovery of the psychological consciousness which corresponds to the empirico-psychological level of consciousness and to the disengagement of a meta-empirical (transcendental) consciousness which is the level of transcendental creative intentionality. They correspond to the two lower hypostases of the Plotinian universe: the empirical consciousness and the metaphysical consciousness. Human consciousness in its normal state is related to the outside world. In Husserlian terms, it sees itself as part of the world, a relatedness which is not an independent ruling, but rather a being subjected to it. In the "natural attitude" we naively believe that our concepts are copies of an independent reality-out-there. But in human consciousness there is also a sphere which has no relation to this outside world, or better a relation which is not undergone but which constitutes the world of meaning. This metaphysical or inner consciousness, according to Plotinus, is the experience of freedom and independence from the outside world. Duméry adopts this view: "In our opinion, the transcendental Ego is less a withdrawal from the world than the superior level of consciousness engaged in the world. The constituting freedom emerges from this level." [33] The similarity between the Plotinian universe and Duméry's interpretation of Husserl is clear. At the origin of Plotinus' philosophy also lies this double insight of the two levels of consciousness and the relation between them. The first insight is the conception of the outside world as a manifestation of an inner principle and the second is

[30] *Ibid.*, p. 69.
[31] *Ibid.*, p. 52.
[32] Duméry, *Critique et religion*, p. 147.
[33] *Ibid.*, p. 146.

the experience of an inward ascent [34] which can be carried out in consciousness and which creates an autonomous viewpoint for the evaluation of the outside world.[35]

Having reached the level of constitutive creation, the reductional movement of unification still discovers a residue of receptivity, of dependence and multiplicity. Hence, Duméry finds it necessary to add a final reduction in order to bring the spirit's need of unity to fulfillment, namely, the henological reduction. The transcendental level of consciousness cannot terminate the spirit's ascent to unity since there is still the duality of thought and being and the consequent intersubjective and interobjective multiplicity of a community of spirits and a system of ideas. On the level of psychological intentionality, we find a plurality of subjects and of systems of determinations. This plurality and duplicity would be completely illusory if it were reduced to the unity of an impersonal transcendental principle. They would only be "modi" of expressions of the transcendental consciousness and would not form a real plurality in which the terms have a certain subsistence. This is clearly contrary to what experience teaches us. We see that there can be no spiritual activity without position and opposition, without determination and negation, and finally without a determination and a determining factor. Furthermore, there is no determination without a system of determinations, since every objective determination exists only through negation which calls for its opposite and so on, until in final analysis every determination implies the whole ideal system. Since every determination calls for a determining act, systems of determinations call for a plurality of determining principles. This duality and plurality of systems of determination and of determining principles must be placed on the level of transcendental consciousness since the psychological is nothing without the transcendental. The result is that there is no "Ego transcendentale" but an "Ego *collegiale* transcendentale." Transcendental intentionality no longer says *I*,

---

[34] Corresponding to these two ways of knowledge, there are two doctrines which we may call the roots of Plotinus' philosophy, viz. the doctrine of "eidos" and "hulè," and the doctrine of "chorizein tèn psychèn apo tou somatos." Plotinus, *Enneads,* trans. Stephen MacKenna (3rd ed., revised by B. S. Page; New York: Pantheon Books, Inc.), I, pp. 1-3.

[35] We have to remember that Duméry follows Trouillard's interpretation of Plotinus, according to which the hypostases are not to be understood as ontological levels but as noetic levels. Every human being possesses three levels: the intelligible, the rational and the sensible. The first one corresponds to the Intelligence of Plotinus, the other two form the empirical consciousness, viz. the Soul. Man can identify himself freely with each of these levels because these levels are an orientation, an attitude, a quality of affirmation. But as long as consciousness did not radically question itself, it remains one order, one noetic level ... The ecstasy, which is the term of the soul's radical question-

but *We*, although the plural must be attributed to each singular." [36] The transcendental level is thus indeed the "one and multiple," the second hypostasis of Plotinus. It is a systematization of diverse determinations and community of a plurality of determining principles. It is multiplicity and unity of a plurality of subjects and essences.[37]

The transcendental Ego cannot satisfy the spirit's radical need of unity, because it is paradoxically one and double, singular and plural. When we trace the spirit's ascent to rigorous unity, we find that, by bracketing all order of determination and the multiplicity of determining principles, it reaches a power of pure spontaneity at the heart of freedom. It is here that the real nature of freedom as pure undetermination is revealed. A power which reduces all determinations without being able to escape all determinations must, therefore, be rooted in a transdeterminational force of an Absolute ONE, which is beyond being a thought.

"Cogito, ergo sum; liber sum, Deus est," would be the formula for exhibiting the irreducibility of the One. The proof by freedom, or by the exigency for unity that constitutes the dynamism of the free act, would be the application, pure and simple, of the reductive procedure.[30]

### c. *Nature of the Relation between the Absolute One and the Spirit*

The important point is that God is thus not an order, but that by which the orders exist. The reduction itself proves that essence and existence have to be overcome in virtue of a transordinal force which is present in the Cogito and which nevertheless cannot be its own since the Cogito cannot completely escape all order and determinations. It is at this point of contact with the Absolute that the intelligible and being appear. Through thinking, the Ego creates the original gap and brings negativity between itself and the ideas and creates as such subject and object, thought and being. They are equally primordial, they are the primal duality: thought makes being subsist by thinking it; and being, as object of thought, makes thought exist.[39] Thought and being co-exist, therefore neither one can be the originating unity. There can be no transition from the One to the level of thought and being because there can be no transition from that which is simple to that which is composed. There is no place for participation by the inferior in the superior. It is here that

---

ing itself, is less an order than the source of all orders. It is preceded by the three noetic levels of contemplative intuition, discursive reason and animal psychism. Jean Trouillard, *La purification plotinienne* (Paris: Presses Universitaires de France, 1955), p. 7.
[36] Duméry, *The Problem of God*, p. 46.
[37] *Ibid.*, p. 47.
[38] *Ibid.*, p. 50.

the fundamental difference between ontology and henology becomes apparent.

The spirit *is* an intrinsically living relation with the Absolute and as such the Absolute is present *in consciousness*. The activity of the spirit reveals a transdeterminational force at work in itself, whereby every determination has to be transcended. It is this transdeterminational force which deserves the name of Absolute. This also means then that the Absolute is completely beyond all determination, that there can be no transition from our order to a transcendental order. "From God to the intelligible there is no transmission of essences, but only derivation of energy...." [40] God does not belong to the realm of created orders, and this is exactly the reason why He can be source of all orders. In an ontology, one maintains that the inferior has something of what the superior IS. In a henology one maintains that the superior gives the inferior the force to be what the superior IS NOT. The One gives only the aptitude to "give oneself being," that is, to posit oneself.

> The One cannot give derived spirituality, of any sort whatever, something of what he is, because he has nothing and is not. The One can only give it the radical aptitude to give being to itself; in other words, to pose itself, to make itself. In this sense, the One creates by rendering self-position possible and participation impossible.[41]

The choice of the Absolute transordinal One is of immeasurable importance for the understanding of Duméry's critique of religion. If no participation whatsoever, no *analogia entis,* is possible between the source of everything and what is derived, then revelation, if such a thing exists, cannot be understood in terms of participation either.[42] If there is no *analogia entis,* then there cannot be an *analogia verbi* either, that is, the word of God in revelation, if there is one, will also have no analogical value. If no transcendent reality of the Absolute can be proven by philosophy, only the immanent transdeterminational *force in consciousness* is given, then the Absolute, in the supposition that He did speak, can only speak through the significations created by the spirit's dynamism in its ascent to the Absolute. The word of God can only be the discourse by which the spirit speaks the presence of the Absolute in itself and which it reaches for in itself. This brings up the very serious question whether this does not identify the giving of the Absolute itself, in a hypothetical

---

[39] Plotinus, *Enneads*, V, pp. 1-4.
[40] Duméry, *The Problem of God*, p. 94.
[41] *Ibid.*, p. 87.
[42] *Ibid.*, p. 89.

revelation, with the exigency of unity which the Absolute creates in man and by which his presence is indicated. "In short, the spirit is relation to God; spiritual life is the concrete 'exercise' of this relation." [43]

This also explains Duméry's insistence upon the falsity of the distinction between a God of philosophy and a God of religion. His fundamental distinction between prospective and retrospective knowledge refuses to give reality to the God of philosophy. This distinction reveals his position on the central problem of philosophy, namely the relation between thought and reality, between the real and the ideal. It seems to us that Duméry in adopting the Blondelian distinction between the reflective and the effective order has rigorized it to such an extent that reflective thought is *pure* critique of spontaneous action, a retrospective recapture which is unable to construct anything. Not even the existence of God can be proven before the option. Conversely, he has stressed greatly the creativity of Blondel's action by transforming it into the transcendental Ego, creator of ideas and values. Only spontaneous thought then reaches God. Everything on the level of reflection is mediating this dynamism of the spirit and has therefore *in itself* no reality-meaning. The real proof for the existence of God, then, is not to be found on the reflective level, but in a non-discursive experience of a theurgic presence in the act of freedom.

> This is why, concerning the Absolute, philosophy has no other task than to criticize *the way thought* (or living spirituality) *proceeds when it wants to prove* the existence of God to itself.[44]

For this reason, Duméry's argument comes very close to the ontological argument. Not that he wants to extract the existence of God from the essence of God, for this is only a caricature of the ontological argument. But the fact that God proves his own existence, that one can only think of God if one receives the force to do so from God Himself.

In accordance with this fundamental epistemological position, Duméry must place the authentic Absolute on the side of spontaneous thought and action, which is the dynamism of the spirit, and conceive of God as that which is most intimate to the self and not as an object of the self. God manifests Himself in the impetus by which the subject posits itself in creating its determinations. He never is an object in front of us.

> God is less in front of us, even as a horizon that extends beyond us, than in us, as a unity richer than we can grasp ... He is an *Absolute of exigency*, not the *object* of an exigency for the Absolute.[45]

---

[43] *Ibid.*, p. 115.
[44] *Ibid.*, p. 61.
[45] *Ibid.*, p. 113.

But this means that just as the spiritual act can never be objectified, although it has to objectify in order to exist, the Absolute who is pure act has to be beyond all objectivation, He is the transordinal One. Reflective thought never reaches reality as "sein an sich," because true reality for Duméry is the spirit in its constitutive relation with the Absolute. This brings us to a hyper-ontology,[46] where neither being nor thought can be first, but where being and thought are posited by the spirit in its dynamic relation with the Absolute. The One is no-thing of what is derived from it; it only gives the *energy* so that the spirit may give itself *being*.[47]

Thus at the core of Duméry's philosophy, we find the dynamism of the spirit which in contesting all determinations reveals the presence of a transdeterminational force beyond all determinations and which is the source of man's spiritual energy. This spiritual dynamism projects this presence in creating determinations as expressions of the spirit's inexpressible need of unity. The expressions, therefore, must constantly be criticized in virtue of what they should faithfully express, namely, the spirit's urge to join the inaccessible One. This fundamental thesis of the mind's relation to God and of the mind's relation to its expressions forms the very heart of Duméry's religious philosophy and the foundation of his philosophy of religion. His philosophy of religion will test the religious categories and schemes on their faithfulness to the religious intentionality of the spirit's ascent to the One. This judgment is what makes his philosophy of religion more than a mere phenomenological description.

Duméry's trend of thought can be summarized as follows. The erroneous distinction between a God of philosophy and a God of religion is the result of not keeping philosophy within the limits of critical and reflective description of spontaneous life. The religious ascent to God appears, when translated into technical terms of rational critique, as the search for an Absolute One. This Absolute One can only be discovered beyond all determinations and is discovered as such in freedom's claim for unity. But since the Absolute is the Transordinal, it cannot create things; it only creates the spirit. In opposition to an ontology of participation where the creature imitates that which God already infinitely is, the henology of procession maintains that the spirit under the influence of a Divine impulse creates radically new orders. The religious discourse is such an order and can therefore be subjected to the critique of reflective thought. Before progressing to the critique of the religious expressions, however, let us

---

[46] *Ibid.*, p. 93.
[47] *Ibid.*, p. 95.

first expound Duméry's theory of the mind's relation with these expressions, namely the doctrine of the Act-Law.

## SECTION III
## THE SPRIT AS CREATOR OF THE WORLD OF DETERMINATIONS. THE THEORY OF THE ACT-LAW

*a. The Spirit as Correlation of Freedom and Order*

Having studied the spirit in its constitutive relation with the One, we now proceed to expound Duméry's doctrine of the spirit's relation with the inferior degrees. As a result of Husserls' transcendental reduction, we saw that consciousness must be conceived essentially as a function of intentionality; it has no substantial content. The different Ego-substances, for instance the Ego-form and the Ego-person, must be surpassed. They are still conceptions of consciousness taken from the standpoint of the "natural attitude" for which the world is still divided in an objective and subjective field and which, therefore, necessarily leads either to psychologism or to empiricism. The naive natural attitude has not de-objectified, de-realized the world and consciousness. It can therefore never come to a correct understanding of the genesis of meaning.

When the word being pretends to reflect factual existence, it indicates one has made a grammatical error. One has taken as noun (and finally as substance) that which has to remain a verb; and remaining a verb serves essentially as a relation.[48]

The discovery of the primitive consciousness as pure indivisible subject-object relation is the first condition of a sound philosophy. "Philosophical soundness is conditioned by the discovery of the transcendental Ego." [1]

Once we accept that the known object is not a thing in consciousness, but consciousness of something, and that consciousness, therefore, has to be conceived as constituting the object as signification, then consciousness becomes an "efficacious look" ("une visée efficace"), without any substantial content. There is no independent world of objects, nor an independent consciousness confronting this world of objects. "There are only intentioned objects because there is no consciousness but objectifying consciousness." [2] The intentional look is an act, a relation, void of any

---

[48] Duméry, *Philosophie de la religion*, I, p. 21.
[49] *Ibid.*, p. 28.
[50] *Ibid.*, p. 41.

substantial content, an attitude in virtue of which everything acquires meaning. "Man is essentially that being through whom there is a problem of being. He creates the significations and values." [3] Consciousness conceived as intentional relation explains the fundamental antinomy of a being which is in things so as to be absent from them and which absents itself in order to remain in them. To exist is to win in losing without completely losing and to lose in winning without completely winning. Everything starts from the fact that we stick ("nous collons") to things. If consciousness adhered absolutely to things, we would not exist any more than the color on the wall, and if consciousness did not adhere at all to things, we would not exist any more than a dream.[52]

This peculiar way of consciousness – to be present to itself in and through an absence – is best expressed by seeing consciousness as negativity. Consciousness is negation of itself in the affirmation of the other-than-consciousness. Thought and thinking are not identical, yet they exist in referring to each other. *What* I think reveals itself in something other than itself, namely, the act of thinking, and conversely, the act of thinking reveals itself in something which it is not, namely that which is thought. When I say, "It is beautiful weather," then these words have no reality nor presence unless they refer to the reality of the clear sky, consequently, by negating themselves (i.e., the words). On the other hand, I cannot reveal the clearness of the sky unless I make it appear in its absence in something which it is not, namely, my words. This presence as negativity, this way of being in things in order to absent oneself from them and of being absent in order to remain with them, is identified by contemporary existential phenomenology with the experience of time. Human consciousness *is* temporality. Time is the experience of presence. This process by which consciousness is at the same time one with itself and scattered is the experience of the transit of time: a unity which exists in a passage. Our being itself is this passage, which cannot accomplish itself but in "tasks" – partial intentionalities which condemn man to a continual transit. "Time," thus writes A. de Waelhens, "is really the subject rising into reality and in it achieving itself. Time is the emergency of negativity in the heart of things. As has been said: 'The subject is time and time is the subject. Time is a person.'" [53]

Duméry disagrees with this thesis of the philosophies of finitude, for he does not want to identify consciousness as such with time. Tempo-

[51] *Ibid.*
[52] Alphonse de Waelhens, *La philosophie et les expériences naturelles* (La Haye: Martinus Nijhoff, 1961), p. 181.
[53] *Ibid.*, p. 183.

ralization is the result of a consciousness which becomes reflective, which becomes knowledge of a consciousness which is anterior or past. By reflecting, consciousness recuperates that which is anterior and thus distinguishes it from what is present and yet links it to what is present. "Reflective conduct is, therefore, the result of a temporalizing Cogito." [54] But this temporalizing and temporal Cogito does not cover the whole reality of the human Cogito. There is still the unreflective realm of the synthetic prospection which is beyond the analytic retrospection. We see here again how our author stresses the atemporality and creativity of the Blondelian "volonté voulante" and the Husserlian transcendental Cogito and at the same time weakens the constructive element of reflection.[55] This leads to his theory of the eternal, creative, transcendental Ego. On the one hand we saw in his natural theology that all determinations must be eliminated from the Absolute, on the other hand we saw that consciousness must be conceived as an unreflective intentional relation and a derived temporalizing reflection. Neither from above nor from below do pre-existing determinations enter the mind. Therefore, the giving of meaning has to be inserted in prereflective consciousness: "it takes place in the direct operation; it escapes reflection which inserts between the Ego and its operation the span from the past to the present, from what is effected to the one who effects." [56]

This pure consciousness, disengaged by the phenomenological reduction or conversion, and beyond psychological consciousness, Duméry calls Act-Law; Act: because this transcendental or intelligible Ego is creative; Law: because it constitutes the first *order*, since the One is not an order but that by which all orders exist. It is the fruit of the processive motion of the One. But since the One is indetermination, there can be no participation in his determinations and, therefore, being cannot receive its being from the One. It has to give itself its own being. An echo of the Sartrian objections against a God creator resounds here:

> Absolute simplicity, pure spontaneity, is uprising indetermination. It does not use any pre-existing matter as does the artisan; it does not even act according to a directive idea as does the artist; it does not preconceive and execute an architectural plan.[57]

Creating according to preconceived ideas is unacceptable because it implies that the essence precedes the existence.[58] The Transcendental Ego

---

[54] Duméry, *Philosophie de la religion*, I, p. 42.
[55] *Ibid.*, p. 43.
[56] *Ibid.*, p. 45.
[57] *Ibid.*, p. 48. Cf. Sartre's objection against a God creator.
[58] "Lorsque nous concevons un Dieu créateur, ce Dieu est assimilé la plupart du

is thus act, auto-position instead of participation. But in this necessity to create itself lies the necessity to create an order. The Transcendental Ego is *order,* in other words, the Act-Law posits itself by inventing its essence, by creating the order of being. Proceeding from the One, the spirit posits itself as a determined order of return-to-the One. It has to use the mediations in order to make its conversion an original recapture of the energy given to it by the One. These mediations are interior to the Act-Law and escape the psychological consciousness. On the other hand, one must not think that these mediations exist in an intelligible space – a Platonic realm of Ideas existing above the real consciousness. They exist in the Cogito itself but on the transcendental level, prior to all self-consciousness. Neither must a distinction be made here between an axiological and a gnoseological point of view. The spirit continually unites values and ideas.

The Act-Law manifests itself in four efforts of conversion, namely: mathematics, esthetics, ethics and religion. But the expressions which prove its presence on the psycho-empirical level are only rational and symbolic transcriptions of the original attitudes and functions.

> The Act-Law engages and mediatizes itself on the most profound and radical level of consciousness. It never exposes itself. We only perceive it through the veil of discursive expressions, often very confused. They form an amalgamation of fragments of intuition, of more or less coordinated reflection, of non-verified empirical observations. In this way, the Act-Law veils and unveils itself in its search for expression.[59]

But on the other hand the intelligible does not realize itself outside of these expressions. This conscious specification happens on two levels: first, the specification of ideas and values as they are thought and lived directly; secondly, when they are understood in a critical systematization. In actual practice one could identify, making abstraction from the categories and schemes which incarnate all determinations, the level of intelligible creation with the level of living specification as found in the prereflective Cogito.[60] The passage from this prereflective specification to the methodical and reflective systematization constitutes philosophical con-

---

temps à un artisan supérieur... Ainsi, le concept d'homme, dans l'esprit de Dieu, est assimilable au concept de coupe-papier dans l'esprit de l'industriel; et Dieu produit l'homme suivant des techniques et une conception, exactement comme l'artisan fabrique un coupe-papier suivant une définition et une technique." Sartre, *L'Existentialisme est un humanisme,* pp. 19-20.

[59] Duméry, *Philosophie de la religion,* I, p. 51.

[60] *Ibid.,* p. 52. Duméry distinguishes between the supra-conscious level of the creative Act-Law and the level of *self*-consciousness. This "self" should not mislead us into thinking that we are on the level of philosophical reflection. We know, he makes the distinction between a first and a second reflection. The first one is "unreflective." He therefore can identify the level of the Act-Law with the first reflection.

sciousness. Mathematics, esthetics, ethics and theology are essentially prospective disciplines, which means that they are not constructed from the standpoint of transcendental consciousness and consequently are based upon a certain objectivation. Reflection in the strict sense of the word is only found on the philosophical level. But it is at the service of the living consciousness and must, therefore, rather than construct a system, work at the purification of the self by retracing the living intentions in the different levels of expression. Doing this, reflection reveals that the ideas and values are not objects, but the objectivation of a fundamental attitude of the spirit applied to an empirical datum. "One must see in ideas and values, not absolute entities, but mediating principles or subordinated norms." [61]

The creation of essences and norms will not lead to anarchy and relativism, because the projection of the essences is the primary expression of the spirit's intrinsic relation with the Absolute. The essences express the necessary relation of the subject with the Absolute: *to be its own norm means to mediate its union with the Absolute.* The more the subject is faithful to itself the more it will realize itself, and this faithfulness is stricter than any extrinsic norm. "The foundation of the objectivity of essences is the intrinsic relation of the spirit to the Absolute; a relation which has for its first expression the projection (or creation) of essences." [62] The error lies more in not recognizing the true nature of the ideas and values than in the refusal to recognize them. By adhering to the lower levels of expression and reverting them into absolute things, the subject never comes to discover the real meaning of the ideas and values. The lower levels are only inverted expressions. Everything must be understood from the viewpoint of transcendental consciousness. One has to see how its formations are the mediations through which the essential relation with the Absolute overcomes the essential limitation which is an a priori condition of the procession.

Duméry will now approach some of the most controversial topics of contemporary philosophy with his theory of the Act-Law: viz., intersubjectivity, freedom and temporality. Here, he will clarify his understanding of the relation between the Act-Law and the psyche. But since we have already indicated above how intersubjectivity must be founded on the transcendental level (cf. Chapter III, Section II), we will here only treat of the two latter ones.

[61] *Ibid.*, p. 53.
[62] *Ibid.*, p. 54.

## b. *Description of the Relation between the Act-Law and the Psyche: Freedom and Determinism, Eternity and Time*

The most important distinction in Duméry's philosophy is the one between the natural intramundane Ego and the transcendental supramundane Ego. The first is receptive and constituted. It undergoes its own ideas and values because its essential characteristic is to alienate itself in an inverted order of expression. Contrarily, the transcendental consciousness knows itself as creator of these determinations in reducing to pure intentional relations what the natural Ego naively thought to register as already there. This means that freedom is installed in the heart of determinism as its source, instead of in the gaps of determinism as that which escapes it. All determinism is subsequent and not antecedent to freedom. "While existence grounds essence and act grounds law, while choice is fundamental (initial and constituting), the determinisms are only subsequent and derived." [63] There is no determinism without determining freedom; there is no order without an ordering principle; there is no necessity without freedom. So instead of endangering freedom, determinism refers and supposes it. To accept an objective determinism chosen by a freedom of indifference or a forcing necessity ratified by freedom would mean to accept an order without ordering principle. Here again it is a matter of raising the philosophical critique to the level of the transcendental consciousness. Then one discovers that an objective indifferentism or an objective necessitarianism with which freedom would be faced is nothing but an ambiguity resulting from the natural attitude. One acts as if the psychological consciousness were the whole consciousness, or as if the psycho-empirical expression could be substituted for the free initiative of the intelligible act. A freedom of indifference results from identifying freedom with psychological deliberation, and a freedom of ratification results from hardening certain principles of experience into blind absolute necessities. The freedom of ratification is based on a scientific attitude which forgets that the experimental structures of interrogation belong to man himself. The scientist has concern only for a determinism which is his work, or is faced with some unclassifiable phenomena. As for the neutral possibles or contingencies on which the freedom of indifference would be based, one has to say that they are nothing but hypostasized fictions. They designate nothing concrete. This view is in the final analysis based upon the henological Absolute. The theory of the One repudiates all virtual and actualizable possibles (the One is beyond all essences),

---

[63] *Ibid.*, p. 59.

whereas the Act-Law has an essence only through auto-position. Therefore:

> Every possible is realized, for every existence grants to itself the essence that it needs in order to be that which it is. In a word, the Act-Law founds the totality of that which it is or will be, of that which it does or will do. Only "chronomorphisms" can abuse the "natural" man on this point.[64]

Duméry contends there is nothing alogical and if the determinisms have gaps this is due to the law of expression by which the determining principle has to objectify and thereby strengthen the opposition subject-object, and not due to the reality as such. Therefore, nothing allows man to give up his free and responsible initiative.

> There is no way, therefore, to set down the burden of freedom. Neither indifference nor resignation will be a motive for laying it aside. There is only a suspect and blameworthy neutrality, only a deceitful and artificial resignation. That is, freedom bears an inadmissible dignity which even reaches to the core of bad faith, error, or one's failings. It has the fullness and intensity of self-grounding; it is noetic and axiological creativity; it is limited by nothing since even its failures presuppose that it has charge of itself, even in renouncing itself.[65]

Duméry justifies the obvious limitations of freedom by referring to the expressive character of the human spirit, in which the fundamental ambiguity of human existence is revealed. The Act-Law is not "aseitas"; it is simultaneously position of the self and position of laws. If there are no determinations without a determining principle, neither can there be a determining principle without determinations. The Act-Law, in positing itself, posits the intramundane Ego whose role it is to manifest the Act-Law and by so doing to awaken the spirit to itself. But this awakening of the spirit lies in assuming all these structures, to discover the psyche and its objects as inverted expressions of the creative freedom of the Act-Law.

> The human condition is recognized in its ambiguity: the menace of facticity, the precariousness of a subjectivity, which cannot ground itself without creating its existence, but which remains exposed to lassitude and torpor to the extent sometimes of chaining itself to its past rather than constructing its future.[66]

---

[64] *Ibid.*, p. 62. Duméry makes a distinction here between the possibles or contingencies and what he calls the possibilities. The latter are the tasks presented to freedom by the imagination which is "un irréalisant efficace" which suspends spontaneous thought and leads to the discovery of freedom.

[65] *Ibid.*, p. 64.

[66] *Ibid.*, p. 69.

The necessity of the detour of expression thus constitutes freedom's fundamental limitation and introduces the notion of receptivity, a receptivity which the Act-Law has to give itself. We will elaborate on the nature of this receptivity of the external world in the next section.

It is hardly necessary to repeat that the Act-Law as creative freedom is not only required to discard all enslaving objectivism of an anterior datum, but also to do away with all objectivism of a superior datum. The autonomy of the transcendental subject imposes itself not only as the result of the constitutive reduction, but also in virtue of the authentic conception of the Absolute. "... the sole means of radically challenging objectivism is to recognize, on one hand, the specificity of a non-hypostasized intelligible order, and on the other hand, the transcendence of an Absolute that is in series with no 'order.' " [67] The creativity of man saves us from projecting our constellation of ideas and values in God and by this from destroying the transcendence of God. Far from leading us to atheism, creativity of the spirit leads us to an authentic theism. "Henology reopens the way to God and dislodges atheistic humanism. Thanks to it, creativity is reintroduced with full rights into the theistic context." [68] Necessity from below and above is thus eliminated and leaves room for a radical human freedom. The only real necessity lies in the spirit's imperative of expression and projection which constitutes a world of objects, in the Husserlian sense, that is, of significations. Because of the fact that the human spirit is an act which has to realize itself – a freedom which has to liberate itself – all determinism and necessity has to be understood as media of realization and liberation.

In such a way that if it is true to say that there is imposed on me, without me and in spite of me, that which enables me to say *me*, it is still more true to affirm that I am not able to receive anything without assuming it (the imposition) and am not able to undergo anything without incorporating myself into it. I cannot lay aside the burden which weighs on me. It is too late. While I resent its discomfort I have already taken it into my account. At the same moment that I ask myself about it, my freedom is awakened. And if it suffers it is an indication that it regards itself as "situating" rather than "situated." The further I go the more are multiplied my duties, and the more does my freedom acquire a sorrowful or courageous lucidity. On the other hand the day when I no longer experience any kind of heaviness will be not a demonstration of liberation but of total alienation. For the freedom of man keeps itself alert when stirred and contradicted ... There is no freedom but liberating freedom.[69]

[67] Duméry, *The Problem of God*, p. 81.
[68] Duméry, *Philosophie de la religion*, I, p. 71, note 1.
[69] Duméry, *Foi et interrogation*, pp. 67-68.

Just as determinism only has consistency in and through freedom, so also time only has meaning in and through eternity. The Act-Law is living eternity, judged and unified temporalization, whereas the psychological ego is eternity made manifest, expressed in time. By eternity is understood the primitive unity by which the spirit unifies and dominates all areas of change. It is the living principle to which all activities can be drawn and saved from disappearing into a solidified soulless past. The spirit as source of permanent actualization, as living recapitulation, as continual rebirth, is in its central point eternity.

It is the unifying unity of which it has need in order to be reborn at each moment from its ashes; or rather, in order to sustain meaning beyond the disconnectedness of discourse and psychological discontinuity. Thus eternity and time, far from excluding one another imply each other; only eternity is temporalizing, only time can succeed in expressing eternity on the level of psycho-empirical consciousness.[76]

Time and eternity are thus correlative terms, one implies the other. Time is that by which the unity of the spirit reveals itself on the psychological level. Without this unifying principle, time would have no substance. Without this central point which recaptures the scattered moments, time would not exist. Sartre in refusing to call freedom living eternity is contradicting himself since his notion of absolute freedom should imply a possible recapture of oneself and everything.

Sartre involves man in time alone which, from that point on, is contradictory since an absolute freedom inserted in a pure duration implies a falling away without a return; this is quite the opposite of perfect and incessant issuing forth.[71]

Time is the phenomenon of eternity. But phenomenon, let us not forget, has to be understood in the Husserlian sense. Usually phenomenon is understood as an inconsistent reflection of a reality, which would mean that Duméry is conceiving history as an illusion from which one has to escape. But phenomenon for Duméry connotes the appearance of meaning (being), its actualization in and through the psychological mediations. Whenever he talks about expression, symbol, manifestation, we should remember the phenomenological implications of these words.

Temporality belongs only to the expressive or symbolizing order; *but this does not mean that it is unreal or inconsistent.* Time is first of all present eternity; it is also manifest eternity; finally it is totalizing eternity.[72]

[70] Duméry, *Philosophie et la religion*, I, p. 73.
[71] Duméry, *Foi et interrogation*, p. 89.
[72] Duméry, *Philosophie de la religion*, I, p. 75.

We wonder, therefore, whether one can accuse Duméry of Docetism if one takes sufficiently into account the phenomenological meaning of the symbolizing role of time. Georges Van Riet nevertheless maintains that Duméry's evaluation of time is Docetic. Van Riet writes:

> Actually time does not have any efficaciousness by itself. Events in their empirical texture have neither meaning nor consequence. Becoming is only the manifestation of the eternal and value-giving fecundity of the Act-Law.[73]

But for Duméry, time and eternity, as we have seen, are correlative terms which cannot be separated; particularly, since eternity has to separate existence in God. Just as God is above the correlation essence-existence, so also He transcends the correlation time-eternity. An absolute eternity is inconceivable; it is always thought of in relation to time. The notion of eternity and time spring from an experience in which we simultaneously envisage our distention and unity. It is impossible, therefore, to consider one of them unrelated to the other.

Neither temporalist nor eternalist, Duméry stands for the indivisibility of the couple time-eternity. The cyclical scheme where everything develops according to the law of eternal return and the linear scheme where all events form a unique and oriented series are both schemes of our imagination and hence do not represent an objective reality. It is important to grasp the intentional nature of history through which it acquires temporal as well as an eternal characteristic. Historicity is the specific human way of existing; it points to the specific human way of creating meaning and signification. It reveals the nature of a being which realizes itself only in and through the realization of a world of significations. Man is freedom which realizes itself in and through determinism; eternity which establishes itself in and through time. It would be wrong, therefore, to hypostasize the second terms since they have value only insofar as they carry the intentional "visée" of the living subject which by nature transcends all its expressions. This is why the cyclical as well as the linear scheme, when considered as objective copies of an existing reality, reveal themselves as ultimately inconsistent. The cyclical scheme is the objectivation of an impersonal and rational order, of a perfect movement. The linear scheme is the objectivation of the individual psychology which uses time as instrument to consecutively order certain events. The linear scheme is thus useful in classifying a certain period of civilization. But one cannot compel it to include time as such, or a prehuman time. The origin as well as the end of time are humanly incon-

---

[73] Georges Van Riet, "Idéalisme et christianisme. A propos de la 'Philosophie de la religion' de M. Henry Duméry," *Revue philosophique de Louvain* (1958), pp. 361-428.

ceivable because they escape the measurement on which scientific representation is based. Time is the form of sensibility and the law of construction, and one cannot find a standpoint from which to capture it.[74] "This is an abuse, this is again beginning to put man in time, rather than time in man; this is one of the most treacherous tricks that language plays on thought." [75] Time, the linear as well as the cyclical scheme, is a means of objectivation. It is that by which the subject perceives, not what is perceived.

Once we have understood the essentially expressive nature of time through a reduction of all chronomorphisms, we are ready to see that time can neither be completely pure becoming with its own empirical efficaciousness, nor a pure becoming without empirical efficaciousness. On the one hand, there is always an original unity necessary to ensure a real continuity, on the other hand a real continuity can only be in time in virtue of an incarnation of an original unity. Eternity, therefore, must be in time, they must form one reality. Only then can we escape the alternative of contingentism and eternalism. Time is neither objective nor subjective; it is signification.

> Time is always more than the palpable stuff of events; it is their meaningful or intelligible web; it is the insertion of unity into diversity, the presence of changing eternity. Thus it is really efficacious, but not by reason of its empirical texture. It unfolds on the phenomenal level the efficaciousness of the eternal Act-Law.[76]

The psychological ego is in time; the intelligible ego judges time. The Act-Law is eternal while the psyche informs the sensible under the sign of time. But this does not mean that the Act-Law and the psyche are two subjects. The Act-Law can only take up its psychological function by unfolding time. The Act-Law does not assume the phenomenon of the psyche accidentally, but by virtue of an intrinsic necessity. The fundamental distention between act and law accounts for the development of the different levels of consciousness. At the summit, there is the undivided presence of transcendental consciousness which provides unity, and at the bottom, the body which is subjected to the injuries of the biological evolution. Temporalization is thus concurrently dependent upon eternity and the body. We can already see how history, being the human creation *par excellence* could be understood as revelation: the place where man speaks about the presence of the Absolute in man. History shows how

---

[74] Duméry, *Philosophie de la religion*, I, p. 95.
[75] *Ibid.*, p. 80.
[76] *Ibid.*, p. 82.

man creates ideas and values in contact with a spatio-temporal world which he gives himself. And when the spirit is understood exigency of the Absolute, then history becomes revelation. This is what the people of Israel have comprehended. The Absolute, being completely transcendent and, therefore, making a speculative revelation impossible, can only reveal itself through a positive revelation. That is, He reveals Himself through the intentionality of history which is the perfect instrument to declare a presence without at the same time objectifying it.

The human dynamic, history, is the only order of reality in which we can express Him (God) in an intentional manner; the only one in which it itself is able to excite, inspire and attract free and responsible intentionalities. Thanks to the process of revelation, Judaism conceives an Absolute which surpasses all expression and which, for that same reason, borrows our expressive ways.[77]

Duméry's religious philosophy is an attempt to translate into a technical, philosophical language the spontaneous thought of the Judeo-Christian religious experience. The central idea of the Judaic religion, on which Christianity is based, is that when it is contradictory for a transcendent God to reveal Himself speculatively, a positive revelation becomes possible. An historical attestation of the Eternal then becomes plausible. God cannot talk in a human fashion; therefore if He speaks He must appropriate our way of talking. But this implies two theses: on the one hand the ineffability of the Absolute and the capacity in man to signify the Eternal in time. Man cannot create the infinite; but if he names the infinite, then it is necessary that the infinite name itself through the mediation of man. "Man becomes the revealer."[78] This was the genius and the special vocation of Judaism to conceive history as the revelation of the transcendent. God can only reveal Himself through his witnesses and, therefore, history rather than nature is the place of revelation. God is never possessed like an object. He is experienced as a presence in man. Now history is the perfect place to harbor the moving presence of God in man because it hides and reveals at the same time, because it does not contain the Absolute in what we see, in what we touch, but in an intentional "visée" expressed in time.

From this standpoint, namely, history seen as the manifestation of the Absolute in time (which was the only concept of history possible for the Jews – there is no such a thing as profane history for him), history becomes

---

[77] Duméry, *La foi n'est pas un cri*. Foi et institution (2d ed.; Paris: Editions du Seuil, 1959), p. 223.
[78] Duméry, *La foi n'est pas un cri*, p. 217.

identified with the process of revelation. History is revelation. "For, finally, if temporality is not referred to the Absolute, there is no more history and no firm orientation for human becoming." [79] We thus see that Duméry's philosophical positions about the relation between time and eternity are indeed the technical translation of his interpretation of the Judeo-Christian religious experience. What is more important, we understand that if revelation is history, if God is the term of an intentional "visée" which man projects and symbolizes in time; if the word of God is a syncopated formula expressing the discourse by which the spirit seeks the presence of the Absolute in itself; then a philosophy of religion which will describe this process of revelation in search for its coherence and which will judge it in virtue of the spirit's exigency of the supra-essential Absolute becomes possible. The nature of the process of revelation justifies the anthropomorphism, the immanentism of the expressions of the intentional "visée" of the Absolute.

Revelation is of a human structure, but from a divine origin, in that it expresses the presence of God in the spirit which speaks this presence.[80]

### c. Empirical Consciousness and Its Universe: Inverted Expressions and Projections of the System of Spirits

Duméry discovers a diversity of levels of consciousness in man, levels which exist between two limits: the upper limit where the spirit reaches for the Absolute, and the lower limit where man meets matter, antithesis of the pure idea. Between these two limits man passes through different levels of consciousness which are different attitudes of affirmation, noetic levels rather than different entities. "Let us remember constantly that the distinction of levels is never equivalent to establishing in consciousness a plurality of subjects." [81] Duméry distinguishes three such levels:

1. The *spiritual level* which is the operative region of the Act-Law, the level of the auto-position or the creation of the ideas and values.

2. The *rational level* which forms the temporal expression of the dynamic relation of the spirit with the Absolute through a constructive (the first reflection or spontaneous spirituality) and a reflective activity (the second reflection or methodical reflection).[82]

3. The *sensible level* which is born through the application of rational activity upon the external world through the mediation of the body. This constitutes the essentially ambiguous level of sensation.

[79] Duméry, *La foi n'est pas un cri*, p. 219.
[80] Duméry, *Philosophie de la religion*, II, p. 277.
[81] *Ibid.*, I, p. 92.
[82] *Ibid.*, pp. 52 and 94.

It is of some interest to observe two other divisions which run through this threefold division of noetic levels. There is first the distinction between the supramundane Ego which is the Act-Law, and the intramundane Ego which encompasses the rational and sensible level. Secondly, there is the distinction between the reflective and unreflective levels. The unreflective level does not mean complete absence of reflection; rather it means only absence of critical systematization. There is a self-consciousness here which is thetic, which is not self-knowledge. We meet here the important distinction between prospective and retrospective activity. By doing this, he grants to philosophy only the power to exercise reflection in the strict sense of the word. The other disciplines constitute a thought immanent in action. The critical method of philosophy is essentially different from the spontaneous method of the other sciences because philosophy uses the reduction, the conversion. Spontaneous consciousness is caught by its object. It considers itself receptive whereas in reality it gives itself receptivity.

The Act-Law gives itself a rational and sensible consciousness. The rational level has no activity which is not applied also to the sensible experience. Here, we approach Duméry's theory concerning sensory knowledge, which, as one might expect, is one of the weakest parts of his philosophy. Seeing the universe as a descending procession created by the Act-Law in its essential relation with the One, he has some difficulty in reconciling the receptivity of sense-knowledge with the creativity of the spirit. At this point, we discover that Duméry's philosophy, which he calls "a spiritual realism founded on the relationship of the spirit to God," [83] is actually a kind of idealism. The idealism we encounter here is not a subjective idealism of the individual consciousness, nor a transcendental idealism that leaves room for a noumenal world, but what has been called "an idealism of signification." [84] (Professor Dondeyne of Louvain). The identification of philosophy as radical thinking with phenomenology implies that the phenomenon, "that-which-is-for-us," is the only meaning of being. "That which is not for us is not." [85] This identification pushed to its extreme results in an idealism where *esse est percipi*, but Duméry seems to accept a certain transphenomenal foundation, which is not a noumenal world, but something against which one collides. He does not explain what this transphenomenal reality means and many texts imply

[83] Duméry, *La foi n'est pas un cri*, p. 233.
[84] Albert Dondeyne, *Foi chrétienne et pensée contemporaine* (3d ed.; Louvain: Desclee-De Brouwer, 1961), p. 102.
[85] Duméry, *Philosophie de la religion*, I, p. 106.
[86] *Ibid.*, pp. 106-107.

an identification of being-for-us and being. He explains this transphenomenal reality away by leading it back to the fact of intersubjectivity. That the world is always already there is true, Duméry says, but this only reveals the fact of intersubjectivity.[86] Objectivity is intersubjectivity.

However, we must remember that Duméry does not conceive of man simply as the paradoxical unity of spontaneity and receptivity. He adds a very important qualification to this by saying that the spontaneity has to use the *detour* of receptivity.

What defines man is not that he is at once finite and unlimited. It is that he imposes upon himself, in order to attain the infinite, the detour of the finite; in order to think, to experience; in order to love, to strive; in order to will, to oblige himself; in order to become free, to take hold of himself.[87]

Herein lies the fundamental standpoint of Duméry. Finitude, multiplicity, matter are not things in themselves. They must be understood as resistances and functions, as means of liberation or of enslavement. They have, in a word, a double meaning.

Sensation is alternately bondage and liberation, slumber and an awakening. The Act-Law which grants to itself a consciousness grants one which is intellectual and sensible; it wills itself soul and body; it chooses for itself activity and passivity, light and confusion, autonomy and conflict, but also self-conquest and liberation.[88]

Everything happens as if each function can only exercise itself by projecting in front of itself that which resists it. It is thus that the superior level gives origin to an inferior level. This principle of resistance, this antithesis in its pure form, is matter, which like the Absolute is not an order. All multiplicity and finitude is derived from it. It is present under different forms on all levels of consciousness and everywhere mixes being with non-being. Gradually this non-being becomes stronger according as one proceeds in the direction of multiplicity. This principle of resistance gives origin to an inferior level by determining the energy of the higher level. The lower is, therefore, the weakened and inverted expression of the higher, because to receive an energy in a resistance is to force it to go in an inverted manner.[89] But this law of expression and inversion has its

[87] *Ibid.*, p. 98.
[88] *Ibid.*, p. 95.
[89] The "inversion" idea is somewhat vague. Henri Bergson compares the inverted movement of the spirit to a creative act which undoes itself, "Pensons ... à un geste comme celui du bras qu'on lève; puis supposons que le bras, abandonné à lui-même, retombe, et que pourtant subsiste en lui, s'efforçant de le relever, quelque chose du vouloir qui l'anima; avec cette image *d'un geste créateur qui se défait* nous aurons déjà une représentation plus exacte de la matière. Et nous verrons alors, dans l'activité vitale, ce qui subsiste du mouvement direct dans le mouvement inverti, *une réalité qui*

application only between the spiritual and rational and between the rational and sensible levels. The intelligible which is the unfolding of an order, starting from the transordinal One, cannot be seen as expression because this would imply a certain kind of participation and analogy. The intelligible order is thus not the reversing of another order (the One is not an order), but auto-position in virtue of a transdeterminational force. It is in the act of creation itself then that man's similarity with the One lies. He is the image of God, because "God creates auto-creators." [90]

Since the law of expression rules from the intelligible level to the sensible level, it becomes possible to realize a differentiated unity of man's scattered consciousness. At the same time, since the lower is the inverted expression of the higher, there is also the possibility of a stabilized disintegration which is the case when one adheres to the lower levels of consciousness. "By expression (in the sense in which we understand it) ambiguity diffuses itself closer and closer, bringing everywhere both the real presence of truth and the veil which conceals it." [91] Man's whole problem is thus to overcome little by little the receptivity and passivity of the levels where they are imposed upon him, in order to discover his own spontaneity and to use this for his effective liberation.[92] It is in this frame of thought that Duméry borrows a term from Simone Weil to indicate this process of gradual overcoming of all determinations towards a pure freedom of undetermination. The process is called "décréation," which means making the passage from the created order to the uncreated order. Whereas, the opposite process is: making the passage from the created order to nothingness.

Thus the situation of man is the following: by creation he inserts himself in a course of determinations; by the fall he becomes complacent in these determinations and places himself in a rut; by conversion he must uproot himself and force himself to surmount these determinations. S. Weil defines the end of conversion in her prayer: "My God, grant me to become nothing for in the measure that I become nothing God loves Himself through me." [93]

In this view, since the creation of determinations belongs to man, the problems of matter, life and the empirical in general do not refer to God

*se fait à travers celle qui se défait.* Henri Bergson, *L'Evolution créatrice* (Paris: Presses universitaires de France, 1962), p. 248. The inversion of the creative movement is responsible for the materiality of the real, for the multiplicity of beings, for the spatialization of things, for the retrospective character of our intellect, for the care (*souci*) which alienates our thought.
[90] Duméry, *Philosophie de la religion*, I, p. 70.
[91] *Ibid.*, p. 100.
[92] Duméry, *Critique et religion*, p. 208.
[93] Duméry, *Philosophie de la religion*, I, pp. 295-296.

but to man. It is the finite spirit, the Act-Law, which mediates itself and which carries the responsibility for its projections. On the one hand, we have to accept the correlation between a universe of things and incarnated consciousness, the idea of intentionality discovered by transcendental phenomenology. On the other hand, the position of finite determinations refers to finite determining principles and not to an infinite determining principle – the Plotinian insight. These two theses lead us to accept a view of the universe as the sensible projection of the intelligible relational chain posited eternally by the collegial body of the Act-Laws. "The theory of a cosmos conceived as an ensemble of inverse expressions or projections of the system of spirits imposes itself at least by title of hypothesis." [94] The external universe is, therefore, never an independent reality existing in itself. What we have is always a dialectic of real antinomies with internal division and resistance. Consequently there can be no pure receptivity. What is received is always assumed, it is given a meaning. The physical object is not full of intelligible forms: it only gives a shock which occasions the giving of meaning by the spirit. The possibility of drawing certain answers from nature, answers which have no meaning outside of a precise interrogation, does not prove the qualitative reality of the natural shocks. The question whether there is an external world is thus senseless.

Receptivity is interpretation from a shock, not a real exchange with exteriority. There does not exist an inaudible sound nor an insensible taste, nor an imperceivable color nor, generally speaking, any object which is not able to be experienced.[95]

No distinction can thus be made between a brute element and intended element. The world is always already given as correlate of our body. We cannot go beyond this. There is no such a thing as matter which would precede all sensible experience. Matter is non-being which manifests itself only under the forms of integrated resistance.[96] These resistances which, through the mediation of the body can concurrently be undergone (receptivity) and assumed (activity), must in last analysis be brought back to the alterity which is necessary for every individual in order to determine itself. If it is true that the Act-Laws are interdependent, then this means at the same time communion and opposition. These two tendencies, identity and alterity, can only be reconciled in the projection, according to the law of inverted expressions, of an outside world which offers itself

[94] *Ibid.*, p. 135.
[95] *Ibid.*
[96] *Ibid.*, p. 108.

to the intentionality of the interrogating body. The world presents itself then as organized and as strange: "The universe is an inverse expression." [97] It is like a tapestry seen from the wrong side. In order to discover its design one has to turn it over. But it is not possible to see immediately things from the right side. One has first to see the sensible sun before one can discover the astronomical sun. "So it is that without perception one would not attain the idea without the idea one would not verify the perception nor validate it." [98]

Because of Duméry's insistence on the necessary incarnation of ideas, we wonder whether Van Riet did not go too far in accusing Duméry's anthropology of Docetism. It must be kept in mind that for Duméry perception has a validity of its own and that only an ascending dialectic is correct and not a mere deduction from the idea to its inverted expression.[99] "It is the world, or better, the experience of 'world' which is commissioned to teach us about what the things are for us the expression; and it is history which reveals to us the interiority of the Act-Laws." [100] That there is receptivity in the sense in which Duméry accepts it, viz. a receptivity which the transcendental Cogito gives itself, is the expression of the fact that each concrete subject is not all the others. In this way, the fundamental limitation of every subject as *part* of a system is made clear and the consequent inexhaustibility of everything experienced.

Everything depends subsequently on understanding that, when the Act-Law "gives" itself a psychè and the world as its intentional correlate, this giving is not to be understood as a gratuitous creation but as a necessary creation resulting from the duality of the Act-Law itself. This necessity to create connotes that the symbolizing function of the Act-Law does not result in a correlate psyche-world which of itself has no ontological consistency. We must remember that what Duméry has in mind is an ontogenesis, an ontology which is continually being made, which can only be founded from above and be completed only through the effective ascent of the spirit towards unification with the One. For Duméry, there can only be talk of an ontology at the end, not at the beginning. In this again, he follows Blondel whose search for an authentic autogenesis led him to the necessary hypothesis of a God who gives Himself in order to fulfill human action.

For Duméry, philosophy is thus by essence religious, and his refusal of the term religious philosophy may well be the result of this conviction.

[97] *Ibid.*, p. 111.
[98] *Ibid.*, p. 112.
[99] *Ibid.*
[100] *Ibid.*

Indeed, the term religious philosophy would imply that there are other philosophical disciplines with equal rights. Philosophy is always religious philosophy because man is essentially religious, because he is constitutive relation with the Absolute. He is procession from the One and his conversion consists in continuing to proceed but knowing that, and whence he proceeds. Procession and not participation is the relation of the spirit with the One. "The inferior is always only that which the superior is not." [101] Participation, as a result of the law of expression, exists only between the lower levels. The spirit as exigency of the supra-essential Absolute will reach its fulfillment by taking determinations for what they are, viz., expressions and projections of the spirit's dynamism towards the Absolute. Passage from auto-determination to *Aseitas* – this is the way Duméry understands grace.[102] Again we encounter a fundamental point of difference between Blondel and Duméry. Instead of talking about a necessary hypothesis of the supernatural, Duméry has recourse to the lived religious experience which affirms the effective reality of the supernatural.

God is supra-essential *Aseitas*; man is auto-determination. We are now ready to broach the study of religion as the expressive body of man's constitutive relation with the One. The aim of this philosophy of religion is to *describe* the religious proceedings of the Act-Law; to *discriminate* the various expressions according to the level of consciousness to which they belong; and finally, to *judge* them as mediations of the spirit's ascent to the One. By doing this, a radical unification of man and his diverse activities will be realized, since in final analysis all levels of existence are expressions of the spirit's most essential urge: the super-essential union with the Absolute. "Religion is consciousness completely brought together around its center and restored to its principle with all levels reunited." [103] Let us proceed now to the critical discrimination (the distinction of the religious expressions according to the three levels of consciousness) of the distributed religious truth – God as *Aseitas* and liberating freedom, and *man as auto-determination in search for Aseitas* – over the different levels of consciousness.

---

[101] *Ibid.*, p. 132.
[102] Duméry, *The Problem of God*, p. 888.
[103] Duméry, *Philosophie de la religion*, II, p. 275.

CHAPTER IV

# DUMÉRY'S PHILOSOPHY OF RELIGION: CRITIQUE OF THE CATEGORIES AND SCHEMES WHICH EXPRESS THE SPIRIT'S CONSTITUTIVE EXIGENCY OF THE TRANSORDINAL ONE

> Macht exegetisch und historisch aus Jesus was ihr wollt, es fragt sich allein was die Idee ist. Hegel [1]

## SECTION I
### THE SCHEME OF TRANSCENDENCE AND THE CATEGORY OF THE ABSOLUTE

*a. Scope of the Reflective Critique in General and of the Critique of the Attributes in Particular*

The previous chapter delineated Duméry's refusal to acknowledge the transcendent and absolute Being of analogical theology, and his substitution of the transcendent and absolute One of negative theology. This choice has far-reaching consequences for his theology of the attributes of God since it implies a special epistemological position; or, since epistemology is inseparable from ontology, his epistemological position culminates in the choice of the One as the ultimate ground of everything. Knowledge, for Duméry, is an imaginative and rational projection of the Act-Law searching for self-identity, which it must recover through externalization and expression.

Everything happens, actually, as if spontaneous man could be certain of his grasp of the world, orient himself, express his total self, only by projecting in the sensible or psycho-empirical level his highest values, including the divine or the holy.[2]

Knowledge as projective activity does not credit the schemes and concepts as such with a reality value, but these schemes refer to reality only

---

[1] "Think Jesus on the exegetic and historical level as you wish, the real question is to know what the idea is."
[2] Duméry, *La tentation de faire du bien*, pp. 106-107.

mediately through the dynamism of the spirit in search for transdeterminational union with the One.

Under the pressure of its infinite and constitutive exigency, the Act-Law is made to give itself a body and a world, obligatory mediations for its self-realization. The supreme intentionality is free and creative, whereas the essences which it posits are objective and necessary. The necessity of this expressive mediation contains an inevitable fall, because the signified is by definition of a higher order than its sign.

The most alert and precision-minded spirit falls back, as soon as he speaks – and speak he must – into dependence not only on the judgment but also on the bondage of psycho-empirical expressivity.[3]

Even the philosopher is thus subject to this partial fall of the law of expression, of the detour of temporal and spatial projection. This law of the fall of expression can be understood to mean the impossibility of incarnated consciousness to reach for the object which it expresses without relating its intentionality and the expression to two different levels. On the first level we find the transcendental supramundane Ego, which in virtue of the intentions recaptures the determinations. On the second level we find the natural intramundane Ego in which the Act-Law becomes body and world. The first transcends the second, which means that the distance between the two cannot be overcome through a continuous movement. Such is the human condition which nobody can escape. "There is no possibility for man to return to himself outside of these two interwoven ways: intention and expression." [4]

One must recognize at the same time both the necessity and the insufficiency of the schemes (imaginative structures) and categories (conceptual expressions). The danger lies in the fact that the partial failure of expression becomes complete when one loses sight of the expressive and intentional character of the schemes and categories. In the field of religion this confusion of the sign and the signified is all the more disastrous since the distance here is insurmountable. God is not transcendent either in the way the world transcends consciousness, or the pure ego its thought. For this reason, Duméry introduced the word "transordinal"; God is completely beyond all order. The schemes and concepts are functional supports of the pursuit of God. They are intentional acts, reducing pursuits which are only valuable for the person who made the concrete religious ascent himself.[5] The act of reduction is thus more important than the

[3] Duméry, *Philosophie de la religion*, I, p. 126.
[4] *Ibid.*, p. 127.
[5] Duméry, *The Problem of God*, p. 105.

resulting expression, though we have to admit the necessity of the expression. Otherwise, religious intentionality, instead of relating itself to its real object, namely, the mystery of God, will fall into an imaginative and rational idolatry of abstract notions and historical events.

Thus superstition is born: in idolizing schemes it enacts them in the name of a magical consciousness ready to change the world without ignoring the laws of objectivity. It is no longer a question of an inevitable faltering; it is a case of a fall which is consented to and willed. It is not a case of a rearrangement within the interior of consciousness but rather of a tentative absence from oneself which is blameworthy and contradictory.[6]

It is the task of philosophy of religion to make this critical and reflective recapture of the entire body of religious discourse (and Duméry has in mind Catholicism), and to show that its true meaning can be understood only in terms of the general law which imposes upon the Cogito the necessity to create determinations and structures on the different noetic levels. They serve the only irreducible reality of God as *Aseitas,* as a source of auto-position and liberating freedom. This founds the original intention of faith and perpetuates itself through cultural forms of different origin and tendency. Religion believes it possible to keep the same intentional view through changing schemes and concepts, because these are nothing but the result of the projective activity of the religious intentionality. The distribution of religious truth over all the noetic levels is the work of faith. This projective activity of religious intentionality gives origin then to the insertion in the organic, cosmic and social world of the spiritual "visée" of the Transordinal One.

Faith transposes the Transordinal into the ordinal; it reduces the Absolute of exigency to the absolute of dialogue and immediately involves this latter in psychological, imaginative, institutional and historical structures.[7]

It would not be correct to think that Duméry talks about the projection of subjective attitudes or of abstract notions upon historical events. Such would mean a return to the natural attitude which imagines the existence of a world previous to our understanding, and thus a betrayal of the idea of intentionality. What he means is that consciousness *is* spontaneously projective, not by giving something of itself to something which is not itself, but by constituting completely significations which it reaches for on different expressive levels. Projective consciousness is but another word for incarnated consciousness, with the understanding that for Duméry

[6] Duméry, *Philosophie de la religion,* I, p. 128.
[7] *Ibid., II,* p. 259.
[8] *Ibid.,* I, p. 98.

incarnation does not so much mean a being *composed* of opposing principles, but a being which *uses* and *imposes* upon itself different forms of finitude.[8] We will have to say more about the projective mentality when we discuss the category of faith and its factual and doctrinal schemes. Here also Duméry's sympathy for Hegel finds its explanation. Man is that being which realizes itself by expressing itself; man is essentially "discourse." Unlike Hegel, Duméry does not think that the discourse can be completed, and that, therefore, philosophy is above religion. But he does agree that the expressions as such are relative and, thus, only means to turn man in the direction of reality.

> Projectivity indicates the necessity for consciousness to project its intention in subsequent levels of expression while it turns at the same time the intention in the direction of the real.[9]

Duméry would be in agreement with Hegel's philosophy of religion had Hegel made a clear distinction between philosophy as the critique of the expressions of life and life as aspiration which escapes all objectivation; that is, had he maintained that the overcoming of the level of representation was not accomplished by thinking only, but also and much more by action.[10]

After this digression on the general scope of Duméry's critique of the schemes and categories of religion, we turn now to the critique of the first two, namely, the scheme of transcendence and the category of the Absolute. It is clear, Duméry concedes, that one could call transcendence a category. The notion of the Absolute also has an etymological reference to space. But Duméry prefers to call transcendence a scheme since it symbolizes the spirit's ascent to God in using and overcoming all orders of determinations.[11] He calls the Absolute a category, a determination on the rational level. The previous chapter established the value of the affirmation of God through religious consciousness. The true God is pure transcendence, not object but rather intended term of the dynamism of the spirit. The existing God is not the idea of God; the scheme of transcendence and the category of the Absolute are only legitimate supports of the spirit's tension towards God.

> Our idea of God is necessarily below God. It has a functional role; for taken as a determination, it is only the conceptual expression of the intention toward God. Thus it remains human, limited, ambiguous, indefinitely purifiable, even when the movement of the soul it takes account of is supported by an Absolute of exigency. This Absolute impels man to place himself

---

[9] Duméry, *Foi et interrogation*, p. 246.
[10] Duméry, *Critique et religion*, pp. 190 and 231.
[11] Duméry, *The Problem of God*, p. 127, note 2.

totally (essence and existence) in question in order to transcend himself in all that he has and is.[12]

It is the coefficient of the relativity of the attributes which has to be determined. Under what condition can we safely use the scheme of transcendence and the category of the Absolute without infringing upon God's transordinality and man's creativity?

### b. Henological Redemption of the Scheme of Transcendence and the Category of the Absolute

The difficulty we face in thinking and using the scheme of transcendence and the category of the Absolute is that in both cases they seem to endanger irrevocably human interiority and freedom. The scheme of transcendence with its reference to spatial exteriority tends to make the Transcendent into a superimposed order which kills human interiority. Here Duméry takes into account especially Brunschvig's opposition to any notion of transcendence. Like Brunschvig, Duméry maintains that the spirit is interiority. He therefore joins Brunschvig in his refusal of any extrinsic transcendence.

No one can simultaneously serve spirituality and transcendence; to be transcended is to be denied. To place pure spontaneity in God is to deprive ourselves of our own light, to evict ourselves from our own home, in short, to commit suicide as a spiritual subject.[13]

These are objections which, knowing the trend of his thought, we feel Duméry will take to heart. So, too, Sartre's objection against the notion of the Absolute will be taken very seriously. Sartre cannot see how an Absolute can be thought which does not at the same time turn into an alter-ego, which, in an objectifying look, freezes all human creativity. This God-witness gives the believer a chance to use the Absolute for his own advantage by substituting his own wishes for God's will. "The orders you pretend to receive, you send to yourself." [14] The notion of an Absolute of dialogue thus gives origin to one of the most enormous mystifications:

The Absolute is used, confiscated and has responses dictated to it at the same time that requests are made to it. This kind of religion is only the apotheosis of man. In deluding God, consciousness, likewise, tries to delude itself; faith coincides with the most pernicious form of bad faith.[15]

Duméry grants that Sartre exaggerates, yet he maintains that Sartre has a very good point, because the notion of a dialogue between God and

---
[12] *Ibid.*, p. 68, note 33.
[13] *Ibid.*, p. 85.
[14] Sartre, *The Devil and the Good Lord*, p. 141.
[15] Duméry, *Foi et interrogation*, pp. 118-119.

man is itself a derived expression. What is original is a radical experience which has no form.

Does this now mean that, in order to escape all extrinsicism and reciprocity, we are thrown back into a certain immanentism? This would not do justice to the religious experience, for without transcendence there can be no intelligent talk about a *real* God whom religious man strives to join. On the other hand, the proof of the existence of a transordinal Absolute has already been given in the previous chapter, so this is not the question here. The crucial question at stake here is to know how the scheme of transcendence and the category of the Absolute are to be properly used without bringing into the picture their fatal extrinsicism and reciprocity. It would seem that the only logical answer is to present the transcendent as the transordinal, and to replace the Absolute of dialogue by the Absolute of complete indetermination. Thus reciprocity is abolished. The dilemma of how to serve human interiority and transcendence simultaneously is overcome by such recourse to henology and negative theology.

The transcendent does not compromise our interiority and freedom since the One, Who is beyond intellect and being, guarantees our autoposition. The transordinal One grants complete originality to derived beings and is at the same time radically transcendent. "No rivalry between the Infinite and the finite is to be feared. God does not steal our subjectivity; he does not stifle the substance of man." [16] The relation between God and the created cannot be defined by a partial or total ontological transmission. The One is No-thing or Nothingness and can therefore be the source of everything. "The Absolute can be the source of all because He is not what beings are." [17] That which is not is the supreme source of that which is. The terms, therefore, which proceed from Him receive nothing in participation. He only provides the *power* to the derived terms to be what He is not. The difference between a system of participation of being and a system of procession from the One is that in the former the inferior is in virtue of what the superior is and in the latter the inferior is in virtue of what the superior is not.

In this manner, the specific nature of the intelligible order is rigorously secured. The replacing of the mechanism of participation by the mechanism of procession does away with all forms of passage between the originating One and the originated orders of determination. The essence of the mechanism of procession lies in its ability to provide a generation

[16] Duméry, *The Problem of God*, p. 86.
[17] *Ibid.*, p. 92.

which is not ontological. There is no ontological communication in direct line since the whole meaning of the procession lies in establishing a completely original order. In the same way, the conversion does not destroy the procession. Rather, it strengthens it. In order to discover his dependence, man must display his independence; in order to relate himself to the One (conversion), he must proceed from Him. "... conversion never abolishes procession, it leans on it and witnesses to it. When conversion attains, procession maintains; when conversion leaps over, procession establishes; when conversion unifies, procession specifies." [18] Thus we are able to reconcile supreme dependence and authentic independence of the derived term. Procession constantly directs the spirit to the interior of its own order where the spirit is creative, and in this act it discovers the presence of the transdeterminational energy of the One.

The scheme of transcendence understood as transordinal does not endanger man's interiority. To conceive the transcendent as transordinal one must purify it from its tendency to represent the Absolute as a superimposed intelligible order of being. The scheme of transcendence is necessary to assure the absolute originality of the One. If one does not apply the scheme of transcendence to the Absolute one runs the danger of confounding the Absolute with the transcendental level of ideas and values which would turn the Absolute into an impersonal principle incapable of founding real personal individualities, reducing them to evanescent modes of the Absolute. The only way then to conceive a real distinction between the Absolute and the intelligible without endangering the interiority of the spirit is to say that *they do not constitute two orders, but are respectively absence of all order and constitution of orders*. "The best way to avoid putting God in series with us is to keep from reducing Him to our level, even the highest one; this means to think Him with reference to no level, that is, to pose Him as *transcategorial*." [19]

The same reasoning must be applied to the category of the Absolute. Because of the intentional nature of human knowledge and because of the transordinality of God, man's looking toward God needs the support of the concept of the Absolute as the notional expression of the radical spontaneity and complete *aseitas* of God. But in accordance with the intentional nature of human knowledge, this expression must be surpassed, in a continual purification, rather than discarded. The category of the Absolute, taken from the psychological realm, may easily lead to the concept of an absolute consciousness – witness or conversation-partner.

[18] *Ibid.*, p. 96.
[19] *Ibid.*, pp. 84-85.

But to posit the relationship God-man in such a way is simplistic and ridiculous. It leads to the conception of revelation as a conversation between two beings and leaves no room for a progressive evolution in man's understanding of this revelation. The relation between God and man is much more direct than this spiritual reciprocity. The Absolute is present as an Absolute of exigency, a presence of animation through which man creates his universe and expresses this presence. Revelation will then be understood as God who *makes* man say His name according to the human mode of expression.[20] "The dialogue no longer goes from the *one* to the divine *alter ego* (that representation would be a distortion). It goes from spiritual singularity to God's productive simplicity which creates the spirit as self-creator." [21]

The purification of the scheme of transcendence and of the category of the Absolute through the henological reduction should not, however, make us forget the necessary character of these expressive mediations. One could ask oneself whether Duméry does not eliminate de facto all objectifying representations of the Transordinal One, since their only meaning is to disengage the dynamic presence of the One in the heart of the transcendental Ego. Is this not a process of demythologization of a rationalistic kind? Duméry does not want to hear of renewing the religious terminology, of changing the dogmatic apparatus, and this, not because of the absolute nature of these expressions, but rather because of the relative nature of all means of expression. This attitude is the result of his paradoxical conviction that religious language is at the same time necessary and relative.[22] The method of the henological reduction does not intend to eliminate representations, but rather to show that they are means. "Representation of God is a way towards God, it is not God. It is the means that the spirit fashions so that it might enunciate to itself the terminus towards which it tends." [23] But these representations are necessary and indispensable, because man, being auto-position and not *aseitas*, has to use the detour of essences. "God can be represented only when

---

[20] Duméry, *Foi et interrogation*, p. 233.
[21] Duméry, *The Problem of God*, p. 119.
[22] Duméry does not agree at all with Bultmann's attempt to demythologize Christianity. Cf. *Philosophie de la religion*, II, pp. 239-247, also *La foi n'est pas un cri*, pp. 236-238. He maintains that the mythological elements have to be understood, not eliminated. But in a way, as will become clear later, Duméry disagrees with Bultmann, not so much, because, in his opinion, the latter goes too far but because Duméry wants to go further. For Bultmann, there is still the saving event of the empirical *kerygma*. Duméry replaces this by the mystical dynamism of the spirit in its attempt to join the One. The empirical *kerygma* has to be founded on the sapiential *kerygma*. Cf. *Philosophie de la religion*, II, p. 45, note 2.
[23] Duméry, *Critique et religion*, p. 196.

projected in the objective determinations of our bio-psychological and psycho-social experience." [24] The attributes of God (and we will see that the same holds for the specific religious expressions) must be concurrently posited and denied. "The notion of God or the attributes of God, without being determinations of the Ineffable, are indispensable road signs for every *itinerarium mentis in Deum.*" [25]

### c. Henology and Negative Theology

A question which still requires an answer is: what, in final analysis, is the value of these representations which at the same time must be accepted and refused. If the attributes of God are nothing but mediations, however necessary, of the spirit's impulse towards the ineffable One, are they not devoid of any reality – and truth – value? If God is superessential simplicity, if He excludes all determinations, if He ceases to be the location of the ideas, if He is really transcendent, are we then not confined to a complete agnosticism? Hence, with the words of Brunschvig, we would have to say that the meaning of a negative theology lies in a negation of theology. On the other hand, we saw how religion confesses the belief in a reciprocity of dialogue between God and man. But we have discarded this kind of reciprocity as irreconcilable with the nature of the transordinal One. So we find ourselves caught by our own critical devices. Trying to do away with all anthropomorphism, we are faced with an equally dangerous enemy, namely, an agnosticism which *au fond* brings us to atheism. Agnosticism or anthropomorphism, are these the only alternatives? Or is there a third one, and if so what is its nature? Here Duméry expounds his theory of the attribute of God.

Indeed we do not know what God is. But He is present in the spirit because He is the source and the principle of the spirit. This relation, however, is not ontological; it is of a purely dynamic nature. Therefore, there is no gnoseological relation between God and man. He is neither the producer of the intentionalities nor the place of the essences. He transcends the distinction essence-existence, object-subject, and can thus never be thought either in the line of objectivity or in the line of subjectivity.

In whatever way one seeks to define the relationship of the spirit with God it is necessary to be on guard against compromising the Absolute whether on the side of subjectivity or on the side of objectivity, both of which belong properly only to man.[27]

[24] *Ibid.*
[25] *Ibid.*
[26] Duméry, *The Problem of God,* p. 99.
[27] Duméry, *Critique et religion,* p. 195.

God is present as the source of the spirit's dynamism and productivity, as a Divine motion which at the same time makes the spirit proceed and convert. The infinite dynamism of freedom which constantly transcends all determinations is the sign revealing God's presence. Hence the science of God instead of being an explicative theology is simply the science of the spirit's effort to join the Absolute. The spirit *is* living relation with the Absolute tending toward ecstatic union with the Absolute, so that the constitution of the spirit, creating ideas and values, is identical with the exercise of this relation with God.

God gives the spirit the possibility of *acting* so it can give itself *being*. To accept the first, to confer the second on itself, to go toward God, are three different ways of designating the same fundamental operation. Thus it can be understood that being turned toward the Absolute (being converted) coincides with correctly performing the tasks of the spiritual function.[28]

It is this relation to God, interior to the spirit, which permits us to have knowledge of the Absolute. The spirit as an intrinsically guided dynamism towards an ecstatic union with the One, and the creations of the spirit as necessary mediations of this ascent to the One, constitute the only possible approach toward a valid knowledge of the Absolute. This is also the only means by which God manifests Himself to us. Because of His super-essential mode of existence, He can become intelligible only by creating spirits which, in relating themselves to Him, create significations, mediations and revelations of an immediate and ineffable presence. "But the ineffable is no less present; and as ineffable it can be expressed only if it gives rise to an expressing being that is below it." [29] To explain this, Duméry refers to Plotinus and Scotus Erigena for whom God, being "Nihil per excellentiam," cannot know Himself unless by creating. The intelligibles are created in the common act by which God and the spirits express themselves. But this does not mean, although the neoplatonic terminology facilitates such misunderstanding, that thus the doctrine of emanation leaves no room for a free transcendent action on the part of God. "The One necessarily transcends his expressions, even if the latter answer to a law of procession that he freely imposes on himself." [30] The great merit of the neo-platonic thought, however, remains its having stressed the self-creating role of the spirit and its intimate relation with the Absolute.

According to Duméry, God reveals Himself not so much on the level

---

[28] Duméry, *The Problem of God*, pp. 102-103.
[29] *Ibid.*, p. 114.
[30] *Ibid.*, p. 104, note 7.

of imaginative and rational expression, but rather in the ascensional dynamism of the spirit itself.

God is manifested in derived terms, not first of all by contingent and extrinsic expressions, but through the processive motion itself. Thus the intelligible bears witness to Him at the heart of self-position.[31]

The real knowledge of God is realized then not by the speculative approach to a God-object, but by the lived ascensional act in which the spirit at the same time posits itself and its universe and becomes conscious of the infinite power by which this act is possible. To know God is to know oneself as spirit,[32] as constitutive relation with the Absolute. Since the henological reduction is nothing but the technical term for this concrete ascent of the spirit, the process of coming to knowledge about God consists in the actual operation of the henological reduction, namely, in making the passage from the one and multiple (the spirit) to the One. Hence there is no knowledge of God possible outside of the framework of a lived religious experience. It is impossible to know the unknowable; therefore the only remaining approach is to *live* consciously the relation of the spirit with the Absolute. Thus an explicative theology is not possible, but only the effort of the spirit to join its source and the critique of this effort. Natural theology is the systematization of the concrete proceedings of the spirit by which it discovers its constitutional relation with the Absolute.

In this context, what becomes of the attributes of God? Again, the attributes are not explicative formulas but contents of reduction. "The attribute is nothing other than the notion in which the result of a reductive intention is inscribed. It witnesses to the success of the intention; but to understand it, one must himself effect the movement that it summarizes."[33] In accordance with his dynamic view of the relation God-man, Duméry prefers to talk about dynamic attributes of the concrete spiritual life instead of conceptual attributes of abstract theology. The attributes of God are the *energies* flowing forth from the Divine source in the determinational and (therefore) manifesting universe of the spirits.[34] The attributes are the different milestones of the spirit's ascent to the One. Some of the classical attributes express what is irreducible (simplicity, unity, spontaneity), others have still to undergo successive purifications (infinity, immutability, omnipresence, intelligence, will, freedom, love,

---

[31] *Ibid.*, p. 121, note 33.
[32] *Ibid.*, p. 104.
[33] *Ibid.*, p. 105.
[34] *Ibid.*, p. 107, note 12.

life and beatitude). The attributes are distributed over the different levels of consciousness through which the religious intentionality passes in its search for absolute unity. They never transcend the human order (all order is created by the human spirit), and can therefore not be conceived as predications of which God is the subject. Finality and causality are simply modes of representation valid only for our world and not based on a system of ideas and values pre-existing in God. In themselves then, the attributes have no reality-value; they are the intelligible mediations which allow the spirit to return to the One from which it proceeds. The aim of the attribution has to be rejected and in doing so may discover the original point wherein it coincides with the One.

God supersedes our categories, but He is not outside of our spirituality. In this way, Duméry at the same time escapes notionalism and agnosticism. We are prisoners of our categories and can, therefore, never expect to make God enter our closed world of determinations; yet He can be discovered as *that by which the spirit constitutes itself and its world of determinations.* Just as the power of sight can never be object of sight, so also the source of all intelligibility and freedom cannot become object of objectifying freedom.

God will not reveal Himself to those who wish to hold Him under their regard. Whereas He does manifest Himself in the impulse which pushes the spirit to self-position . . . He is an Absolute of exigency, not the object of *an exigency for the Absolute*.[35]

His presence is revealed in freedom's absolute power to contest all determinations. Therefore, the best way to God is the methodical deciphering of the spiritual experience, since in final analysis the spirit possesses the power to express the inexpressible. The only way in which the finite can imitate the infinite is by diversifying the finite insights *ad infinitum*.[36] This power of infinite diversification *in actu exercito,* not the deversifications themselves, is what reveals the Absolute.

The spirit is thus the word of God in that it speaks about its constitutive relation with the Absolute. "If, then, the Absolute does not speak, the spirit and the world, taken charge of by the spirit, can speak to us of Him and for Him." [37] And religion is nothing but a series of expressions, which, distributed over the different levels of consciousness, mediate the spirit's exigency of absolute unity.

[35] *Ibid.*, p. 113.
[36] *Ibid.*, p. 123.
[37] *Ibid.*, p. 116.

When the spirit is understood as relation to God, religion and spirituality are identified, provided that the life of the spirit can receive from God not only a capacity for self-determination, but the still better aptitude of liberating itself from all determination.[38]

But this absolute freedom of indetermination can only be recovered through the initiative of the Absolute promoting us to the state of divine *aseitas*. It is this possibility which is expressed by the category of grace and the schemes of the supernatural.

SECTION II

INTERPRETATION OF THE CATEGORY OF
GRACE AND THE SCHEME OF THE SUPERNATURAL

*a. Is There a Philosophical Problem of Grace and How Can Philosophy Deal With It?*

These two questions are intimately related to each other. The first one is a question of doctrine; the second one, a question of method. Duméry's method of discrimination [39] not only describes the different levels of the religious discourse, but also allows him to apply a discriminative judgment of these different layers of religious consciousness in virtue of his religious philosophy. We saw how he defines the spirit as an axiogenic dynamism and mechanism which reveals the pure spontaneity of the One present in the transcendental *Ego cogito*. It is because of the fact that he chooses this axiogenic dynamism that his philosophy of religion is not merely descriptive but also critical. Indeed if the subject is primarily free act which posits orders in order to achieve self-identity (in last instance union with the One), then the expressive orders can be judged according to the index of unification which should be theirs. Since religion is nothing but the exigency of the Absolute represented to consciousness under the forms of ideas and images, its whole expressive body can be *described* and *judged* from the standpoint of this ascensional dynamism of the spirit.

Religion is an exigency for the absolute which is inscribed in the heart of freedom and which is expressed on all levels of consciousness, from the highest to the lowest, penetrating at once thought and sensibility, judgment and sentiment.[40]

How can Duméry maintain this transphenomenological standpoint when it comes to grace? It requires an introduction of the very notion of grace

[38] *Ibid.*, p. 102.
[39] For definition of Duméry's method of discrimination cf. Chapter II, Section III.
[40] Duméry, *Critique et religion*, p. 217.

in his philosophical discourse. Up to now, Duméry's exposition remained within the boundaries of traditional natural theology. He treated, though in a very original way, the traditional questions of natural theology ("*An* Deus sit" and "*Quid* Deus sit") in his henology and negative theology. But from now on he intends to go further and to expound what we could call a "Christian metaphysics." This term, which Duméry does not use, is not an extrapolation gratuitously affirmed, for the good reason that his philosophy of religion is not and does not intend to be a mere phenomenology of religion.

Where, precisely, does Duméry insert the problematic of grace in his religious philosophy? We have seen how he maintained, in opposition to Sartre, that our inventive and efficacious freedom is not incompatible with the affirmation of God. The axiogenesis excludes only a God-object, a Divine constellation of ideas and values imposed from above upon man, an Absolute of alienation. A transordinal One, Who, by the very fact that He is not an order, cannot infringe upon human creativity and its order of ideas and values. But if Sartre should accept the existence of a transordinal One as ground of man's freedom, it seems equally imperative that he should also concede that freedom's power of contestation is, in final analysis, a quest for participation in the supreme power of contestation of the super-essential One. Human spirituality not only means auto-determination. It also aims at complete possession and interiorization of its determinations. This transdetermination is what is called grace. Human freedom implies the One as source of the created spirits and, what is more, human freedom cannot be exercised without considering a possible deification of man. Man cannot achieve the task of liberating this freedom without the help of God. Freedom and grace then are one and the same thing insofar as the first is human autonomy as seen from the standpoint of man, and the second, human autonomy as seen from the standpoint of God.

Basically this freedom is grace and this grace, a perfect indetermination, is God. We should not reproach Sartre for his ethics of pure freedom. On the contrary we would call to his attention that this freedom is divine or divinizing. To insist on it as a human privilege is to advocate self-deification, self-redemption. Such an apotheosis is rather hasty for a philosophy which sees in the idea of God a mere mirage.[41]

It is thus still by thinking in the line of Sartre's absolute freedom that Duméry is led to insert the notion of grace in his philosophical discourse. The recognition of the Absolute's presence at the heart of freedom, even

---

[41] Duméry, *Philosophie de la religion*, I, p. 281, note 3.

henologically understood, still contains a danger of alienation. Even if Divine transcendence cannot be said to create the spirit like a thing, but to create auto-creators, there still remains an undeniable dependence. Therefore, the Absolute will only be accepted in view of a possible passage from auto-position to the *aseitas* of the One. Then the freedom of man would be completely established.

A God who is merely a benefactor will remain always paternalistic; this is an improvement over a tyrant but it is still a subtle alienation. Only a God who is capable of granting a share in his spontaneity can assure the salvation and dignity of the spirit.[42]

Anxious to satisfy Sartre's demands to respect human freedom and interiority, Duméry proposes a participation in the Absolute divine spontaneity, a promotion to the statute of the freedom of God Himself.

How, in this promotion, Duméry is successful in securing the freedom of the Divine initiative is an absorbing problem, but space does not permit its discussion here. It is clear, however, that some serious doubts about this will have to be raised. Not only the gratuitousness of the supernatural but the supernatural as such seems to be in danger. Duméry does not fail to raise this question, but he answers it by turning to the question of his descriptive method. Yet this is not the whole answer, since in view of his attempt to go further than mere description of religious categories, he had to bring the notion of a supernatural gift within the immanent philosophical discourse. How he does this is not clear, and many of his phrasings imply a dangerous naturalization of the supernatural. For the present we adhere to Duméry's own answers to this question. When one asks how such promotion is possible, he says, one is not asking whether it really exists. The question of its existence is left to the option of the living spirituality; all the philosopher is concerned with is its immanent coherence and the conditions of its possibility. "But this participation in divine spontaneity concerns living spirituality. Te task of the critique is limited to defining the conditions for the possibility and validity of such an exaltation." [43]

The philosopher of religion finds the Christian dogma of grace, of a real living relation between God and man. This relation presents itself first as an alliance with a certain people. Then appears a man called Jesus who interiorizes and universalizes this alliance and on whose life a mystique of salvation is founded. Through identification with Christ, man acquires participation in Divine life. He enters a process of deifi-

[42] *Ibid.*, p. 70.
[43] *Ibid.*, pp. 70-71.

cation by becoming another Christ. This process of deification realizes itself in and through a community of prayer, cult and teaching. This is what the philosopher of religion is faced with. For somebody who is not acquainted with religion, this is indeed a strange and mysterious world. Only in faith can one truly appraise this mysterious universe. But the philosopher as philosopher has no faith. He relies on reason only. Do we have then to turn away from religion and give up all attempt to subject it to a philosophical critique? No, certainly not. What we have to remember again, so Duméry claims, is that there is a safe distance between the living spirituality and its means of expression. We are sufficiently familiar with Duméry's thought to know that this is not just a matter-of-fact distinction which everyone accepts, but that this implies and is based upon his philosophy of the subject as transcendental intentionality. From this transcendental standpoint, he is able to grasp the intellectual and practical structures of the religious consciousness without having to deal with their reality content. All he has in view is the "significations," mere noematic correlates of noetic acts. The engaging freedom, acting under its own law or in relation to God, always remains beyond this critical reflection.

Everything is hidden in the act of faith except for that which its performance implies within the immanence of consciousness, that is, the meaning which it accords itself and the expressions of this meaning... The rational critique examines what the meaning of those data is and how this meaning is incarnated in order to be lived.[44]

In this way our author is able to study the category of grace and the schemes which support it in the imagination, without straining the irreplaceableness of the Divine action. The universe of religious meaning has an immanent law of coherence. It is this coherence, or incoherence, of the religious affirmations and attitudes which requires elaboration. The affirmations as such are always beyond the range of the philosophical critique.

The complete difference which exists between the two critical analyses and religious experience is the same as that which is found between the reality of spirit and analytic retrospection. Each time we affirm that philosophy is a critique of spontaneous behavior we suggest the irreplaceable originality of effective action.[45]

As already stated, when the question of the Divine transcendence and initiative arises, Duméry always refers to this distinction between living

[44] *Ibid.*, p. 143.
[45] *Ibid.*, p. 144.

spirituality and reflective critique, between prospective and retrospective knowledge. But this does not really answer the question. It serves merely to arouse further suspicion. Where is the distinction between faith and reason, between the spiritual and the supernatural, between revelation and the ascensional dynamism of the spirit?

We will have to return to this crucial distinction between the supernatural elevation of man and his natural expansion according to his innermost exigencies. All we want to clarify here is that Duméry conceives grace as complete freedom, absolute indetermination, fundamental negation of all external data. Grace gives man access to the absolute simplicity, to the absence of all orders, to the Divine spontaneity. But human freedom is by nature bound to its determinations. Therefore this super-essential existence can only be achieved through the initiative of the Absolute itself. "When the spirit exceeds its limits and approaches the super-essence, only the super-essence can carry it." [46] This communion with the super-essential Absolute, just like the spirit's foundation in the One, may not be understood in terms of participation. Where grace is concerned, Duméry prefers to talk about a passage from auto-position to the *Aseitas* of God.

Everything considered, supernatural grace is "participation" (in the technical sense defined above) no more than natural illumination (with different degrees of gratuitousness) is. It is preferable to conceive it as a passage from *self-position* to *Aseitas*.[47]

This position, namely, Duméry's concept of grace as superessential freedom and his refusal of the participation idea, points again towards his main concern. This concern is to secure human freedom from all alienation and human interiority from all exteriority. This is the norm by which he determines the relative value of the schemes of the category of grace. How far does this scheme express the intentional life of the human spirit to the super-essential One? The final goal is the overcoming of all imposed determinations.

Man's entire problem is to surmount little by little receptivity and passivity on those levels in which he is subjected to them in order finally to discover his own spontaneity and to make use of it for his effective liberation.[48]

It is this possible freeing, though realized by God, we envisage when talking about grace. With what degree of success do the different schemes imaginatively support this super-essential liberation?

[46] *Ibid.*, p. 282.
[47] Duméry, *The Problem of God*, p. 88, note 22.
[48] Duméry, *Critique et religion*, p. 208.

Before advancing to this discriminative judgment, Duméry gives a historico-phenomenological description of the different representations and concepts of grace. He questions successively the Biblical schemes of the Old Testament, of the Gospels and of St. Paul, the patristic schemes, and, finally, the supernatural schemes of the theological age. He finds the schemes of Divine son-ship – recovered human integrity – forensic justification – gift of God and supernature. We will not reproduce this historical phenomenology of the schemes of the category of grace, but we will, in the following pages, present his discriminatory judgment. He determines the noetic level and the degree of dignity of the recovered schemes. In a final point, we will proceed to Duméry's exposition of what the Ego reaches for through these different schemes. Here he reapplies his henological reduction in order to disengage the irreducible core of the category of grace. This last point constitutes his specifically philosophical concept of grace.

### b. *Discriminative Critique of the Different Schemes of the Category of Grace*

Grace, as the deification of man, has been expressed through different schemes. Unless one recognizes the difference in value of these schemes, no philosophical judgment is possible, and religion approaches superstition.

> Judgment can only be discrimination; religious intentionality can only be the aiming at the only Absolute, and therefore the preservation of the inherent illusion found in the relative and incomplete. The sorting out of representations, the graduated arrangement of schemes, their division according to differentiated noetic levels can take place only in the light of and under the responsibilities of the critical spirit.[49]

The kind of schematism which one adopts is in accordance with the perspectives of the subject. Every man chooses religious representations in accordance with the purity of his religious intentionality. It is important then to take a critical attitude with respect to these religious expressions in order to purify one's religious intentionality. This purification, however, is not achieved by eliminating the means of expression or even by replacing one mode of expression by another. Every order of expression has its value. What remains to be done is to realize on what noetic level each mode of expression exists. The real fault is to favor one exclusive mode of expression and to disregard the others. In doing this, one makes an absolute of a particular expression instead of seizing each level *as ex-*

[49] Duméry, *Philosophie de la religion*, I, p. 267.

*pression*. Duméry does not intend the inferior level of expression to be abandoned in favor of the superior. He only wants to distinguish the different levels of expression and their respective value. The discrimination of these different levels of expression is achieved by means of the norm of greater or lesser interiority.

> Intentionality ... unless it be deviated or set back, scales the different schemes in the use it makes of them. It hierarchizes them by instituting the only legitimate gradation, viz., the one which leads from exteriority to interiority.[50]

In this way, one makes a history, personal and collective, of the spirit's quest for the Absolute. Gradually consciousness transcends its cosmological, biological, sociological and psychological projections of the Absolute in order to discover finally the intrinsically sanctifying and freeing God. But to adore successively this cosmological, sociological and psychological God does not mean that one, at least by intention, does not adore the same God.

> God never changes. To set out on a journey towards Him across immense spaces (the transformation of self) or to ascend successive peaks (the noetic levels) is not to modify the term towards which one is tending, but rather to situate it beyond all grasp and, nevertheless, to continually multiply the means of apprehension.[51]

Every scheme thus expresses the same truth on the level which is its own. The filial scheme of Divine son-ship with its correlate of God the Father expresses on the psycho-sociological level the condescending love of a liberating God. This familial scheme, by the fact that it transcends a mere biological utilitarian altruism, suggests real self-devotion. Of course this scheme presupposes the reciprocity of God and man. It is based upon an Absolute of dialogue. This basis must be kept in mind, since we are concerned with a reducible expression, not on the same level of the trans-ordinal One which does away with all reciprocity.

The scheme of a lost and recovered integrity translates in terms of a chronomorphic representation the belief in the existence of a noumenal ground, an authentic freedom which man desperately tried to reach. As such it expresses the spirit's exigency of absolute freedom. By means of the psychological schemes of temptation and original fall, of happiness and unhappiness and the mythical projection of a golden age, man strives to know his own identity.[52]

[50] *Ibid.*, p. 274.
[51] *Ibid.*, p. 275.
[52] We will present Duméry's theory of the religious myth in the third part of this chapter.

The scheme of integrity (lost and found again) is less a particularized scheme than an ensemble of structures through which with the help of mythic projections, a moral and religious intuition which regards spiritual reality as its center crystallizes itself.[33]

The scheme of justification through grace is a juridical scheme. This legalistic characteristic has, however, been overcome by Jesus' interiorization of the Law. The connected schemes of imputation and regeneration are therefore of a different nature. The first one remains juridical and empirical. But the second one indicates the moral conversion of man and a passage to the interiority called forth by grace. Forensic justification is weakened by extrinsicism. Only justification-regeneration takes place on the level of human freedom and interiority. Yet the danger of extrinsicism is evident even with the scheme of justification-regeneration. It is by essence a soteriological event, which means that it links together a spiritual and a historical process. Hence another division will be made according to a philosophical notion of history applied here.

Since history can be envisaged either as an expression of interdependent freedoms or as the course of contingent events (and in its extreme form, without an immanent law), one finds oneself in the presence either of a manifestation of spiritual acts or of a disconcerting flow of empirical facts. In the latter case interiority will be maneuvered from without – something a philosopher will not grant. In the first case soteriological history would be understood as the sign of properly spiritual mediation exercised throughout time.[54]

This text exemplifies Duméry's concern to avoid all extrinsicism and the danger of a certain immanentism resulting from this concern. Forensic justification, Duméry maintains, is endangering human interiority. At the same time it is clear that the scheme of forensic justification exemplifies more clearly the sovereignty of the saving God than the scheme justification-regeneration.

The scheme of the "gift of God" expresses clearly the gratuity, the liberality of the divine Giver. But it is essentially a sociological scheme and therefore evokes the idea of a particular gift-object rather than communion with the Undetermined, with the Absolute of pure freedom. Certainly, it has the advantage of pointing towards the *real* presence of a divinizing principle in man (*gratia creata*), but at the same time it suggests that grace is something that can be manipulated as a thing. But this disadvantage can be overcome by purifying it of its empirical ties. This is

[53] Duméry, *Philosophie de la religion*, I, p. 269.
[54] *Ibid.*, p. 271.
[55] *Ibid.*, p. 272.

done when one says that God gives *Himself* in grace. "The gift of God is precisely not *a thing given by God* but *God giving Himself.* Objectivism is thus emasculated or overcome." [55] This illustrates again the difficulties Duméry meets whenever the scheme expresses the Divine sovereignty. God's free action is always translated in extrinsic schemes. The philosopher shuns them, because they cannot enter his rational discourse. How can he reduce them without falling into an idealistic pantheism? Duméry is aware of this.

Emanationism is too often confounded with necessitarianism (which leads to immanentism) ... We are anxious to affirm with absolute clarity the gratuitous character of creation and to give the greatest possible prominence to the notion of transcendence.[56]

He has similar problems with the more recent scheme of the supernatural. Its cosmological origin characterizes it with a serious extrinsicism, difficult to overcome. He makes the distinction between the supernatural of addition and the supernatural of super-essence. The first one, by conceiving the Divine gift as an extrinsic addition, leads to the representation of man as a being with two stages. On the one hand, we have a static closed nature; on the other hand, a supernature imposed upon the first and open to Divinizing grace. This leads to a dualism of nature and supernature which first reifies the human essence and then adds another superhuman essence. The consequences are fatal. It forces the Transcendent to place itself in opposition with consciousness.

This provokes the belief that the presence of God remains imprisoned in the category of otherness and that the supernatural is alienation. In reaction to this, humanism can only be atheistic. If it is discovered that certain unbelievers were only atheists refusing a tacked-on Absolute, their atheism would be an homage to the true God; while supernaturalist theism (that is, naturalist in a double respect) would be an offense to the One.[57]

The only way to escape this spatial and substantialistic mortgage is to interpret the supernatural scheme through the spirituality of the super-essence of a Pseudo-Dionysius. Super-essence has nothing to do with a superior essence. It indicates the absence of order and essence. We are back here to the fundamental distinction between ontology and henology.

When one says essence, one states the ensemble of determinations; that is, in the technical sense, order. On the other hand, when one says super-essence, one states the negation of all determination, the absence of order; in short, the super-essence is the transordinal One.[58]

[56] Duméry, *The Problem of God*, p. 104, note 7.
[57] Duméry, *Philosophie de la religion*, I, p. 273.
[58] *Ibid.*, p. 233.

One has to choose between these two alternatives: a dialectic of participation and a dialectic of procession; between *Esse* and *Unum*. The choice made here results in an extrinsic or an intrinsic notion of transcendence. Only the last one surmounts the spatiality of the scheme of transcendence.

But is it not impossible to assimilate the supernatural into the super-essential? The supernatural necessarily entails, in a metaphysics of the substance, a splitting of the human existence into two orders. Natural faculties correspond to supernatural faculties, and immanent finality of the natural order to a transcendent finality of the supernatural order. To the extent, however, that the supernatural is understood not as an order, but as that which transcends all order, it comes closer to the super-essential and becomes the best scheme to support the category of grace. "If one is careful to place the principal accent on the chief acceptation (the one we have finally delineated: a beyond every nature, understood as determination and order), it appears that there is no longer any reason to oppose its usage." [59] As soon as one passes the last order, or better, the very notion of order, Sartre's fear of a superimposed order which would crush human intelligence becomes unfounded and his abhorrence of a divine moloch demanding unconditional obedience unsubstantial. The intimacy between the One and the created order is so great that alienation of the created is out of order. On the other hand, the distinction between the created and uncreated is so strongly marked that the naturalization of the transordinal cannot be conceived. The supernaturalization of man, understood as the access to the freedom of supreme indetermination of the One, is a promise which a philosopher like Sartre should take into consideration.

This pure freedom of the Undetermined may not be understood, however, as if man would surmount completely all determinations. If this were so he would lose his singular individuality. "To be deified is not to be diluted in the supreme indetermination; it is to enter into it in order to take hold of it again at the source of all determination and have the initial power to posit determinations." [60] In the communion with the super-essence, the spirit will still be linked to the determinations which it gave itself. But there the spirit ceases to see the determinations as an objective screen. The spirit, united to the One, will see the determinations in the perspective of their spiritual genesis. "My determinations themselves become, so to speak, *transparent*; they have but sufficient reality to permit me to subsist and to remain a unique individual, even after

[59] *Ibid.*, p. 235.
[60] *Ibid.*, p. 235, note 5.

universal charity has penetrated me." [61] The super-essential existence of grace will thus be the final establishment of man's transcendental consciousness, the standpoint from where man knows himself as the creator of his universe and the infinite power in virtue of which he is auto-creator. This also is the standpoint from where Duméry judges the religious discourse. This will have to be examined more minutely when he gives a properly philosophical interpretation of the category of grace. Then the degree of consistency he gives to the religious schemes of the category of grace will be more clearly demonstrated.

*c. Philosophical Critique of the Categories of Grace and the Supernatural*
Duméry's discriminational critique of the schemes of the category of grace was completely directed towards the henological reduction. The schemes are valuable as far as they can suggest the passage of finite freedom to the super-essential freedom of the One. Now we have to ask for the final metaphysical value of this idea of a divinizing freedom. This, however, does not mean that we want to determine the intrinsic value of the act of faith. This escapes the range of the philosophical inquiry.

We should ask ourselves if this idea (of a deifying freedom) is anything other than a dream, a consoling illusion. We do not have to share in the truthfulness of the fact of Christian testimony. We leave the option of belief to the initiative of the subject ... We ask ourselves if grace and the supernatural are coherent ideas which answer to the motion of conversion of the spirit.[62]

On what conditions can the gift of grace become meaningful? To what fundamental characteristic of the human situation does this possible elevation correspond? In what sense can this divinization proposed by the idea of grace be seen as a legitimate evolution of man's innermost aspirations? These questions indicate the direction of the metaphysical inquiry which will follow. They anticipate how careful we will have to be so as not to harm the "supernatural" nature of grace. Yet, we have to agree with Duméry that, in some way, the possible gift of grace has to correspond to something in man. Otherwise how would the idea have arisen in the history of mankind?

Duméry again commences with the fundamental intuition of his philosophy: What is man? *"Man is freedom existing through a nature."* [63] The essential feature of this definition is that the two terms form a transcendental correlation. Their correlation is more important than their

[61] *Ibid.*, p. 296.
[62] *Ibid.*, p. 277.
[63] *Ibid.*, p. 280. (Italics mine.)

respective definitions. This correlation of freedom and nature must also be seen in the frame of a dynamic process, which gives the notions different meanings. At the lowest level, nature is that which is dead and crushed upon itself, absence of all spontaneity. But this is a limit-idea, in the sense of a mathematical limit.[64] The idea of a completely determined nature is never equaled by its duplicate in reality. There is no such a thing as pure facticity. As soon as we talk about nature, we imply an internal principle of production present in nature, indicating a lower or higher form of organization.

The word nature connotes, therefore, a way of existing which implies different degrees of determination or self-determination. At the initial point of departure, there is a product entirely enclosed within its determinations. Then enjoying little by little a certain play between its power of determining and the objective effects of this power, it finally becomes capable of releasing the vise when the internal principle becomes present to itself, that is, at the precise moment when it takes consciousness of its act; but then at this supreme moment nature returns completely to its radical origin, grasps itself, changes its name and is now called freedom.[65]

This process of progressive self-possession is what we call human nature. Man is freedom emerging from cosmological, biological, and psychological determinism. But again this does not mean that in the end we reach an absolute freedom. Freedom, just like nature, is also a limit-idea. Its reality never equals its idea. In this limit-situation lies their reality. Facticity would not be real facticity without the leeway of freedom, and freedom would not be real freedom (possibility of freedom) without the boundaries of facticity. Freedom at the same time suffers and profits from its limitations. Man is freedom-in-the-making.

Freedom exists only in assuming a body, it lives through opposition and confrontation, it is nourished by contraries, its history is a long series of conquered failures. Man is not free as God is free; he frees himself. What characterizes his freedom is struggle, rebellion, negativity; it *is* not, but it happens and is never complete.[66]

It is in this context that Duméry introduces the notions of grace and supernature. He starts by stressing that the supernatural union with God is completely the work of God Himself. God, being incommensurable, cannot be reached in created nature. Since God has to be conceived as

---

[64] A limit is a fixed value or from which a varying value or form may approach indefinitely but cannot reach. For instance, an irrational number is the limit of the different fractions which give an ever closer equivalent of the number.
[65] Duméry, *Philosophie de la religion*, I, p. 278.
[66] *Ibid.*, p. 280.

the transordinal One, man, whose existence *is* an order, cannot transcend the orders. Man's freedom is by its very essence linked to determinations.

> Man, the intelligent creature, cannot surpass the level of a freedom circumscribed in a nature. In order to arrive, not at an order more exalted, but at absolute simplicity (which is the absence of order), it is necessary that this latter accounts for the uplifting of our determinations. When the spirit overcomes its limits and approaches the super-essence only super-essence itself can carry it.[67]

The proceeding term is necessarily linked to finiteness, to determinations and multiplicity. Therefore, it is impossible that the finite term should overcome its own finiteness through its own forces.

On the other hand, this passage to a super-essential existence would be unthinkable if this super-essence did not already in one way or another support our existence. Man has to be defined as intrinsically tending towards the One. We should not be misled by the contingent schemes which introduce extrinsicism and make us believe that the super-essential existence is super-imposed on a nature which does not expect it in any way. In other words, we should not confuse the necessary extrinsicism of the schemes supporting the category of grace with the gratuitousness of grace. If the super-essence were not present in our spirituality, in the Act-Law, the supernatural existence would be a second creation, a new spiritual dimension, completely heterogeneous to our deepest being.

One can therefore hold – abstraction being made from representations – that the supernatural would never enter into man if the super-essence did not ground spirituality; it is necessary that it be eternally present in order one day to awaken the spirit to that which is more noble within it yet without being itself. Everything is adventitious yet absolutely gratuitous. We must not permit ourselves to be deceived by language or by the historicist illusion.[68]

But what happens to this view of man, as oppositional unity of freedom and nature, and of religion as freeing force, in the context of Duméry's axiogenesis? If human freedom creates the values, is freedom's servitude to nature not already overcome? This would mean that the consideration of a possible passage to a super-essential existence becomes superfluous. Axiogenic freedom already has a complete mastery over its determinations since they are its own creations. It is here that Duméry accuses atheistic axiogenesis of not being consequent. If one bestows an absolute power of contestation upon human freedom, then one should also accept

---

[67] *Ibid.*, p. 282.
[68] *Ibid.*, p. 284.

that this negative power of contestation calls for a positive power of complete overcoming of all determinations. But this refutation of Sartre's refusal to accept any communication or communion with a transcendent Being does not answer the question by which Duméry introduces the question of axiogenesis versus grace. It only aggravates the situation. Maintaining that Sartre should discover a power of absolute indetermination present in freedom's power of contestation, one makes the danger of immanentism become only more imminent. Let us have a closer look.

We have already presented Duméry's fundamental objections against Sartre's atheistic axiogenesis.[69] He accuses Sartre of not being concerned with the salvation of the axiogenesis. This term "salvation," as one may expect, has no specific religious meaning. It merely implies that Sartre should be more concerned about making man's freedom meaningful. Duméry makes the option for a meaningful human existence, whereas Sartre chooses the opposite position. The latter maintains that man is free not in spite of, but because of, his limitations. Human freedom as negativity rebounds on its empirical situation, without ever being able to grasp it. This leads us directly to Sartre's final conclusion: life is a useless passion. Man *is* an absurd project: attempt of the for-itself to conquer the in-itself, entailing the destruction of the for-itself.

> Human life can be reduced to an escape doomed to failure, to absurd alternation of destructive and rejuvenating blows, triumphs and dejections; everything takes place, is consummated and exhausted in the sterile pride of constantly renewed struggles.[70]

But this is not the whole truth. There is more, so Duméry writes, in freedom's refusal of all determinations than this senseless Sisyphean alternation of accomplishment and destruction. If freedom displays a power of infinite contestation, then freedom really overcomes finitude in that it judges its situation without thereby evading all "situatedness."

> It disengages itself from everything and yet remains involved; it is at the interior of its determinate situation, of its psycho-empirical situation – let us say of the incarnate and worldly consciousness – so that it surpasses nature, situation, the world of sensation or of perception.[71]

One must thus maintain that freedom is infinite and transcends all "situatedness" and, at the same time, that it has to reconquer itself continually with respect to the finite. Here, two roads are open to man. Either he loses himself in fascination of the objectified world, or he wins himself

---
[69] See Chapter I, Section III.
[70] Duméry, *Philosophie de la religion*, p. 287.
[71] *Ibid.*, p. 289.

in a radical relativizing of the whole phenomenal world. In the last case, man reaches real liberation. He transforms the obstructing determinations into pure mediations; he makes transparent the opacity of the objects. Remaining present to the world, he overcomes every determination. He uses the determinations as if he were not using them. "Perfection does not consist in a negative renunciation; it exists in serene, calm, disinterested usage; it is not an attitude of evasion but of simplicity and acceptance." [72] But this is only possible if man, on a certain level within himself, is allowed to live by the power of Undetermined Himself. Only then are the determinations transcended, not suppressed – since the Divine energy continues to make proceed what is converting itself.

Duméry talks about this passage to the super-essential existence in terms of ecstasy. If the scheme of the category of grace pointed to an experience of deification, ecstasy is the transitory acquisition of pure freedom. Ecstasy is the result of a complete openness of man to the immanent presence of the spontaneity of the One.

> It is the discovery that one makes himself only because God grants to us the possibility to make ourselves; in a word, it is to discern that spirituality, inasmuch as it is a process, is through the reality of super-essence and that intelligible self-constitution is only through the divine *aseitas*.[73]

Duméry seems to imply that the ecstatic experience of the mystics is necessary to reach a decisive liberation. Through the night of the senses and through the night of all objective light (rational objectivations), the spirit joins, or rather communes, with its source. In terms of love:

> To love everything *with* the love of God is to confide in God, to adhere to Him, without touching Him, or trying to experience Him; such is the expression all at once of devotion, freedom and love.[74]

Ecstasy brings God present to man in a new manner. God is present in two complementary ways. As creator, He is present in man as the power of man's power (procession). The second presence is one of "decreation." This means a presence which is the result of man's conversion. In converting to the One, man turns the created into nothingness. In other words, decreation is thus the reversing of creation by refusing to delight in it.[75] Decreation is "the definitive redemption of all limits which creation imposes in its contingence and finitude." [76] Man has to become nothing-

---

[72] *Ibid.*, p. 291.
[73] *Ibid.*, p. 283.
[74] *Ibid.*, p. 294.
[75] As already mentioned, Duméry takes this insight from Simone Weil: *La pesanteur et la grâce*, p. 36.
[76] Duméry, *Foi et interrogation*, p. 27.

ness so that God may love through him. Sartre makes the movement of decreation without discovering its real meaning. His philosophy is indeed a theology without God.[77] He should discover the presence of the pure freedom of the One in freedom's power of contestation. Since he does not do it, he gets caught in a senseless fanaticism of the effort. "To be free by God, in God, and as God, or to remain inauthentic: such seems to be the stakes of the human condition." [78]

In order to reach fullness of existence, man has to activate these two presences: the presence of creation and the presence of decreation. By decreating ourselves, we take part in the creation of the world. We discovered some beautiful pages on this theme in S. Weil's other work, *Attente de Dieu,* which gives us a better insight into what Duméry means here. She interprets the act of creation of God as an initial act of renouncement. God, Who in His love wants man to participate freely in His divine life, withdraws in creating so as to give man possibility to choose. In this sense creation is a retreat, rather than an expansion, of God. The creatures reveal God's absence, a *willed* absence for him who discovers God's love rather than His presence.

> Creation on the part of God is not an act of self-expansion but of retreat and renouncement. God and the totality of creation is less than God alone. God accepted this diminution-creation. He emptied Himself of a part of being. He already emptied Himself in this act of His divinity; that is why St. John says that the lamb has been slaughtered at the constitution of the world. By the creative act He denied Himself as Christ required of us that we deny ourselves. God denied Himself in our favor in order to give us the possibility of denying ourselves for Him.[79]

This way of conceiving creation as an act of withdrawal suits the purpose of establishing a rigorously immanent human world. It is what Bonhoeffer calls the powerlessness of the Christian God which man increasingly has come to realize since man's coming of age which started in the thirteenth century and came to completion in the modern concept of man's autonomy.[80]

We find a strikingly similar approach in Blondel's theory of the two gifts. Blondel also brings together the distinction between nature and supernature and the distinction between the gift of incarnation and

---

[77] Egon Vietta, *Theologie ohne Gott. Versuch über die menschliche Existenz in der modernen französischen Philosophie.* (Zurich, 1946).
[78] Duméry, *Philosophie de la religion,* I, p. 291.
[79] Weil, *L'Attente de Dieu,* pp. 132-133.
[80] Bonhoeffer, *Letters and Papers from Prison,* p. 200.

redemption. But Blondel also uses the notion of the *kenosis* [81] in his understanding of creation and our response.

*Deus seipsum exinanivit.* God, in order to create, has not produced externally and outside of Him a new region. A less deceiving explanation is to depart from a completely merciful intention on the part of the Creator Who prepares not in space nor in His substantial plenitude but in His fecund love, a capacity for a life of happiness, a life of transforming union for other "Himselves." [82]

To this Divine *kenosis* corresponds a human *kenosis* by which man also empties himself of his divinity, i.e., his autonomy.

In order to make us, God, as it were, withdrew Himself. *Se ipsum exinanivit* ... It is therefore up to us to restore to Him on ourselves the empire of which He voluntarily divested Himself in order to allow us to restore it to Him in freedom as well as in love; it is therefore a radical mortification of natural and human being which prepares the advent of supernatural divine being.[83]

But getting back to Duméry, a summary of his discriminative and henological critique of the schemes of the supernatural and the category of grace has now been completed save for the fact that proper attention could not be given to his treatment of the positive and historical incarnation of the schemes of the category of grace. Up to now we did not recover much of the religious expressions of Christianity. Christianity does not teach a certain kind of purely intellectual supernaturalization. It is also and much more a *historical* revelation and redemption. "The Christian religion claims to tie together, in a special way, the interior liberating mediation within the spirit and the external projections of consciousness." [84] How can Christianity link these two together? This is what Duméry has to explain in his critique of the category of faith whose function it is to distribute on all levels of man's spatio-temporal existence the religious truth of the spirit's passage to the super-essential existence of the One.

---

[81] Phil. 2, 6-11. Well-known text where St. Paul describes how God emptied Himself in Christ.

[82] Blondel, *L'Etre et les êtres*, p. 310.

[83] Blondel, *Exigences philosophiques du Christianisme* (Paris: Presses Universitaires de France, 1950), pp. 137-138. This text and the previous one we found in the work of Claude Tresmontant, *Introduction à la métaphysique de Maurice Blondel* (Paris: Editions du Seuil, 1963). He has a very beautiful chapter on Blondel's theory of the two gifts: Chapitre XVI, "Le problème capital de la métaphysique chrétienne," pp. 253-305.

[84] Duméry, *Philosophie de la religion*, I, p. 299.

SECTION III
CATEGORY OF FAITH, FACTUAL AND DOCTRINAL SCHEMES

*a. Descriptive Phenomenology of the Judaeo-Christian Religion*

The irreducible core of the Judaeo-Christian religion is very simple. Religious man reaches for the transordinal One in an attempt to join the Absolute, his super-essential foundation. The scheme of transcendence and the category of the Absolute, the schemes of the supernatural and the category of grace, are proven by means of the henological reduction to be translations, on the different levels of consciousness, of the spirit's constitutive exigency of a passage to the super-essential existence of the One. In this way, the creation of a supernatural interiority is envisaged through a mystical union with the One. But this interior presence of and communion with the Absolute in a mystical *apophasis* seems to establish a religious philosophy which makes religion as such superfluous. The ecstatic union with the Absolute, even if it employs the mediations of psychological and mythical expressions, does not at all indicate the necessity of an historical and institutional mediation. Yet this is exactly what Christianity proposes. "Faith is not a cry!" [85] Christianity is a positive, an historical and institutional reality. By this, we do not mean simply that Christianity is an historical fact; of course not. The essence of Christianity is to reach and witness that God came into time, that He became history, that He rendered Himself visible. This indeed constitutes an enormous difficulty for the philosopher of religion. The reduction of the representations of the spirit's exigency of a super-essential existence is nothing in comparison to the reduction [86] of the historicity of Christianity, which our author will now attempt.

How will Duméry be able to absorb the positive historical elements of Christianity into his mystical interpretation of Christianity as search for and passage to an ecstatic union with the Absolute? Without doubt, Duméry, like every philosopher of Christian religion, here meets the supreme test. Will he, too, like so many other philosophers of religion find herein his Waterloo? We do not know. But regardless of our final appreciation, we must, considering the enormous difficulty of the problem, be sympathetic. We can already indicate vaguely how Duméry will face the problem. His critique of the category of the Absolute and the category of grace displays how he continually applies the principle that freedom

---

[85] *La foi n'est pas un cri*, Duméry.
[86] Whenever we talk about reduction, we are talking about the phenomenological reduction – not reductionism.

has to make a detour of psychological expression in order to realize itself. Interiority is reached through the mediation of exteriority. He applies the same principle here by saying that the historical reality of Christianity is the necessary detour of an incarnated religious consciousness. This is why a theory of man's deification, including the notion of grace, is not necessarily Christian. Duméry thinks that the general notion of grace is probably not a Judaeo-Christian invention. This is an interesting remark because it exemplifies once more Duméry's hellenizing tendency. Such a deification process can be found, for instance, in Plotinus. The Christian supernatural, however, is an historicized, instituted supernatural.

> The Christian notion of the supernatural does not refer to the category of grace in general (which goes beyond Christianity and imposes itself in every doctrine of transcendence); it refers to a certain manner of instituting grace, that is, to render it manifest in a certain course of history with the aid of certain schemes and rites. Positivity is essential here. To suppress it is to suppress faith itself. In these conditions the institution does not appear as something added on: it is constituting. It is precisely this which is the cause of disquiet to many philosophers.[87]

The positivity of the Christian religion is the great scandal for the philosopher of religion.

> The historical element is what poses for the philosopher the most embarrassing problem. Why abide in the historical element when history has rendered the service which was expected of it? If Jesus has revealed love and justice it suffices to receive his message; it suffices to strive to love, to become just, thereby forgetting the contingent occasion which provoked the questions . . . Are there, therefore, two ways to salvation: religion with its rites, narratives, and symbols; philosophy without a practical cult, without statuary faith, without imaginative projections?[88]

Duméry could not express the problem in a more acute form: do we have to make the choice between philosophy and religion; how keep both as disciplines in their own right and still come to a certain philosophical insight into what religion is? Duméry answers: by keeping in mind that human consciousness is essentially projective and that, even when the philosopher overcomes this projective mentality, this projective mediation remains necessary and salutary on account of man's incarnation. This is why a religious philosophy of man will never do away with religion.

---

[87] Duméry, *Phénoménologie et religion* (Paris: Presses Universitaires de France, 1958), p. 74.
[88] Duméry, *Philosophie de la religion*, II, p. 224.

Faith is not summarized completely in the engagement of profound freedom. If it did reduce itself to this it would raise but a single problem: the liaison with God on the level of pure interiority. But in man pure interiority does not exist, it is an abstraction. The regime of the spirit is one of incarnation. Freedom is only exercised when it mediates itself by body, world, society; in a word it is consciousness. Every man is a complex being, engaged in different levels in different networks of relations, meanings and values. Consequently, it is not surprising that faith extends itself to this totality. This is especially true of faith since it does not admit of any division and is, as every human act, a diversified totality.[89]

The problem is to investigate whether the necessity of projective mediation explains why grace has to be historically and not only psychologically mediated. For Christianity, history is truth. Philosophy, however, tries to found truth on the interiority of universal and necessary meaning. In its extreme form, this may lead to exactly the opposite postulate, namely, the more an event is meaningful the more chances there are that the event is product of a legend. How is the opposition between truth as factual history (Christianity) and truth as transparent meaning overcome? Everything of course depends on what is understood by history. In the final analysis, the answer to the question, "What is history?" will provide the answer to "What is revelation?" The philosophical mind has a hard time believing that there is anything outside its own operation. On the other hand, the Christian religious mind does not merely believe because the Christian dogmas are true in themselves, irrespective of whether what they say happened or not, but also just because they happened. This is the opposition Duméry will try to surmount. Again, let us not underestimate the difficulty. So often one thinks a solution is reached because one does not realize the consequences of the Christian option for an historical religion. Pascal was aware of this when he wrote: "Believing that the Incarnation is a reality is a very serious option; few Christians have weighed all that this option supposes." [90]

One cannot understand Christianity without going back to its Judaean source. Christianity is a Judaism. It was the genius of Judaism to discover that *the great revealer of the Absolute is human history,* because only through history can man relate himself to the Absolute by means of the principle of intentionality. For the pagan religions, the great revealer was nature. Of course this also was the result of a hierophantic procedure [91] which the religious consciousness uses in order to represent the

[89] *Ibid.,* p. 20.
[90] Pascal, *Pensées,* number 201.
[91] Hierophantic process is the process by which the religious consciousness makes the sacred *appear* and *present* by imparting a sacred quality to profane objects.

Absolute. But everything changes once man begins to realize that he, himself, is the great revealer of the Absolute. The theophany becomes anthropomorphic, the gods assume a human face. But the divine can be humanized in two ways. The first one proceeds by deifying legendary personalities or historical personalities who soon lose their concrete references. This is the way pursued by Greek and Roman mythology. The divine, however, can also take real historical personalities as its expression. This is the method followed by the Jewish religion.

It (Hebraic mysticism) does not regard as a source of revelation either external nature as did archaic paganism, or even the nature of man (in the psycho-rational sense) as did Greco-Roman paganism. For it, history alone reveals God; only the historical subjects express by their deeds the divine wishes.[92]

The important point here is that a pure speculative revelation becomes impossible. The Bible declares that all human wisdom about God is vain. The wisdom of God is of another order. It cannot be grasped by the human intellect. Only a positive revelation, therefore, remains possible. God cannot communicate in our fashion; consequently, He has to let man talk *about* Him. Human history, therefore, becomes the means par excellence of revelation. It has the advantage over a revealing-nature of escaping all superstitious objectivations of the Absolute. On the other hand, it enables man to respect the mystery and transcendence of the Absolute. In this, historical revelation is superior to speculative-mythological revelation. The superiority of an historical revelation over the two other kinds of revelation (nature and thought) lies in its intentional character. History incarnates free intentions and, in its religious form, it manifests in time the "presence" of the Absolute, "presence" which at the same time allows for an "absence."

Intentionality alone permits this manifestation. Since God cannot show Himself openly, He decrees that He be sought. He beckons to a long undertaking, offers Himself as the term of an infinite quest and a ceaselessly renewed effort. On his side man cannot grasp Him; he can only aim at Him. God is never possessed as an object. He presents Himself as a presence – a presence which is even more exciting in its sustained mystery. Now history lends itself marvelously to this aiming at God by man, to this moving presence of God within man.[93]

To understand Duméry, we should recall that phenomenological existentialism, the atmosphere in which he thinks, identifies almost com-

---
[92] Duméry, *Phénoménologie et religion*, p. 8.
[93] Duméry, *La foi n'est pas un cri*. Foi et institution (2d ed.; Paris: Editions du Seuil, 1959), p. 218.

pletely historicity and man's creative freedom. Both ideas point to the fundamental fact that man is not a natural being but a cultural being. At the same time, they also indicate that man lives under the law of incarnation. He does not belong to an eternal and completely intelligible realm. Historicity indicates man's peculiar way of bringing a world of meaning into existence. By inventing the category of history, Judaism discovered the specifically human creativity. It overcomes the naturalistic attitude which believes in a pre-human world. The world is always already human; it is invested with meaning. On the other hand it does away with all disincarnated concepts of the human mind. In the idea of historicity, Israel expressed the most fundamental experience of human existence on which everything else is based.

> Israel has recovered for the benefit of its own culture and for the benefit of culture as such, the original experience from which every man departs and to which every man remains bound: by his presence in the world the human subject invests all reality with anthropological predicates. This is true to the extent that the world is only a universe by and through the attention of man; it only becomes the occasion and matter of history by and through the action of man.[94]

But Israel invented the category of history for religious motives. According to the biblical writers only God makes history and consequently only the men of God, the men united with God, make history with God and for God. If man is the maker of history, and if this history reveals God's designs, it is because man's ultimate vocation is union with a God Who is Invisible. There is no profane history, man's life is ascent towards the Absolute. Yet this sacred history is completely human. God does not talk. This paradoxical notion of a sacred history which is at the same time radically human, results from Israel's rigorous notion of transcendence. In its essence, Judaism is iconoclastic, a religion without altars and images. God is the Ineffable and Invisible. " 'But, my face,' He said, 'thou canst not see; mortal man cannot see Me, and live to tell of it.' "[95] This deep consciousness of the heterogeneity of God allows us to speak about Him in anthropomorphic terms. Man talks about God because God Himself cannot talk. Man talks because he cannot intuit the Absolute. "Man is a speaking being" serves as an adequate definition of man.

Man is incapable of experiencing anything *without speaking it*. Each of his experiences, and included here that of the holy, requires that it pass to expression. Hence the rigorous paradox: *because* it (religious experience) is an

---
[94] Duméry, *Phénoménologie et religion*, p. 9.
[95] Exodus, 33, 20.

experience of the invisible, man bestows representations of it. It is the experience of the inexpressible and *this is why* expression is given. Of all religions Judaism doubtlessly has employed this mechanism with the most precision. Yahweh is the hidden, inaccessible God. For this reason he becomes the close and familiar God. He is the non-manifest and impenetrable God. This is why he becomes the manifest and revealed God.[96]

The originality of Judaism consists in accepting as expressions of the Divine only those which are intentional: history, human acts. An intentional reality at the same time is and is not its content. Therefore, when it "intends" the Absolute it reveals and hides the Absolute. It reveals the Absolute insofar as its tending signifies the Absolute. It hides the Absolute insofar as its tending cannot contain the Absolute. Revelation can never become speculative insight. When we say "revelation," we say that man is the "speaking" being. When we say "divine revelation" we say that this speaking being has the presence of and the yearning for the Ineffable One. The application of the idea of intentionality to the category of revelation is one of the most valuable insights of Duméry. Intentionality applied to revelation prevents us from understanding the word of God either in a too physical way or in a too speculative way. It makes us understand that the equation, "What the sacred author says is what God says," is after all not so simple. Revelation cannot be reduced to a collection of clearly defined concepts and categorical affirmations coming ready-made from heaven. The word of God, which is the foundation of Christianity, may not be conceived in a naturalistic or intellectualistic manner.

History, the intentional reality par excellence, is not only successful in revealing the Absolute without infringing upon the transcendence of God, it also leaves room for a radically human world. This idea of an independent human realm is very dear to our author. If historicity as the institution of meaning and not the discovery of a ready-made sacred meaning constitutes the mechanism of revelation, then historical religion is a radical humanism. Not nature but humanity and the becoming of humanity reveals God.[97] Therefore, the revealing act of God through man falls together with the meaning-giving act of man. The world left to itself has no meaning; its meaning has to be made. Human history becomes meaningful by referring it to the Absolute. Similarly, the meaning-giving activity of man becomes a progressive recreation of the world in order to bring perfect harmony between man and nature.

[96] Duméry, *Phénoménologie et religion*, pp. 11-12.
[97] It might be useful to point out to the reader the Hegelian overtone of this recurring theme: Man creates himself in a historical process.

Israel has chosen to give to history the sense of a progressive consecration of creation, of a recreation of the world until the day when the world will express by peace and harmony the only ideal worthy of this name: union with God which for man involves, together with the realization of self, the accomplishment of everything.[98]

Union with God is realized through the mediation of bestowing meaning upon nature. According to the Bible, there is conflict between man and nature. Suffering and death, the resistance of things, the inner conflicts of freedom are so many expressions of this fundamental hostility which man must overcome. This aim is expressed in the biblical projection of an original harmony which has to be recovered in the future. The eschatological vision of a world where the wolf and the lamb will live in good understanding (Isaias) constitutes Israel's messianic hope.

For the Jew, to make history, to assign an end to it and to work towards the coming of the Messiah, coincide. Messianism is nothing but a program of action. It is a question of finding a meaning in history. This meaning will consist in the progressive elimination of every cause of division. Lived history coincides therefore with the transformation of the world in the hope of inaugurating a complete refashioning of its elements.[99]

This intramundane process of meaning-giving *is* at the same time man's ascent to the Absolute. By this, Judaism is able to reconcile man's duties in time and his eternal vocation. Israel's doctrine of salvation holds a middle position between a completely this-worldly liberation of man (Marxism, atheistic humanism) and a completely other-worldly salvation (religion as salvation of souls, liberation of the spirit from the body). The salvation of man can only be realized in an action of transforming nature. This action, however, receives its efficiency from an alliance and union with God. Grace, therefore, is the ultimate moving force of history. Union with God is at the same time the goal of history and that which makes the realization of this goal possible. This union with God is mediated by man's effort to bring meaning and harmony into this world. This is what historical (constitution of meaning) religion (union with God) means.

When it is a question of *historical religion* one means this effort, on the part of man in alliance with God, to transform nature in order to prepare for the coming of grace within history and by means of history. Israel invented the category of *history* the day she understood that her vocation was to witness the beyond in the here and now. But this vocation implied an extremely forceful idea which is: the beyond has no effective expression in the here and now unless in the witnessing of men among men.[100]

[98] Duméry, *Phénoménologie et religion*, p. 67.
[99] *Ibid.*, p. 14.
[100] *Ibid.*, pp. 17-18.

History is at the same time radically human and totally divine. It is also simultaneously a constitution of meaning and harmony; it is revelation of the sacred design immanent in time. History, in the final analysis, is sacred. It is only through the hypertrophy of technology that man's transformation of the universe lost its sacred character.

Once it is admitted that history, and not nature, is revealing, then history is also *typological*. This is the second essential characteristic of the Jewish religion. The events and personalities of history, which is revelation, are types in which the alliance of Israel with God is expressed. Through the extreme immanentizing of Divine revelation, the concrete history of the insignificant tribe Israel becomes the concrete expression (type) of the Divine. History became Judaeo-centric the moment it became anthropocentric. Israel is "the light shining among the nations." The collective history of Israel, the great religious events (the exodus, the passage of the Red Sea, the crossing of the Jordan, the exile in Babylon) establish a concrete historical exemplification through which Israel can recover its fundamental vocation. Not only the history of Israel as such, but also certain privileged individuals provide the believer with incarnate ideals in which he recognizes his religious intention. Typology means that what is presented is always a concrete lived religious value. In order to express what sin, faith, patience in suffering is, the Bible never gives a learned definition. It always introduces historical heroes (Adam, Abraham, Isaac, Moses, David, Job . . .) and through these gives concrete lived examples of what is meant by the great religious categories. It also typifies human beings of vision and anticipation, through whom the final union with God will be reached (cf. Isaias, the man of suffering; Daniel, the son of man). These prophetic and eschatological typifications, however, are also centered around an historical Messiah. One might think that the typification process of the Bible is the result of a primitive way of thinking, of an incapacity to think a general idea. Yet this is not true. Israel's predilection for the lived and concrete is a deliberate choice: a refusal to advance the general over particular cases.

This leads to a third essential characteristic of the Jewish religion. The historical and typological character of Judaism reveals the fundamental thesis that *the universal can only be reached through the particular.*

In biblical literature there is a distinctive art: elaborating religion in history, thinking about ethical and mystical matters in the concrete situation and only in this situation . . . Thus typology is a suitable manner, though not very learned, of reading the universal directly in the particular . . . Furthermore it denies completely that the universal can be perceived otherwise than in its expression which is always particular and quite ambiguous. Today phenomenology develops an analogous thesis.[101]

Judaism is a universal religion with a particular expression. It is universal at least by intention, since it adores the unique God, creator of the whole universe. It also sees its vocation as the beginning of a salvation of all nations. Jerusalem is the real center of the world.[102] The God of Abraham has to be recognized as the God of mankind. One cannot believe in Israel's God, the only true God, without accepting the essential points of the Jewish Law (the pagan who accepts these points is called a "God-fearing man"; for instance, Cornelius in Acts 10, 2) and even circumcision (the pagan who accepts the circumcision is called a "proselyte"). This particularism is not just accidental, but belongs to the very essence of Judaism. It is based upon its principle of revelation. If God is transcendent, if He is ineffable, then only a human witness can bring us the "word of God"; consequently, the teaching of revelation is identified with a particular word.

An historical, typological religion, realizing the universal in a particular expression: such is the essence of Judaism.

The boldness of Judaism can be summarized in a few propositions: The transcendent is accessible only by way of the immanent; the universal is conquered only through the particular; if the letter kills, if the spirit gives life, the spirit lives only by the spirit of the letter ... Only the religious institution pretends to reconcile the infinite and the finite, the absolute of the spirit and the relativity of history. Judaism is not stranded in history since it has established a school. Christianity has taken from it its principal institutional features.[103]

Christianity like Judaism is an historical religion. It accepts the idea of a divine revelation inherent in Israel's history. It ratifies the idea of a chosen people and the general scheme of the Alliance. Yet, Christianity is not just a Jewish sect, for it constitutes an original creation. This originality consists in the fact that the disciples of Jesus inaugurate a new doctrinal object pertaining to worship: the risen Christ. This faith in the risen Christ will gradually change the tone and the nature of the messianic spirituality.

The specific meaning of the Jesus-fact is that through Him the anonymous messiah of Judaism is given a name and that consequently the eschatological expectation of the Jews is halted. The final result is a

---

[101] *Ibid.*, pp. 24-25.
[102] Cf. the famous Chapter 60 of Isaias on the universalism of the Jewish religion.
[103] Duméry, *Phénoménologie et religion*, pp. 29-30.

profound transformation of the Jewish prophetic futurism in the Christian actualism of salvation.

Official Judaism remains actually a messianism with an indeterminate maturity. On the other hand, Christianity is a messianism with a dated maturity. Similarly, Judaism claims a revelation which is poured forth in the time of history which will end only with the end of the world. Revelation closes only in the beyond. Christianity on the other hand limits and interrupts revelation at the interior of history; it declares that it is terminated when there remains no longer a direct witness to messianic events.[104]

We can now anticipate the direction which Duméry will follow in his interpretation of the Jesus-fact which is the foundation of Christianity. Faith in Jesus will, in last analysis, be the discovery of the capacity to interiorize the religious values of Judaism. This interiorization is initiated by the Rabbi of the sermon on the mount.

Jesus succeeded in turning the futurist expectation of the Jews into the actuality of salvation. Jesus truly made present and interiorized the elements in messianism which remained projective. By that He has not delivered us over to history, but has delivered us from history.[105]

This capacity of interiorizing Jewish religious values is nothing else but the capacity to come to a vision of the Absolute (One) beyond all representative determinations of the mind and the imagination. But since the incarnate consciousness cannot do without the intellectual and imaginative expressions, Christian faith will again project this perfect revelation of the Absolute in Christ, in religious categories and schemes: the scheme of resurrection and glorification, the category of logos, the doctrine of Incarnation and Trinity.

The important point is to disengage the essential fact that Jesus directed the messianic expectation to His person and that He interiorized the Jewish ideal of justice. By this He reacted against the tendency to escape into an unrealistic and futuristic messianism and against the legalism of the material observance which implied blasphemous self-salvation. Jesus is supreme and actual theophany. He shows that the Absolute is present and that, therefore, the messianic kingdom is at hand. He teaches that the union with God is the result of a complete self-immolation of man through charity.

Jesus is the founder of the absolute religion because the Absolute cannot reveal itself in a more complete manner than in Him, i.e., under the sign

---

[104] *Ibid.*, pp. 35-36.
[105] Duméry, *Foi et interrogation*, p. 42.

of total disinterestedness, of charity in thought and deed. This is the basic message of the Gospels.[106]

Historical revelation finds its completion in Jesus. Therefore, He also focalizes in Himself all the typological revelations of the past. He is the type of the realization of all promises represented in the previous types. Since revelation is historical, the typical is the revealer. Jesus, therefore, is the supreme revealer. He is theophany in act. To imitate Jesus is thus to unite oneself to the God of Jesus, the God present and revealed in Jesus. By applying to Jesus the laws of the Jewish typology, Christianity imposes upon itself the obligation to keep a positive reference. This will prevent Christianity from being absorbed by its successive and different cultural expressions. Yet the meaning of the Christian typology of Jesus is different from the Jewish typology of the Old Testament. Behind the Christian typology stands the actualized and realized Promise: Jesus. Therefore, the different typifications of Jesus become, as it were, transparent, they lose some of their inner consistency.

> Christological typology is no longer a screen; it is transformed into a transparent mediation. It allows the soul to reach God *directly* by the exclusive effect of an understood mediation.[107]

The Jewish schematism found its completion and fulfillment, and becomes, therefore, when applied to Jesus, a mere mediation through which one can discover the perfect revelation of God in Christ. What Duméry seems to imply is that the Jewish schematism has been transcended by the very fact that its expectations became reality. This actualization is now considered by our author to be mainly an interiorization of the religious ideals of the Jews. In order to understand this we have to give further attention to this fundamental thesis of Spinozian inspiration.

> In our opinion the merit of Spinoza, as paradoxical as it may seem, is to have suggested that Christianity after the manner of Jesus, the historicity of which is not contested by Spinoza, is formed, from its origin, by a spiritual interiorization of messianic futurism.[108]

We have to recall Duméry's deep concern to discard any form of action coming from the outside and imposing itself upon man and thereby doing harm to human interiority. When talking about the historicity of the Jewish revelation he was able to save the interiority of the religious consciousness by understanding revelation as an immanent process of

---

[106] Duméry, *La foi n'est pas un cri*, p. 30.
[107] Duméry, *Phénoménologie et religion*, p. 70.
[108] *Ibid.*, p. 15.

ultimate meaning-giving. He avoids talking about a direct intervening action of God in history. He prefers to speak in terms of Israel in search of its vocation as unique revealer of God. It is for this reason that one may not be deceived, Duméry says, by the primitive way in which God's intervention is expressed in many passages of the Old Testament.

The divine unforeseeable intervention that it (O.T.) celebrates in a lyrical manner has nothing to do with a voluntarist theism which would be the consecration of the arbitrary. Its function is to note the rupture between the order created by freedom and all natural order. It does not destroy the historical human order; on the contrary it confirms it and restores to it its proper originality.[109]

This text clearly indicates Duméry's decision never to let the Divine action become foreign and thus infringe upon the autonomous universe of human freedom. One can imagine the difficulty he faces when it comes to the doctrine of incarnation which is at the origin of Christianity. How can one here avoid the implication of a Divine action intruding the order of human history? He has to understand the incarnation in conjunction with his concept of immanent historical revelation. By seeing in Jesus a unique case and culmination of the discovery that God reveals himself in and through man's capacity to *create* meaning, to *make* history and therefore to render God present, Duméry found a philosophical equivalent of the dogma of incarnation.

The greatness of Jesus was in teaching man to discover an *absolute presence* within his *interior presence*. It is by that, it seems to us, that he has liberated us from history, at least from its servitude. We have to change ourselves *here and now;* and to change ourselves is, in making ourselves, to make history and not to undergo it.[110]

How does he arrive at this interpretation of the scriptural sources? It is evident that the historical person of Jesus cannot be clearly elicited from the Gospels. The Gospels are intrinsically religious books, they are not historical documents. We deal with religious history, historical recollections penetrated by a religious intention. Duméry further grants to the historical critique that primacy is to be given to the believing community over the individual preaching of the Gospel. It is in the Church that the Gospel has been formulated. Scripture is the product of tradition.

If it is the case that the Gospels are not a biography of Jesus and the apostles, if they are rather the product of the original faith, they assuredly teach us about the milieu which gave birth to their redaction. At the same time they

[109] *Ibid.*
[110] Duméry, *Philosophie de la religion*, II, p. 71, note 1.

distance themselves, as it were, from their historical source: Jesus. What they present is less the fact of Jesus than this fact reflected in the consciousness of the first believers.[111]

Has the Jesus-fact then been constructed by the faith of His followers? The thesis of the *Formgeschichtliche Schule* which sees the Gospels as the product of the collective religious consciousness of the first Christians is, according to Duméry, a psychological impossibility. Collective consciousness never reaches such a high level as is necessary to initiate a religious revolution such as Christianity.

A personal melody is necessary to animate and guide the collective symphony. Religious intuitions, as every intuition, belong always to an individual consciousness before being grasped and orchestrated by groups. The collective never replaces personal initiative even in the case of religious inventiveness.[112]

Duméry thus accepts the historicity of Jesus.

What is this personal initiative, this fundamental intuition which is at the source of Christianity? The point of utmost importance is to understand Jesus' attitude as a continuation and completion of the ancient biblical tradition. One should not be misled by the later adopted categories and schemes which come from the Hellenic milieu. One must look for the original inspiration which directed and assumed these expressions of non-Jewish origin. Christianity has its roots in Judaism. The essence of the Christian message is to be found in its reinterpretation of Judaism. This, however, does not mean a break with the past but continuity. Jesus has the intention of realizing the Law not of abolishing it,[113] nor of abrogating it but of maintaining it.[114] The only means to confirm the Law without abolishing it is by replacing the outward justification by an inward one, as St. Paul explains.[115]

It is a question of surpassing the law, not adding to it; a question of returning from its exteriority to interiority. Jesus does not bring a fulfillment in the sense of a quantitative addition. Rather He simplifies the law; He introduces a new quality or rather He uncovers in biblical religion a quality which was never suspected to be there.[116]

Duméry adds the last remark to justify his reading of the Old Testament in which he interprets the historicity of Judaic revelation as an immanent

---

[111] *Ibid.*, pp. 44-45.
[112] *Ibid.*, p. 49.
[113] Mt. 5, 17-18.
[114] Lc. 16, 17.
[115] Rom. 3, 31 Heb. 8, 10.
[116] Duméry, *Philosophie de la religion*, II, p. 52.

search for the Absolute and progressive consecration of the universe. In Christ, this immanent revealing religious intentionality of history reaches its full completion. By the same token, Israel's futuristic messianism undergoes a spiritual interiorization. He founds the absolute religion of interiority by transcending all factual positivity.

Duméry quotes texts of St. Paul and St. John in favor of this thesis. But it is obvious that Spinoza is his main inspiration here. We know that Spinoza sees the opposition between Judaism and Christianity as an opposition between exteriority and interiority. Spinoza is convinced that Jesus extracted from a legalistic and nationalistic Judaism full of exteriority a Christian religion which is all interiority culminating in the command of love of God and neighbor. In the light of this opposition Judaism appears as subjected to the passions of the soul and as ignoring authentic freedom.

> The Hebrews were not able to raise themselves to the level of spiritual freedom; they obeyed by fear and constraint; they were incapable of making an autonomous judgment... The Jews generally could not reach universality (they remained bound by the mosaic alliance) or interiority (submission to law by love of recompense or fear remained the principle of the ancient faith).[117]

Christ, as opposed to this, by teaching the universality of love, has discovered the essence of religion. He extracted the final and definite form of religion from the Jewish tradition by actualizing and interiorizing the external and futuristic messianism. Spinoza does not deny the historicity of the religious events. He only rejects that the event as event is saving.

> Exteriority would not know how to ground or to justify interiority. Interiority, in a rigorous sense, can only be grounded on itself. It is an immense mistake to secure for it extrinsic supports and then to believe that these sustain it... Now for Spinoza, the religious genius who has best rid religion of all carnal and complacent historicism is Christ.[118]

Jesus has revealed to the world interiority, and, therefore, He deserves the title of philosopher as much as Socrates. Spinoza called Jesus "le philosophe par excellence." [119]

Is the Christ of Spinoza a faithful picture of Christ of the Gospel? Duméry thinks so. When we open the New Testament, we are immediately faced with a most astonishing observation. The Messiah, expected by the Jews for ages, has appeared in the person of Jesus of Nazareth.

---

[117] *Ibid.*, pp. 55-56.
[118] *Ibid.*, p. 63.
[119] *Ibid.*, p. 64. This was a saying of Spinoza recorded by Tschirohaus.

This reversal of the Jewish messianism is a spiritual revolution whose daring one can hardly imagine.

> Messianism halted in its full élan, actualized, interiorized, is Judaism at once fulfilled and contradicted, accomplished and surpassed. A very bold enterprise perhaps. The New Testament affords witness to it and attributes its origin to Jesus.[120]

Hence, so Duméry continues (and here we meet again the rather strange way of establishing the historicity of Jesus), we can discard all doubts about the historicity of Jesus. The Jewish messianism could only be reversed and actualized through the intervention of an individual not of collective consciousness.

> The historicity of Jesus is drawn from the necessity of placing at the beginning of Christianity a qualified person – qualified by the characteristics of boldness and discernment to effect the definitive interiorization of Jewish Messianism.[121]

Jesus has existed because to spiritualize and actualize the messianic hope supposes a spirit capable of lifting itself up to the level of interiority. Such a creative intuition always springs from a personal consciousness.

Spinoza, so Duméry maintains, has thus correctly understood the intuition of Jesus which stands at the origin of Christianity.

> Jesus is the herald of spiritual interiority and by that He delivers us in the course of history from history... By inviting His contemporaries to stop projecting before themselves their ideal of justice and by urging them to realize it immediately with God's Grace by themselves, Jesus substitutes for the alibi of tomorrow, so convenient for the conscience, the urgency of the present moment.[122]

Jesus liberates us from history because He enables us to see that the only adequate valorization of history lies in the conviction that man's freedom is capable every moment, and, with the help of grace, to escape the sway of evil. But it is much easier to return to a religious futurism than to keep inventive freedom awake. We recognize the ghost of Sartre ever present in the wings. Religion as mere celestial eschatologism is betrayal of human freedom and responsibility. Man is responsible for his salvation here and now. Religious futurism is too often an alibi of courage.

Jesus escaped the traps of imagination. He made us see that the alternating hope-realization-and again hope is a schematism which supports the notion of time. Judaism became victim of a mere projection into the

[120] *Ibid.*, p. 65.
[121] *Ibid.*, p. 67.
[122] *Ibid.*, p. 69.

future of something which is really here. This projection is only an imaginative scheme through which an eternal and present reality is intended.[123] It confused language and reality, means and goal. Jesus proclaimed the effective presence of God at all times, and the purification of the heart required to recognize this presence. This is the essential point of Christianity. All the categories and schemes of Christianity applied to Jesus are but the result of the projective mentality of the religious consciousness. The ideal of an actualized and interiorized justice realized in Jesus will be expressed through mental and imaginative representations coming from the Judaeo-Hellenic world. They are valid only as far as they can lead us back to the original intuition of Jesus.

### b. *The Jesus-fact Assumed by the Hierogenic Consciousness of the Early Christian Community*

The foregoing pages demonstrated how Duméry attempted to disengage the essential element of the Christian faith. He brought faith in Jesus back to its core: the discovery of Jesus' capacity to interiorize the religious values of Judaism. In Jesus, the historical revelation of Judaism came to its completion. The immanent revelation in history, the only way God can converse since He is completely transcendent, culminates in Jesus' discovery of the principle of interiority, of the presence of God in history and of eternity in time. This becomes apparent in his philosophical critique of the Christological dogmas. These dogmas are to be seen as an imaginative and mental projection by the religious consciousness of the ideal of interiority. Here Christianity follows the same laws of religious consciousness as found in all other religions, the laws of emotional and intellectual expression.

> The superiority of Christianity is to possess as its main contention an undeniable historical reference. But for the lesser facts it seems that their constitution requires only the application of common laws.[124]

Duméry distinguishes seven Christological stages leading up to the full development of Christology. The first stage is the assumption by Jesus of the concept of messiah in order to define His vocation. His meditations on Isaias incline Him to conceive His messianism as not simply glorious, but glorious because of His suffering. The first stage thus encompasses only the life and passion of Jesus. Between this phase and the following phases,

---

[123] Duméry objects violently against any notion of a linear time. "L'éternité est à l'intérieur du temps vécu, de l'histoire concrète; le temps comme pur flux, comme simple devenir, n'est qu'une abstraction." (*La foi n'est pas un cri,* p. 267.)
[124] *Ibid.,* p. 74.

there is the distance between the historical fact and the religious consciousness starting its projective sacralization of this fact. The resurrection is the first stage this side of the distinction. Through faith in the resurrection, Jesus' shameful death can be reconciled with His messianism. To have believed in the presence of God in Jesus meant that death could not have conquered Him. Jesus' resurrection is postulated in virtue of His theophanic quality. God's presence in Jesus, as far as the Christian realizes this attitude in his life, is then not only the assurance of Jesus' victory over death, but also of the human condition as such. "In proclaiming that Jesus has risen, really risen, the Christian faith merely projects into a typical case that which is ruled out for the general human condition." [125] The resurrection is a Semitic way of expressing belief in the immortality of man.

The martyrization of the deacon Stephen indicates another phase. By indicating how the passion of Jesus realizes the type of the Son of man described by Daniel,[126] St. Stephen makes the passage from the suffering and humiliated Jesus to the glorious Lord Who will come to judge and to establish an indestructible reign. This leads to a radical reversal. He Who announced the kingdom of God becomes the object of this announcement. Stephen praying to the "Lord Jesus" inaugurates the Christocentric piety. St. Paul reasons along the same lines. His Christology is completely centered around two terms: crucifixion and resurrection. Like St. Stephen, he understands that the cult of the temple is outdated. Jesus on the cross has atoned once and for all. It suffices to join His sacrifice, to be co-crucified in order to be co-resurrected. St. Paul's Christology is not only soteriological but it is also daringly theological. Christ is the "Image of the invisible God, the first-born of all creation. . . . Everything has been created through Him and for Him. He takes precedency of all, and in Him all subsist." [127] This deification of Christ will allow the transition from Jewish messianism to Greek theology. We are here on the dividing line between Jewish schematism and Greek categorialism.

The fourth Gospel provides us with a more adequate concept to qualify the eternal pre-existence of Christ. The term "logos" indicates that the author is a hellenized Jew.[128]

---

[125] Duméry, *Phénoménologie et religion*, p. 39.
[126] Acts 7 and Daniel 7, 13-14.
[127] Col. 1, 15-17.
[128] The commonly accepted opinion that the author of the fourth Gospel was a hellenized Jew is not universally accepted. Father Daniélou writes: "There is conclusive proof that the Johannine logos is the Hebrew 'dabar' – the word as creative of what is spoken: it has no point of connection with the Stoics' 'logos,' reason. And 'pneuma' in the New Testament is the Biblical 'rouah,' the image of God in a strong

Only an Israelite of the Diaspora could master both the Jewish and Greek cultures. In every way it is a happy choice. For a Jew, "logos" recalls "dabar," the word, here the word of God. For a Greek it recalls the teaching of Philo of Alexandria. It is thus understood by each in his own tongue – the strange phenomenon of glossolalia which permits two idioms, two mentalities, to be joined together without losing their originality.[129]

The process of deification is completed. From now on the believer speaks of Jesus-Christ, the simple hyphen placed between the name of a man and a transcendent attribute signifies the joining of the finite and the infinite.

By greeting Jesus with the title of Logos, by declaring that the Logos resides in God from all eternity, that it is God become man, the fourth Gospel accomplishes the bringing to the absolute of the "type" of the Messiah. From the outset, he elevates Jesus to the heights of the divinity.[130]

The theology of the Logos will necessitate the construction of the trinitarian theology.

Many other typifications followed. Successively messiah-prophet (Jesus' own understanding of Himself), messiah-lord (resurrection), messiah-judge (St. Stephen), divine messiah-savior (St. Paul) and messiah-logos (St. John), Jesus-Christ receives many other typifications coming from the myths and ritual schemes of the Hellenic world. Some even believe that these mystery-cults influenced directly the accounts of the Passion and Resurrection, or at least St. Paul's interpretation. Duméry thinks, however, that no convincing proof of this has been given.

No one has furnished proof of it. And, moreover, the differences are such that the resemblances themselves are not convincing. However, by reason of atmosphere, if not by way of expressions, it is possible that they helped to understand the redemption by Christ.[131]

---

gale of wind – not the common Greek 'pneuma,' a breath, the figure of incorporeity." Jean Danielou, *The Lord of History* (2d printing; Chicago: Henry Regnery, 1964), p. 117. He bases his theory of the Jewish origin of the Johannine logos upon the recent discoveries of the Dead Sea scrolls. There is a definite connection between St. John and the community of Qumran. St. John's gospel is entirely constructed around the theme of the conflict between light and darkness. Now this is also the leitmotif of Qumran. There are many more parallels. Danielou concludes: "This is a discovery of capital importance which shows that the backdrop of John's thought is Jewish, and thereby a breach is made in the theses put forth by the two most important recent commentators on John: Dodd, who interprets him as stemming from Hellenism; and Bultmann, who links him to the Gnostics. As Albright has stated, the debate on the original background of the Gospel of John appears to be definitely closed." Danielou, *The Dead Sea Scrolls and Primitive Christianity*, trans. Salvator Attanasio (Baltimore: Helicon Press, 1958), pp. 108-109.
[129] Duméry, *Phénoménologie et religion*, p. 44.
[130] *Ibid.*, p. 44.
[131] *Ibid.*, p. 46.

Finally, the messianic type receives its definite formation through a metaphysical reflection. The councils of Chalcedon (451) and Constantinople (553) decree that Jesus-Christ is true God and true man. This definition greatly differs from what we perceived as the original intuition of Christianity. By identifying the doctrine of incarnation with his interpretation of the process of biblical revelation reaching its culmination in Christ (Christ is Emmanuel: God with us), he is able to show that there is continuity, no break with the point of departure.

The question one should ask here, perhaps, is whether it is correct to see only a difference in degree between Christ and all the other revealing personalities of the Bible. We think that this cannot be done. It infringes upon the uniqueness of the incarnation of the Word of God in Christ.[132] Here, Duméry again reflects Spinoza who has a special theory of inspiration. According to Spinoza, there is no specific difference between the revelation through the prophets and through Jesus. The only difference lies in their way of expression. God revealed Himself in Christ immediately, without the intervention of parables and images as in the case of the other prophets.

> Whether it be a question of Moses, of the prophets or of Jesus, they are all bearers of revelation. But nevertheless they do so in different manners ... Christ was not a prophet, but the mouth of God ... thus there is a major difference between Christ and the prophets. They received their inspiration through an imaginative form; Christ, on the other hand, received His, without any detour, from the foundations of consciousness; as if He had only to recollect Himself in order to rejoin the source of all thoughts, the font of illumination for every spirit.[133]

Duméry's concern about freedom-alienating extrinsicism keeps him from conceiving any real action of God in history. We do not see how Duméry's understanding of revelation is anything more than an immanent coming to consciousness of man, even though a religious consciousness. This complete consciousness is reached in Christ. Is Christ anything more than the *ideal of* interiority? Is the historicity of Christ still an essential part of

---

[132] Duméry holds the uniqueness of the incarnation. Yet he is aware that, once we reduced the incarnation to the supreme degree of interiority realized in Christ, it is not clear any more why there should be only one incarnation and not many as in the Hindu religion. "Pourtant cette unicité de l'Incarnation est l'un des meilleurs services que le christianisme ait rendus à la religion dans l'humanité. En faisant de l'Incarnation la théophanie suprême, définitive, la foi chrétienne a condensé le divin dans un seul être; elle l'a retiré de la nature et des objets, elle l'a confié à une conscience humaine privilégiée. Par là, elle marque un incontestable progrès sur toutes les religions naturistes ou fétichistes; elle fait émerger la religion de l'esprit." Duméry, *Philosophie de la religion*, II, p. 105, note 3.

[133] *Ibid.*, p. 58.

the faith in Christ, as much as the dogmatic truth of Christ? Could it not be said that Christ is the truth regardless of whether He existed or not?

The separation of Jesus' resurrection from His life and passion is significant. It implies that His life and passion constitute the sector of positive science and history, whereas His resurrection belongs to the sector of faith and mythologization. There is some reason for such distinction since it is clear that the resurrection is not a fact in the same sense as Jesus' passion. It is very important to take into account what Duméry calls the polyvalence of the factual basis to Christianity. Taking his inspiration from Blondel's article, "De la valeur historique du dogme," [134] he distinguishes three kinds of religious facts. There are first of all historical phenomena among which Jesus' temporal existence is included. Then there are the historical facts which have a religious value. The relation between their historicity and their doctrinal value can be either extrinsic, the case of certain facts of Jesus' life which have no direct relation to His message, or intrinsic, facts which are essential to the Christian doctrine. These intrinsically religious facts call for a verification of a special nature. Duméry quotes Blondel:

If it is true that these different kinds of facts are all able to be considered and criticized, according to this ascending or progressive operation, as "historical phenomena," one must equally recognize that the facts of an intrinsic religious nature bear simultaneously proofs and verifications of a different kind and that their certain reality is not unilaterally proportionate to their demonstrated historicity.[135]

To understand the resurrection correctly, it must be treated as a religious affirmation. The spiritual initiative responsible for this affirmation must be given more weight than the empirical projections which accompany it. One must distinguish a factual and a spiritual element in the religious category of the resurrection. The spiritual element is the affirmation that Christ has been glorified, that He has entered the sphere of the divine and the eternal. The factual element of the psysical resurrection is the imaginative formulation of Jesus' transcending time and space, death and suffering.

The factual element is the representation of an empirical resurrection; left to the popular imagination it becomes in the end the reanimation of a corpse. The spiritual element is of a different order: it is the affirmation that the resurrected has entered into true life; something which no biological pattern of growth and decline can attain.[136]

---
[134] *Bulletin de littérature ecclésiastique* (February-March, 1905), pp. 61-77.
[135] Duméry, *Philosophie de la religion*, II, p. 132.
[136] *Ibid.*, p. 82.

The correct understanding of the resurrection requires the subordination of the empirical scheme to the idea of glorification. To believe in the resurrection is to overcome the resurrection-event by the resurrection-glorification. It is to believe in the presence of God in history, the presence of eternity in time. This echoes the interiority idea.

> To believe in the resurrected is to surpass the resurrection-event in the sense of the resurrection-glorification; it is to subsume the sensible manifestation under the ideal and normative meaning; in a word, it is to believe that God does not die and that those to whom He communicates His life do not die any more.[137]

One may not understand this empirical projection as the projection of a mere subjective conviction (Auguste Sabatier) or as an allegorical expression of a spiritual reality (Spinoza). It must be kept in mind that the imaginative schemes are indispensable to the religious consciousness. In virtue of the law of the incarnation of the idea, the glorification idea of Jesus could not have been understood without the scheme of an empirical resurrection.

> Without the scheme of the resurrection, the faith in the eternal Christ would never have been able to be implanted in Semitism. Nor would it have been able to be sowed in the spirit of the majority of men since they are not capable of keeping together, distinct and interdependent, the intelligible and the sensible.[138]

In other words, the scheme of the resurrection corresponds to the exigencies of the Ego present to a world. The incarnated Ego cannot translate the completely internal truth of faith on the inferior level of psycho-empirical consciousness without using its sensible schemes. The Semitic mind, which could not and did not want to think the spiritual in a separate state, could not think survival in terms other than a certain physical survival.

> One recognizes in the resurrection a procedure proper to the Semite. The Semite is unmindful of any dualist anthropology. He is not able to conceive that a man could be said to be living or surviving in the beyond if his soul was separated from his body. Entrance into eternity became a synonym for the resurrection.[139]

This refusal of any realistic dualism does not mean, however, that one should not distinguish between the empirical projection and the spiritual meaning. The refusal to cogitate the spiritual separate from its expression

---

[137] *Ibid.*, p. 83.
[138] *Ibid.*, p. 95.
[139] *Ibid.*, p. 89.

is legitimate, because the meaning realizes itself in the expression. But this refusal should not be an incapacity to think of them apart because this would lead to an empiricism of the brute fact. The resurrection is a religious fact, which means that it is a transphenomenal reality which can only be seen by the believer. As such, faith in the resurrection is nothing but the certainty that God cannot be defeated. "The announcement of the resurrection is, perhaps, only the normal conclusion of a course of events which presuppose the presence of the action of God in the history of Jesus." [140]

The disciples of Jesus were convinced that Jesus would fulfill the messianic expectations. His death, however, constituted an insurmountable obstacle to the Jew who believed in a material messianism. The overcoming of this obstacle fell together with the discovery of Jesus' fundamental intuition: the interiorization of the Jewish messianism. To understand that Jesus' death meant the entrance into His glory ("oportuit pati et ita intrare in gloriam") was for the first Christians one and the same thing as to interiorize in their turn the Jewish messianism. The realization that God was present in Jesus, that He was the supreme revealer of God and thus like God Himself, led to the conviction that Jesus did not die.

This spiritual certitude that God had committed Himself in Jesus and that hence He could not die projects itself, so Duméry continues, in the christophanies of the disciples of Jesus, by which they visualize their own certainty. Would this mean therefore that the belief in the resurrection is a mere imaginative construction? No, it only indicates that man is a psychosomatic unity and that the spiritual must have its sensible expression. We encounter here another example of Duméry's decision to make of the religious universe a rigorously immanent universe.

The psycho-physiological phenomena which accompany mystical exaltation seem less disconcerting today for science than they used to be. Psychology of religion can give an account of them. Actually today one can see that in certain bio-psychic realms, religious fervor is capable, by utilizing in a maximal fashion the *normal* (i.e., free of pathological irregularity) psycho-physiological mechanisms, of bringing to light its own evidence. Nothing illuminates better the psychosomatic unity of the human being. If one cares to see a "miracle" in such fact, the miracle should be ascribed to the utilization, by grace, of the psychic immanence, not to this immanence itself.[141]

The certainty of Jesus' victory over death objectifies itself, finally, in the argument of the empty tomb. In itself the absence of the corpse is not a

---

[140] *Ibid.*, p. 87.
[141] *Ibid.*, p. 80, note 1.

convincing argument for the resurrection. It is rather a consequence than a cause of the belief in the resurrection.[142]

The most logical reconstruction is thus: certitude of Jesus' glorification, God fully committed to Jesus could not have failed Him, therefore, He is alive again. This certainty translates itself into the anthropological style of the Semites: He is risen. Finally, the religious consciousness projects this on the psychological level (apparitions) and the empirical level (empty tomb). Gradually one came to organize this process according to a chronological scheme. Slowly, little bij little, they arrive at a knowledge of what happened since the burial on Friday night and His resurrection on Sunday. The three days may have their origin in the Talmudic belief that the soul waits three days to leave the body. This interval is used to give the glorified Jesus time to establish His kingship over all of creation by His descent into hell and ascent into heaven. (There is in St. Luke a tendency to place the Ascension on the same day as the resurrection.) So everything is reduced to a very small historical core: the apprehension of the perfect interiority of Jesus by His disciples. "Faith in the resurrection is the index of death as a change of life . . . a universal certitude of the presence of God in the history of mankind, of eternity within the duration of time." [143]

### c. *The Four Means of Expression of Hierogenic Consciousness*

Consciousness is hierogenic as well as axiogenic. It creates its religious as well as its axiological and intellectual universe of expression. We saw the hierogenic religious consciousness at work in the fully creative period of the constitution of the first Christian schematism and categorialism. The scheme of the resurrection and the category of the logos applied to the Jesus-fact from the original expression of the Christian translation of the spirit's intrinsic relation with the Absolute. Jesus' passage to an actual and interior salvation provokes man's attention to the presence of the Absolute. His attitude, therefore, coincides with the spirit's most fundamental impulse, namely, his exigency of the Absolute.

---

[142] The two arguments we find in the Gospels for the resurrection of Christ exemplify most interestingly the two fundamental tendencies of our human mind and how they have to be combined. The argument of the empty tomb is the realistic argument, whereas the apparitions form the idealistic argument. If one takes only one of the arguments as valid, one is forced to an agnostic position. *The empirically inclined mind* (for instance, Strauss) accepts the historicity of the empty tomb and interprets it as the beginning of the legend. The disciples of Jesus took his body away. *The idealistically inclined mind* chooses for the apparitions. He turns the resurrection into an idea, a myth, which however is considered as highly valuable, as the whole truth. The idealist's faith is beyond facts. (Duméry.)

[143] Duméry, *Philosophie de la religion*, II, p. 94.

To believe is to grant to a series of facts (the history of Jesus, the noblest shoot of Jewish prophecy) the affirmation of an intrinsic relationship of the spirit to God. It is to judge and declare that the attitude taken by Jesus manifested spiritual interiority; it is to recognize and proclaim that, in the events of His life, taken as an exemplary ensemble, and in the principal points of His message, grasped as normative ensemble, the eternal mediation, immanent to the spirit, has been unveiled. In a word, it is to bear witness that the theandric bond has been rendered visible in the action and teaching of Jesus.[144]

This text illustrates very well the scope of Duméry's decision to apply the henological reduction to the whole body of the Christian expressive discourse. From the philosophical standpoint of the hierogenic consciousness, nothing can resist the henological reduction. We must remember that this is Christianity seen from the standpoint of the creative free spirit. From this vantage point, it is freedom which has the initiative. It commands its projections and determines the meaning and value of the adopted schemes and categories. But there is also the standpoint of the psychological Ego for whom everything is imposed from the outside. On this level the living religious consciousness accepts the schemes and categories as indexes of reality and truth. It is essential, however, that the constituting philosophical consciousness does not abolish the constituted living consciousness. They both have their truth and need each other.

From one point of view the schemes are prescribed as an expression of intentionality; from the other they are the means which enable the aiming at (la visée) of intentionality to be incarnated in order that it can be realized. For example, in a certain sense the fact of Jesus is "constituted" by religious consciousness; in another sense it is this fact of Jesus which gives to religious consciousness the possibility of exercising itself. This reciprocal causality is nothing other than the flow of constant exchange between spiritual spontaneity and psychological consciousness.[145]

Yet, the distance between the original Christian experience of the interior and actual presence of the Absolute in the spirit and the huge doctrinal and cultic body of established Christianity is so great that Duméry, as philosopher, wonders whether the religious consciousness is not victim of its own creations. After having discovered, through the attitude of Jesus, the eternal saving process in the heart of man, why return to the numerous temporal expressions of this eternal presence? The only answer is that consciousness is essentially projective. "Consciousness only exists in projecting itself (in expressing itself) on a succession of levels, where categories

---
[144] *Ibid.*, pp. 111-112.
[145] *Ibid.*, p. 111, note 1.

and schemes arrange themselves." [146] There are three ways of accepting this projective mentality of consciousness. One can understand this projective mentality and use it. This is the case of the philosopher who, in virtue of the creative transcendental standpoint, can evaluate the imaginative structures of the mind. Secondly, one can exert the projective mechanism and not know how to do it. This is exemplified by the superstitious believer who confuses the different orders and who identifies thought and language. Finally, one can utilize the projective mechanism without knowing it, yet by a certain practical knowledge apply it correctly. This is the authentically religious man. Without the help of the philosophical consciousness he is able to fulfill the spirit's need of unification through the detour of empirical and psychological projections. His concrete action realizes with one stroke the ideal of unification which the reflective mind reaches after hours of painful analysis.

If all spontaneous behavior, especially the religious one, is dominated by this projective mentality, one should not be surprised then to find its universal structures also applied to Christianity. To illustrate this fact, Duméry takes the idea of redemption and shows how the principal mechanisms of the projective mentality distribute this idea throughout the different levels of consciousness. He visualizes the idea of redemption, invented by the religious consciousness, as a remedy for guilt feelings. In the context of the Christian faith, this scheme is exploited in order to express the conversion of the guilty conscience into a conscience of forgiveness and purification. The expression takes place on the psychological, mythical, institutional (ritual) and historical levels.[147]

On *the psychological level,* the guilt-complex objectifies itself successively in social prohibition (taboo), in moral evil and finally in the religious notion of sin. The notion of sin implies the notion of an Absolute of dialogue.

Without a God Who says *I* in the manner the soul says *I*, and Who is his interlocutor and his witness, his Father and his Judge (indeed, his justifier),

---

[146] Duméry, *Philosophie de la religion,* II, p. 182.

[147] Duméry notices that Whitehead confirms this division in his book, *Religion in the Making:* "Religion, so far as it receives external expression in human history, exhibits four factors or sides of itself. These factors are ritual, emotion, belief, rationalization." Alfred North Whitehead, *Religion in the Making* (2nd printing; New York: Meridian Books, 1961), p. 18. Duméry likewise sees in the ritual the primordial factor. He reserves, however, the term "belief" for the major affirmations of the faith and uses the term "mythical scheme" for the auxiliary affirmations. Furthermore, he gives special importance to the historical level since history is essential to Christianity. Whitehead's philosophy of religion is rigorously immanentist and thus leaves no place for a revelation. As such it illustrates very well where Duméry's concern to safeguard human autonomy at all costs might lead.

there would not be sin in the sense of a personal offense. There would only be faults, blunders, mistakes, excesses, inconsequences.[148]

Thus there is in sin a specific reference to God: "Thee only my sins have offended; it is Thy will I have disobeyed." (Psalm 51.) Man is overwhelmed by his sinfulness. He longs for forgiveness. Now, on the psychological level, the only way to appease this need for atonement is the experience of an innocent one who takes upon himself the sins of the others.

Here the idea is that the truly guilty makes satisfaction poorly, precisely because he is guilty and his act of repentance is nurtured therefore out of his very guilt. The innocent party, on the other hand, owes nothing and is completely disinterested. Furthermore, his integrity is the sign that grace dwells within him; he is agreeable to God; he can obtain from Him all that he asks of Him.[149]

It is the idea of the scapegoat, but on a higher level. The projection of man's sins on an animal lacks the free initiative of the pure conscience accepting the sinfulness of others. Guilt can only be conquered by innocence, hence the conviction that salvation becomes possible only when an innocent man gives himself as voluntary victim. It is this psychological mechanism which is applied to Jesus. He is considered as the innocent one offering himself freely to God for the sins of humanity. As a result man comes to the certainty of being forgiven and purified.

The Passion is received, on the psychological level, as a sentimental shock which is at once violent and salutary. To this shock corresponds a brusque awakening of religious consciousness. It discovers in the spontaneous offering of the innocent the certitude that it is pardoned and purified. The innocent leads religious consciousness from the without to the within, thus permitting it to perceive within itself the invisible but real sphere where the divine contact subsists.[150]

Duméry's understanding of religion as lived form of the presence of the Absolute in man is again the key to his notion of sin and forgiveness. Sin is a fascination by what is external. Forgiveness is identical with the discovery of the interior and actual presence of God in man.

But the psychological level does not suffice to express the idea of redemption. Not only the sensibility but also the imagination must be shocked. The idea of redemption is projected on *the mythological level*. The imagination is spontaneously chronomorphic and, in a religious context, creates the sacred time. This sacred time, Duméry, in imitation of

---

[148] Duméry, *Philosophie de la religion*, II, p. 186.
[149] *Ibid.*, p. 188.
[150] *Ibid.*, p. 190.

Eliade and Van der Leeuw, calls the "illud tempus," which means both the original and terminal time. The religious consciousness tries to transcend profane time and inaugurate an a-historical existence. This life-giving eternity can be conquered by reconciling the origin (genesis) and term (eschaton) of humanity.

In the longing to begin again a new life at the center of a new Creation – a longing which is manifestly present in all the ceremonials at the end and beginning of the year – the paradoxical desire to inaugurate an a-historical existence, that is, the possibility of living exclusively in a sacred time, is the penetrating dynamism. This entails projecting a regeneration of all time, a transfiguration of duration into eternity.[151]

The instauration of an "illud tempus" by the mythological consciousness as reason for man's culpability and his hope of liberation also has its application in the Judaeo-Christian religion. The cause of culpability is objectified in a time before time duration, which can only be attained by an imaginative reascending towards the origins. Conversely, the cause of salvation is projected in a time beyond time which can be shared by an imaginative ascent towards the "eschata." St. Paul's theology of the first Adam, source of sin and death, and the second Adam, source of redemption and life, is a perfect expression of man's need to objectify his personal experience of sinfulness and need of grace, of death and aspiration for life. This should not be understood as an illusory attempt to escape one's sinfulness and to dream a salvation, but as an attempt to discover the "meaning" of one's culpability and from there to overcome it.

This return to the primordial Adam and the eschatological cycle opened by Christ function only to render an account of a decisive transformation of the human condition. There is an extremely lucid attempt, taking shape in the projective structures, to make manifest that which man discerns with so great difficulty: the meaning of his own culpability.[152]

In other words, the myth of sinfulness at the beginning of time and of salvation at the end of time expresses in a temporal scheme the discovery of the eternal presence of the Absolute in the heart of man. The first Adam cannot be understood without the second Adam, because the meaning of man's culpability is discovered the moment he discovers the sign of salvation in Jesus.

It is afterwards, with the possession of the remedy, that religious man has realized the extent and depth of evil; it is from the heights of Jesus' cross

---

[151] Mircea Eliade, *Traité d'histoire des religions* (Paris: Payot, 1959), p. 343. Text quoted by Duméry in *Philosophie de la religion*, II, p. 158.
[152] Duméry, *Philosophie de la religion*, II, pp. 191-192.

that the attitude of rebellion, Adam's, appears in its intrinsic harmfulness. Inversely, it is from the viewpoint of human culpability, of that which originated in the adamic complex, that appears the marvels of the grace of redemption.[153]

Duméry's idealistic philosophy appears clearly in his interpretation of the doctrine of redemption. He tends to conceive the knowledge of the Absolute present in man as the very means of salvation. Then the Christian notion of grace is identified with the consciousness of the actual presence of the divine spontaneity in the Ego. Conversion is not so much an act of the will as the ascent of the spirit. This can be done because the source of man's being coincides with eternity. This is aligned to the main thesis of pantheism which conceives eternal wisdom as salvation. This pantheistic-idealistic inclination in Duméry tends to replace the eschatological Christian faith by a mystical faith culminating in an ecstatic union with the One.[154]

The experience of conversion, in order to grow to its fullness, has to explicate itself also on *the level of cult*, viz., on the level of the sacrificial institutions. The Christian sacrificial institutionalism is rooted in the Jewish one.[155] The Jews, a pastoral people, favored the immolation of animals as sacrificial rites. Because of this, the law of expiation by blood could easily be applied to Jesus' violent death on Calvary.

The redemption through the crucifixion of Jesus respects and accomplishes a law held in honor in many religious societies and particularly that of the Jews: the law of expiation by blood. This explains how Calvary has been able to become the rallying sign of all those who spontaneously tie together in thought satisfaction and blood.[156]

This institutional law of expiation by blood results in a rather extrinsic form of redemption. This exteriority, however, is characteristic of the institutional. The institutional is made of a solidified collective psychology, crystallized in juridical norms, rites and customs. Like all objectivations they have an ambiguous meaning. They can be degraded projections of intersubjectivity, or salutary detours which the collective consciousness

[153] *Ibid.*, p. 193.
[154] Not all idealism is pantheistic by nature. But the idealistic position easily leads to pantheism, or monism of the spirit. Indeed, if one affirms that all things exist only in and through the spirit, then one is hard put to distinguish the human spirit from the divine spirit. The idealistic, creative spirit is unique. There is no place for finite spirits. Yet one does not necessarily reach pantheism in an idealistic system, as is clear in the case of Descartes' and Kant's philosophy which leaves room for a transcendent God.
[155] Duméry is opposed to the opinion that the Christian sacrificial theology is born of transformed hellenic mystery rites. The Jewish sacrificial economy suffices to come to a sacrificial interpretation of Jesus' death.
[156] Duméry, *Philosophie de la religion*, II, pp. 193-194.

imposes upon itself in order to reconquer its interiority. The institution is thus a mode of communication and obligation and an overcoming of objectivation so that every subject can become subject for the other.

The self, who is a subject for himself, becomes an object for others as soon as he is expressed. This objectivity for the other, correlative to the subjectivity for oneself, leads to social density. However, if interpersonal relations are correctly lived, each subject should become a subject even for the other. The mutual recognition of subjects as subjects is an ideal of reciprocity which marks a limiting point. It is only promised in love.[157]

Duméry interprets the sacrificial act of the community as sign and realization of an intersubjective liberation. By relating directly to God, the community as community comes to a deeper intersubjectivity.

The shedding of blood with the accompanying attitude of oblation and the spirit of sacrifice is the sign of reconciliation between God and between brothers. Sacrificial activity by bloody immolation is spontaneously a doing together. By it the Israelite community is directly related to God and draws close together in its own unity. By this each consciousness is freed and united to all the others.[158]

The Christian community, for the purpose of strengthening its ties with God and its members, followed the Jewish institutional law of expiation by blood, by establishing the cult of Jesus' Passion. To formulate the character of "doing-together" the Christian religious consciousness unified in a liturgical manner the eucharistic last supper and Jesus' death. Thus the eucharistic sacrifice became the new conventional sign of the conscience of forgiveness released in the believer, who, like Jesus, gradually interiorizes religious values.

By taking hold of the deeds and gestures of the Lord, the sacrifice in the Cenacle and on Calvary become again for every Christian an authentic "doing together" ... The faithful, reassembled for the sacred repast, assume themselves the Victim's sentiments of oblation and renunciation; they climb Calvary, they permit themselves to be nailed to the cross, they die, they arise as did Christ and with Christ. These are not fictions but *attitudes;* not imagined representations but concrete intentions, personal determinations, the significance of which surpass all symbolism. To adopt the attitude of Christ, to reproduce His actions, is to make one's own the intentionality which bound Christ to God; it is for oneself to become Christ; in the language of metaphysics it is to adhere to the Absolute, spirit to spirit, to achieve interiority and universality; in a word, it is to enter into the order of charity.[159]

[157] *Ibid.*, p. 194, note 2.
[158] *Ibid.*, p. 195.
[159] *Ibid.*, p. 198.

Man who at the same time lives in a spiritual and sensible world cannot accomplish anything in the first unless it be signified in the latter. The consecration of the host is a perfect example of the hierophantic process, by which the sacred cannot be reached by the religious consciousness unless there is a sensible support.[160] Religion, therefore, is by essence a matter of cult and Catholicism stands by its Mass.

Yet, it may not be forgotten that in the case of Christianity this universally valid institutional law of sacrifice in community, this mythical construction of an original and eschatological time and the psychological projections of justification through an innocent, are sustained by an *historical level*. The historical person of Jesus, Who profoundly interiorized the Jewish economy of salvation, was the determining factor in the origin of Christianity and the disappearance of the Greco-Roman religion. Without the influence of an historical person such revolution would not have been possible.

Let us not believe that this religious revolution would have been accomplished by itself. No, for the dynamism of history, since it is a question of the discoveries of the spirit, resides in the power of invention and the radiation of certain exceptional men. Jesus belongs to this elite, in fact He marches at the head of them: His example is the only one which was able, across the extremely different civilization, to coincide with the human universal.[161]

Christianity could not have come into existence without a personal initiator. We know that this is the way in which Duméry proves the historicity of Christ. Again, the question arises whether Christianity does not mean more by its historical foundation in Christ. Christianity teaches that Christ *IS* the truth, by which a much deeper evaluation of His historical existence is implied. The difference between Socrates and Christ is not just the difference between an idea presented in an intellectual and moral language and the same idea presented in imaginative and mythical projections. Yet, Duméry seems to favor this opinion.

The idea of salvation, based upon the idea of love, would not have conquered the world had it been proposed with eloquence in the intellectual and moral order... By having drunk the hemlock one April evening, Socrates raised up the Platonic message which still occupies us. Though this is a profane example it is quite moving. But by commissioning the cross for His torture, also one April evening, Jesus raised up this enormous movement of faith which came to shake Judaism and to cause to vanish Greco-Roman paganism.[162]

[160] *Ibid.,* p. 140.
[161] *Ibid.,* p. 200.
[162] *Ibid.*

There is more to the historicity of Jesus, as understood by the believing Christian, than the mere fact that Christ existed. The truth of Christianity does not lie in Christ's teaching only, but in the very existence of Christ. One has the impression that for Duméry the truth of Christianity lies on the mere ideal level. His faith in Christ is beyond facts.

This should not surprise us. The historical foundation of Christianity is that which persistently resists all attempts to reduce Christianity to a mere speculative system. Duméry, however, is mainly concerned about eliminating all extrinsicism and false objectivity. He wants to prove that on all levels, as also on the religious level, man posits his own values in positing himself; the negative as well as the positive values. He is able to do this to a great extent by applying the findings of religious phenomenology. The religious consciousness has its universal laws of objectifying the sacred. These laws are also valid for Christianity. We cannot but approve of Duméry's courageous attempt to integrate these in his interpretation of Christianity.[163] This procedure, however, by the very fact that it proposed universal laws of religious expression, contains the danger of eliminating the uniqueness of the Christian religion. Christianity claims to be the truth of religion as such. Duméry is well aware of this. After having shown how Christianity follows the laws of universal religious consciousness, he raises the question whether Christianity is not after all just one religion amongst others: a mythological mode of presenting universal truths.

The philosopher of religion returns to inquire if the Christian faith, based on a minimum of historicity, is anything other than a myth with great powers of assimilation, better founded than the others, more supple and large, but finally able to be related to an inferior noetic order. If the response is yes, Christianity can be reduced by philosophy and transcended by it. Religion, in its precritical enunciation, would only be the infancy of reason. The adult spirit would cast it away along with the explanations of his childhood days.[164]

---

[163] In this sense, Duméry's philosophy of Christianity could be called a "Critique of Pure Religion." Like Kant in his *Critique of Pure Reason* showed the conditions of the possibility of science, so Duméry investigates the conditions of the possibility of religion. The "Grundsatz" is also that the conditions of the possibility of the religious consciousness are at the same time the conditions of the possibility of the religious objects. The problem is that Duméry does not accept Kant's thesis that everything has two independent explanations: one on the deterministic and immanent phenomenological level and one on the level of transcendental freedom. If he accepted this dualism of phenomenon and noumenon, then everything might become acceptable. This, however, would mean that Duméry should call his book "Phenomenology of Christianity," and not "Philosophy of Christianity." The transition from phenomenology to ontology is *the* problem!

[164] Duméry, *Philosophie de la religion*, II, p. 113.

What, in final analysis, is the truth of Christianity? This is the question Duméry must now answer.

### d. Projective Mentality and Truth of Christianity

What must be thought of the plasticity which the Christian consciousness displays in its assumption of the fact of Jesus? Religious consciousness builds and freely reconstructs a coherent system of salvation with quasi-historical value on a minimum of historical data. This plasticity has a name; it is what we call a *myth*. It is here that we discover the universality of the laws of the religious consciousness. Christianity does not have the privilege of a completely different approach to the sacred. This universal law, according to Duméry, is the projective mentality of the religious consciousness as such.

The main characteristic of religious consciousness always consists in this effort to project on the level of psycho-empirical data a movement of searching which originates in a transcendent presence: that of the Absolute.[165]

It is this mechanism which we have observed at work time and again in the reconstructive assumption of the Jesus-fact. What is the value of these projective and mythological elements? If mythological thought is nothing but the childhood of adult reason, as is very often maintained, then it will be difficult to defend its validity for contemporary religiosity; then we would, indeed, have to agree with Bultmann's attempt to demythologize Christianity. We must prove that mythical thinking survives the age of reason; we have to qualify the myth as contemporary with reason.

That man is a being who makes myths, whether or not he has crossed over the threshold of criticism, must be shown. Therefore mythology risks the possibility of changing its meaning, especially in the religious order. If man fashions myths, it is not only because the idea is too exalted, it is because the idea is essentially an attitude and must be appreciated in all the articulations of the incarnate person. One day it will emerge vertically and dominate its own gesture; but even then it must continue to be a sign, a stance, a behavior, as well as an ideal norm or spiritual goal. The myth is therefore at least a part of the mental organism.[166]

The trend of thought Duméry adopts here is appealing. He seems to imply that myth, that imaginative thinking, is the creative source of ideas and values. But how can one reconcile this with his thesis that the creation of ideas and values takes place on the intelligible level of the Act-Law? We have the impression that we have reached the core of the difficulty

[165] *Ibid.*, p. 148.
[166] *Ibid.*, p. 157.

that the henological reduction applied to the religious schemes and categories reduces them too stringently, leaves them no consistency of their own. At the same time, Duméry stresses the necessity of the schematic and categorical expression so strongly that one feels inclined to accept his critique of religion. The ambiguity of the henological reduction of the religious schemes to the mystical union with the One *and* the counterbalancing assertion that these expressions are essential to the religious consciousness accounts for the alternating feeling of agreement and disagreement one has when reading Duméry. How else could it be that everybody attacks Duméry for his philosophical reductionism vis-à-vis religion while he himself, on almost every other page, vigorously maintains the necessity and in a sense irreducibility of the religious schemes? His interpretation of the mythological elements present in Christianity brings out his conviction of this irreducibility in a vivid way. Perhaps, our final critique of Duméry should be that the theory of the Act-Law be placed not on the intelligible level, but on the imaginative level. This would discard the Hegelian character of his philosophy of religion which tends to see religion as the truth on the emotional and expressive level which has to be transcended by absolute philosophy. On the other hand, it would destroy once and for all the latent implication that the essence of philosophy lies in its rebellion against religious tradition.[167]

Duméry, in imitation of M. Eliade, sees the myth as an attempt to abolish profane time in order to come to a total regeneration in a sacred time. This sacred eternal time is reached by retrojecting to the origins (genesis) and projecting to the end of time (eschaton).

Whatever the possible deviations might be, the fundamental intention is clear: the subject creates the myth only with the end of representing, in his own way, the eternity he envisages, or in order to realize, with the help of this instrumental schematism, his longing for renewal, for refounding himself and everything.[168]

[167] Very interesting in this regard is the thesis of Paul Tillich that the meaning of mythological thinking does not consist in man's need to express on the imaginative level what he intellectually understands, but in the fact that in final analysis reality resists conceptualization. This comes closer to a correct evaluation of the myth than Duméry's concept of the myth as product of the necessary projective structure of human consciousness. Tillich applies his concept of the myth in an interpretation of Plato's use of the myth of metempsychosis. "Following [Plato] the Orphic description of the human predicament he teaches the separation of the human soul from its home in the realm of pure essences. Man is estranged from what he essentially is. His existence in a transitory world contradicts his essential participation in the eternal world of ideas. This is expressed in mythological terms, because *existence resists conceptualization. Only the realm of essences admits of structural analysis.* Wherever Plato uses a myth he describes the transition from one's essential being to one's existential estrangement, and the return from the latter to the former." Tillich, *The Courage to Be,* pp. 126-127.
[168] Duméry, *Philosophie de la religion,* II, p. 160.

This attempt to reach eternity by means of the original time gives rise to a curious exemplarism of repetition. The eternal has to be seized *in time*, and, therefore, religious consciousness sees the eternal according to the imaginative chronomorphism of its spatio-temporal existence. This results in an infinite repetition of the inaugural event which happened in the Great Time. The question which arises here is whether the myth is really coming to grips with reality or whether the religious consciousness is victim of an empty imaginative play. Is mythical thinking a childish illusion as so many rationalists maintain, or has it some lasting value even for the man who came to age? Duméry thinks that the myth has its own specific value, because it immediately grasps a necessary essence through its image and is not a victim of its own images.

Far from speaking in the manner of images, as if to transpose an objectively constituted thing into a mystical meaning, the spirit who fashions the myth has in mind, from the beginning, that which he is led to enunciate and then drawn from that the images to apply them to the data ... If this is the case, if the essence is what is attained first and the images are only derived from this, the myth is not the operation of a deluded man as has been said. (Let it be clear, this distinction, applied by the analysis, should be objectified into a chronological distinction. – The aiming at the essence and its expressions are contemporaneous – one cannot separate them.) On the contrary, it is the first penetration towards the idea, the first conquest of value, and – who knows – perhaps the only way of penetrating ideas and values at the foundation of consciousness, even when rational control intervenes to sort out and purify.[169]

This interpretation of the myth may imply more than Duméry generally admits in his critique of the projective elements of religion. It suggests, perhaps, that mythical thought is *always* prior to reflective thought, and this not in a mere temporal sense, but with respect to the inner origin of reflective thought. Even Duméry himself accepts this, if we understand him correctly.

This is why one can maintain that the first (and most fundamental) undertakings of the subject, such as religion and mythogenesis, bear in themselves, in a global and confused state, the essence of the values, which eventually will be redistributed in a distinct state by an evolved and separate reflection.[170]

And from this standpoint Duméry disagrees with the demythologizing of Bultmann, and rightly so. Because of the intimate relation between insight and its expression (*la visée de l'essence et ses expressions sont contempo-*

---

[169] *Ibid.*, p. 162.
[170] *Ibid.*, p. 162.

*raines*) one cannot separate them and give another expression to the insight. It is impossible to redeem language completely:

> Human language is an organism which does not admit a complete biological reconstruction. This is why the old schematism is never completely redeemed; something of it always remains and therefore one can say that the total eclipse of the myth is a serious illusion.[171]

Duméry rejects the demythologization of Christianity in virtue of the necessity of the imaginative expressions and of the preference given to the original expressions.[172] Yet, as far as Duméry replaces Bultmann's *kerygma* by his mystical search for the Absolute and also sees the level of expression as only secondary, we must say that his position comes very close to Bultmann's. To maintain that the level of expression is to be surpassed by the apophatic vision of the Absolute,[173] even if one stresses the necessity of the original level of expression, is to propose a certain kind of demythologization of Christianity. His mystical view of Christianity is too philosophical and leaves insufficient consistency to the religious expressions. In this sense, Duméry goes even further than Bultmann, because his immanent religious world leaves no room for the sovereignty of grace through the preaching which Bultmann still accepts.

On the other hand, it would be unfair to Duméry to interpret his theory of the necessity of the level of expression in terms of a necessity which can be completely made transparent. Certainly the tendency is there to treat the projective level as something merely accidental and which eventually can be disregarded in an ecstatic vision of the One. Yet, as has been seen, his understanding of the myth seems to imply that the image is contemporaneous with the essence: they are inseparable.

---

[171] *Ibid.*, p. 165.

[172] "When it is a question of genesis and eschatology – those two perilous and indispensable genres to morality as well as to religion – it is useless to suppose that one will improve the aim which is proper to them by renewing the symbolic surrounding. The only reasonable course is to seize this aim in its original symbol, for it is by this that it has taken shape." Duméry, *La foi n'est pas un cri*, p. 237. "A theory of demythologization as Bultmann's cannot satisfy us. What authorizes the extraction of the original *kerygma* from its imaginative context is not at all evident. What has taken shape in a schematism ought to be able to continue in this schematism since it was spawned there. One might object that it is better to replace an outmoded schematism by one better suited to the modern mentality. But this substitution, so delicate to realize, only apparently. improves the situation. The schematism gained by the substitution, like the primitive schematism, remains an imaginative structure, even if it is taken from a symbolism which has currency in our day." Duméry, *Philosophie de la religion*, II, p. 243.

[173] This position is implied in Duméry's understanding of the reductions. To reduce for Duméry means to transcend all objectivations. Knowledge *of itself* has no reality-value. It is a projective act of the dynamism of the spirit. "On peut dire que la réduction est *intrinsèquement* apophatique, au sens dionysien: les théodicées objectivistes ne peuvent l'être qu'accidentellement." Duméry, *Le problème de Dieu en philosophie de la religion* (Bruges: Desclée-De Brouwer, 1957), p. 64, note 1.

Human consciousness does not reach any idea or value which is not mediated by its relation to the world. It attains the essence in striving to go beyond that which is given, so that it stirs up an image by varying its grasp on the same given datum. The essence is thus its goal and the image its prop, the one is rooted in its intentionality, the other in its schemes. Now the myth which bears both of these at once is able to be quite definitive in its orientation and revisable in its representations. Immutability would reside in it with the exchange of symbolic forms. The problem of the fixity of norms and the relativity of images would thus be resolved.[174]

The mythical consciousness, in virtue of its capacity to maintain the immutability of its essential vision throughout different mentalities, does not endanger the faithfulness of the religious consciousness to Christianity's original intuition. It is a great relief to know this, in view of the many mythological elements present in Christianity. There is no reason for being dissatisfied as long as we forget the rationalistic prejudices about mythological thinking.

As a precaution we repeat that the myth is not for us a fiction, an allegory, a kind of recital by which an expert pedagogue adapts a spiritual lesson to his children. No, the myth is veridical, serious, concrete; it is more than an adaption and is not a transposition; it is the expression of total consciousness in its taking hold of the world and itself, in its first and definitive élan towards the highest values. Defined in this way, the myth is obviously freed of puerility.[175]

Does the universe of the Christian religious discourse, understood in its true sense, belong completely to the category of religious myth? No, the mythogenesis of the Christian consciousness is based upon the historicity of Jesus. In dealing with its expressive schematism and its historical foundation, Duméry uses a neologism of Van der Leeuw: [176] Christianity is a *mythhistory*. Christianity is a mythology applied to an historical fact in order to disengage and express the signification of Christ's religious attitude.

In advance of and after Jesus, it has projected means of giving a context to his attitude that it might define, seal, and designate it as the model. From this point of view, the myth (in the fuller sense of this term) has not destroyed the historical, nor has it given it undue emphasis. It has simply served it, taken hold of it, and saved it. In a word, there would not have been a Christian "myth" – meaning the Christian schematization and axiology – if Jesus had not intervened in the interior of the Jewish tradition.[177]

---

[174] Duméry, *Philosophie de la religion*, II, p. 163.
[175] *Ibid.*, pp. 163-164.
[176] Van der Leeuw, *L'homme primitif et la religion* (Paris: Alcan, 1940), p. 128.
[177] Duméry, *Philosophie de la religion*, II, p. 168.

Duméry understands the myth-historical character of Christianity in the sense that pre-existing religious structures were projected by the religious consciousness on to historical facts. These structures are created by the transcendental Ego. There is, for instance, the psychological structure that the faults of the sinner can only be destroyed by the free expiation of the just. This process is necessary to turn the guilty conscience into one of forgiveness. This structure was projected by the primitive religious consciousness on the historical fact of the suffering and death of Jesus. From now on the faith in the redeeming death of Christ refers not only to a religious myth, but to a mythhistory. "When fact and structures coincide, faith is born." [178] The same happens to all the other mythological schemes of Christianity as: the resurrection of the body, the virginal conception of Jesus, the assumption of Mary, etc. . . . In every case there is a reference to a certain factuality, be it factualities of different natures.[179]

It must not be forgotten, our author contends, that the mythological consciousness is at the service of the religious consciousness. Religious consciousness is not a prisoner of its mythological representations. This is also the point where Christianity surpasses all religions. One might be able to show that Christianity from the standpoint of its representations is superior to all the other religions of the world. This would, however, not prove that Christianity transcends the other religions, that it is the truth of religion. In order to show this, one has to turn from its immense expressive body to the soul of Christianity. Then what does one perceive?

You see what Bergson has himself noted apropos of mystical experience: a final transcendence of all representation. For the term of religious intentionality is the identification of the human will with the divine – beyond all conceptual or symbolic projections . . . But between the soul and God there is no longer an adequate means of representation, there is no longer the displacement of projection; consciousness, folded back on its center has done away with the surroundings which masked the absolute presence . . . God has become purely present because the soul has ceased looking without. The detour of the exterior was indispensable but it is now completed and surmount-

---

[178] *Ibid.,* p. 123.

[179] The factuality of the virginal conception of Jesus, for instance, is "une factualité présentée comme phénoménale, mais inaccessible comme telle." The scheme of the virginal conception can only be understood when seen in its own context. It is biomystical reality, not completely biological. Referring to C. G. Jung, who, in the interpretation of the function of the archetypes, poses as first principle that all structural analysis of the images has to take place from within, Duméry writes: "L'interprétation d'un mythologème, quel qu'il soit, doit se faire en fonction de son économie interne et ne point recourir à des types d'explication étrangers." *Philosophie de la religion*, II, p. 135, note 3. This again leads to our conviction that a method is required which would allow the mythological language more consistency than Duméry's method of henological reduction allows.

ed; projection has fulfilled its office; it has resulted in possession under the regime of interiority.[180]

This text reiterates the ideal of interiority as the core of the Christian attitude, as the summit of religion which justifies everything that helps to bring about this apophatic union with the transordinal One. Spinoza's insight in the specificity of Jesus' attitude is correct: the primacy of the actual over the prophetic, the primacy of the direct interior relation to God over the indirect projective relation with the Absolute; this constitutes the essence of the Christian religion. All that was lacking in Spinoza's philosophy of religion was a theory of the maintenance of the imaginative structure. The "amor intellectualis" did not respect the spatio-temporal incarnation of man: "The, 'viator,' for him, is absorbed into the 'sapiens,' who is already a kind of 'beatus gloriae.'" [181] But apart from that, Spinoza's conception of the relation between God and man is correct. It is not affected by schemes of contingence: salvation is not conceived as an accidental decision nor the theandric relation as a dialogue. He keeps the imaginative elements on their proper level and does not confound the different levels of expression. Spinoza's philosophy "is a system which is carefully cleansed and scoured." [182] Duméry does not hide his great sympathy for Spinoza's idealistic pantheism. Indeed, it corresponds to Duméry's philosophical inclination towards idealism.

The constantly recurring question is: why do we have to institute, to organize man's exigency for the Absolute on an imaginative, doctrinal and factual basis. This is the main stumbling block for the believer as well as the unbeliever.

When one desires to become a Christian, when he strives to remain one, there is no hope of being one in any other way than according to the institutional canon. Such is the paradox of positive religion: it institutes the universal itself, love itself, even grace; therefore it situates them, dates them, particularizes them. Is not this contradictory? This will be the case only for those for whom the universal would not be more ideal if it became real. Can one, should one, realize the ideal? Finally we have reached that into which the religious problem resolves. For faith, it goes without saying, the answer is yes.[183]

Christianity believes that the realization of the ideal has taken shape in Christ: the incarnation. Duméry's theory of the essentially projective structure of conciousness tries to account for this. Of course, the philosophy of religion does not have to decide whether or not such a thing hap-

---
[180] Duméry, *Philosophie de la religion*, II, p. 170.
[181] *Ibid.*, p. 176.
[182] *Ibid.*, p. 173.
[183] Duméry, *La foi n'est pas un cri*, p. 172.

pened. It only attempts to prove that it is not a contradiction. It has been shown that Duméry has no problem with the *idea* of incarnation.

> The joining of the finite and the infinite is the very essence of religion; it can only be a theandrism. For the rest, the presence of the Absolute in no way hinders philosophy, if it is situated in interiority... On the other hand, the presence of the Absolute in history, its projection in time, its passage through factuality (having become expressive or even realizing), this is what causes a problem for the philosopher.[184]

Duméry as a first-rate philosopher cannot but be concerned about the scandal of an historical incarnation. He tries to explain the historicity of Christianity through his theory of the projectivity of religious consciousness. It is here, primarily, that his theory proves its inadequacy. Christ becomes merely an example to be imitated, and this is certainly not what is meant when the Christian believer affirms that he has been redeemed through the death and resurrection of Christ. For Duméry, Christ is just the occasion through which the religious man comes to the realization that his salvation is from within through the presence of the One at the source of his being. In Christ, the Christian projects the saving presence of the Absolute in him. This impinges on an auto-salvation of man. By the same token the existence of Christ is almost superfluous.

> The Christian attitude effectively makes the law of love, which was proclaimed by Jesus, its law. At the same time *it takes the fact of Jesus as the scheme* of its intention towards the God-love. The cross-checking of this law by this fact is Christianity.[185]

Thus Duméry brings the historicity of Christ, the greatest obstacle to his interiorization process, onto the level of the projective consciousness and from here on all problems disappear.

The answer to the question, "Why adhere to the historical once it has served its exemplary purpose?" can thus be solved in the same way as he accounted for the presence of mythological elements in Christianity.

> Why, it can be asked, should one remain in the historical when the historical has rendered the service that was expected of it? If Jesus has revealed love and justice, it suffices to receive His message; it suffices to strive to love, to become just, thereby forgetting the contingent occasion which provoked these lessons... To this objection there is only one response. One grants or does not grant that consciousness has a projective structure.[186]

This reduces the historicity of Jesus almost to nothing, or rather to a scheme, to an idea.

[184] Duméry, *Philosophie de la religion,* II, p. 100.
[185] *Ibid.,* p. 223, note 1. (Italics mine.)
[186] *Ibid.,* p. 225.

In a sense, from the point of view of its internal structure, one could say that Christianity is the *idea* of the perfect man, the *idea* of man identified with the Absolute; in a word, the *idea* of the man-God applied to the Jesus-fact.[187]

It does not recognize faith in the uniqueness of the incarnation of Christ. One does not see why, if such is the meaning of the incarnation, there is only one incarnation?

As soon as there is admitted the necessary and normal role of a hierophany to mediate the actuation of the divine in humanity, the case for a central theophany, by individual incarnation, will re-enter into a general law, and from this theophany will follow rigorously the belief in the personal divinity of the theophanous subject.[188]

Once one recognizes as irreducible only the spirit's dynamic relation with the transordinal One, the relation of man to God becomes merely spiritual, super-temporal and super-discursive. But because of the projective nature of consciousness, this relation is translated in different expressive languages: the historical, the institutional, the mythical and the psychological.

There is an authentic religious intentionality which, taking its point of departure from the body and psychology which serve personal and social existence, and moving across mood, sentiment, imagination, collective thought (thus through a physiological, affective, mythological, institutional and historical reality) forces itself to intend efficaciously the Absolute.[189]

Such is, in final analysis, Duméry's definition of Christianity. The henological reduction of his religious philosophy has been able to reduce all of Christianity to the very simple truth: man is immanent exigency of the transordinal One. All extrinsicism has been eliminated. Duméry can congratulate himself. He attained his goal. Sartre should no longer have any problems with the existence of God and even with the existence of a God Who saves through history. The problem, however, is that even if Sartre accepted all this he would still be far away from Christianity. The harmony between the Transcendence of God and Duméry's religious anthropology is too great. One does not see what grace and revelation could add to this natural religion. In purifying the concept of the God of dialogue and replacing him by the God of intellectualistic mysticism to please Sartre, Duméry has destroyed the God of the Bible whose main characteristic it is that man stands *BEFORE* Him.[190] Without this notion

---
[187] *Ibid.*, p. 105, note 2.
[188] *Ibid.*, p. 104, note 3. Cf. Chapter IV, p. 286, note 1.
[189] *Ibid.*, p. 228.
[190] Duméry's concept of Christian mysticism is faulty. He understands it too philo-

of "before," there is no real concept of faith and sin, of prayer and witnessing,[191] of sacrifice and adoration. Kierkegaard has most clearly seen this:

> The opposition sin-faith is the Christian one, which in a Christian way transforms the definition of all ethical concepts, giving them one distillation the more. At the bottom of this opposition lies the decisive Christian concept "before God," a determinant which in turn stands in relation to the decisive criterion of Christianity: the absurd, the paradox, the possibility of offense. And that this should be indicated in every definition of Christianity is of the utmost importance, for the offense is Christianity's defense against all speculation. In this instance where is the possibility of the offense? It lies in the fact that man, as a particular individual, should have such a reality as is implied by existing directly in the sight of God; and then again, and as a consequence of this, that a man's sin should concern God. This notion of the particular man... before God speculative philosophy never gets into its head, it can only universalize the particular man fantastically.[192]

---

sophically. It is not so that authentic Christian mysticism completely discards whatever is historical, institutional and psychological. Christian mysticism must be conceived in the line of St. Paul's doctrine of the Mystical Body of Christ, a physical yet mysterious union of all mankind in Christ. This realistic, physical characteristic forms the decisive distinction between Christian-biblical mysticism and mysticism of the natural religions. The Christian mystic sets up external to himself *the definite God of the Bible*. At the same time he sets up within his soul *the disincarnated God of the Pseudo-Areopagite, the One of Plotinus*. The first is his guarantee of the orthodoxy of the second, and prevents him from losing himself in an indistinction which is non-Christian. The confused God within is highly dangerous. We are afraid that something like this also has to be said about Teilhard's "Dieu d'en avant." It is the God of natural religion, a mysticism of the earth, but is there place for the transcendent God of Judaeo-Christianism?

[191] There is no place for the important Christian notion of witnessing in Duméry's concept of Christianity. The Christian martyr should constitute a real objection to Duméry. Indeed, could one undergo martyrdom for an immanent idea? Is not the difference between a man who dies for an idea and one who dies for a person (or supraperson) that the former one dies in victory and the latter... well it does not matter whether he is right or wrong. The real martyr is above that. Witness is more important than mystical insight! "Les états mystiques vous donnent les impressions que vous donne la pratique de la vertu, dans le cas où l'effort plait. Et pourtant, *dans l'Eglise, le martyr passe avant le mystique*. La pratique avant tout. Il y a des mystiques rudement dévoyés." Guitton, *Dialogues avec Monsieur Pouget*, p. 82.

[192] Soren Kierkegaard, *Fear and Trembling. The Sickness Unto Death* (New York: Doubleday Anchor Books, 1954), p. 214.

EPILOGUE

# HUMAN AUTONOMY AND FINITUDE

> Just to be is a blessing
> Just to exist is holy.
> (A. Heschel)

Henry Duméry's philosophy of Christianity is centered around the problem of reconciling human autonomy and creativity with the heteronomy and dependence of religion. This is what is most valuable in Duméry's philosophy of Christianity. Religion understood as "feeling of absolute dependence" (Schleiermacher) clashes with modern man's conviction that he is the author of his world. The movement towards the autonomy of man – a movement which began about the thirteenth century – has reached its completion in this our day. Contemporary man thinks that knowledge and life are perfectly possible without God. Man "come of age" according to Bonhoeffer, "has learned to cope with all questions of importance without having recourse to God as a working hypothesis." [1] This view that God is no longer needed as final explanation of things is exemplified by Laplace's conviction as against Newton's. While Newton deduced from the order of the planetary system the necessary existence of an intelligent First Cause, Laplace came to the opposite conclusion. Asked by Napoleon when he did not mention the Creator in his *Mécanique céleste*, Laplace is recorded to have answered: "Sire, I have no need of that hypothesis."

For Duméry, God is the force of man's force, rather than the stop-gap for man's incomplete knowledge or the liberation from cares and needs, fears and longings. For too many, religion is an alibi for a lack of courage to live on the human level. The God Sartre denies is a God-refuge from earthly tasks and difficulties. To Sartre, man's faith in God is cowardice, revealing man's incapability to endure the frustrations and uncertainties inherent in the human task. Man's coming of age makes superfluous any recourse to a transcendent God. Sartre, following Nietzsche, concludes that God is dead: "He spoke to us and now is silent; all we touch now is

---

[1] Dietrich Bonhoeffer, *Letters and Papers from Prison* (London: S. C. M. Press, 1953), pp. 106-107.

his corpse." [2] Duméry agrees with Sartre, yet the silence of God is for him not a sign that there is no God but an indication of a radical new interpretation of man's religiosity. It indicates that "a Christian philosophy founded on human freedom should be worked out." [3]

With a genial stroke, Duméry convincingly reconciles Sartrian atheism with Plotinian mysticism. He thus eliminates the atheistic implication of the existentialist axiogenesis. The Dionysian tradition in Christianity conceives the human axiogenesis as the very way God creates man. God creates auto-creators. Man's creativity thus becomes co-creation of the spirit united with God. In this view freedom has nothing to fear from divine dependence since this dependence is the real source of its creative autonomy. The dilemma of either reducing freedom to a mere ratification of an anterior or superior datum or condemning man to create evil is overcome. God, in the Plotinian-Dionysian tradition, is creative force rather than pre-existing order. Plotinus' One is above being and thought, time and eternity, determinism and freedom. He is the transordinal One. The finite spirits are fully responsible for the universe of ideas and values, yet their creative freedom is grounded in the undetermined spontaneity of the One.

Duméry did extremely well in outlining a philosophy of Christianity which respects human autonomy and creativity. Intellectual dogmatism and moral defeatism no longer find place in religion. Thus Duméry has satisfactorily replied to the fundamental critique of modern times that religion saps the energy of creative freedom. This is the lasting merit of Duméry's work.

Man is free, yet finite. We find here the fundamental weakness in Duméry's philosophy of Christianity. His concept of man as exigency for the absolute ignores the bio-social context of man and thereby tends to alienate the religious man from his world. Thus Duméry ignores the general trends in philosophy to put man squarely in the world and in time. Duméry's philosophy is largely Hegelian – a "crashcourse" in becoming God. Thus, in the process of giving primacy to human autonomy, strangely enough, Duméry loses the human altogether. This is serious. It means that the second great objection against religious philosophies viz. idealism, is not answered satisfactorily.

The idealist tradition – represented most influentially by Hegel and the conventional religionists – may do justice to the human aspiration but cannot give any intelligible account of the worldliness and historicity of

---

[2] J. P. Sartre, *Situations* (Paris: Editions Gallimard, 1947), I p. 153.
[3] Henry Duméry, *La tentation de faire du bien* (Paris: Ed. du Seuil, 1965), p. 124.

man. Aristotle's fundamental criticism of Plato's theory of forms, that the theory involves the "chorismos" (separation) of the true world from this world, is also our criticism of Duméry's philosophy of Christianity. One should not take lightly the Nietzschean indictment that "Christianity is Platonism for the people"; or Merleau-Ponty's saying that: "The metaphysical and moral consciousness dies when it comes in contact with the absolute." [4]

In so far as religion remains idealism it will stand no chance of being accepted by contemporary thinking. "The precise meaning of modern atheism in its thousand forms is to abandon the heavens of ideas for the earth of men." [5] If there is one trait of contemporary philosophizing that is common to all schools of philosophy, it is the stubborn refusal to leave the human, the relative, the finite. Man is fundamentally finite and so is human truth and value. Therefore, contemporary philosophy wants to take the bio-social context of man seriously. It categorically denies the existence of absolute truths and values. If they exist, they form the habitat of God alone. All man has are truths and values which are the result of a praxis which is world- and time-bound.

Duméry's idealism plays havoc not only with the contemporary decision to adhere to the finite, but also, we believe, with what constitutes the essence of the Christian religion as history and fact. We agree with Oscar Cullman when he objects to every attempt to eternalize and de-historicize the temporal structure of the life of Christ. Every attempt to reduce Christ to some kernel of ideas without a historical frame goes directly against the genius of the Gospel – to save man *in* the world and *in* time. "Salvation is bound to a *continuous time process* which embraces past, present and future. Revelation and salvation take place along the course of an ascending time line. Here the strictly straight-line conception of time in the New Testament must be defined as over against the Greek cyclical conception and over against all metaphysics in which salvation is always available in the 'beyond'; and we must clearly show how according to the Primitive Christian view revelation and salvation actually 'occur' in a connected manner during the continuous time process." [6]

"Just to be is a blessing, just to exist is holy." To put the meaning of life outside of life is to make life itself empty. The difference between Bonhoeffer's theism of the "beyond in the midst" and Nietzsche's atheism

---

[4] Maurice Merleau-Ponty, *Sens et Non Sens* (Paris: Ed. Nagel, 1950), p. 187.
[5] Jean Lacroix, *The Meaning of Modern Atheism* (Dublin: Gill and Son, 1965), p. 57.
[6] Oscar Cullmann, *Christ and Time*, (Philadelphia: The Westminster Press, 1949), p. 32.

of "ideallessness" may not be as great as we think. They both call our attention to the fact that true meaning is accessible only in the actual lived concrete and not through reflection, however profound, upon the lived concrete. "The tree of knowledge is not the tree of life" (Lord Byron).

# BIBLIOGRAPHY

## I. WORKS AND ARTICLES BY HENRY DUMÉRY

*Works*

Duméry, Henry. *La philosophie de l'Action.* Essai sur l'intellectualisme Blondélien. Paris: Aubier, 1948.
—. *Les trois tentations de l'apostolat.* Paris: Editions du Cerf, 1948.
—. *Foi et interrogation.* Paris: Téqui, 1953.
—. *Blondel et la religion.* Essai critique sur la "Lettre" de 1896. Paris: Presses Universitaires de France, 1954.
—. *La tentation de faire du bien.* Paris: Editions du Seuil, 1956.
—. *Regards sur la philosophie contemporaine.* Tournaix-Paris: Casterman, 1956-57.
—. *Le problème de Dieu en philosophie de la religion.* Bruges: Desclée-De Brouwer, 1957.
—. *La foi n'est pas un cri.* Tournaix-Paris: Casterman, 1957.
—. *Critique et religion.* Problèmes de méthode en philosophie de la religion. Paris: Sedes, 1957.
—. *Philosophie de la religion.* Essai sur la signification du Christianisme. I. Catégorie de sujet, Catégorie de grâce. II. Catégorie de foi. Paris: Presses Universitaires de France, 1957.
—. *Phénoménologie et religion.* Paris: Presses Universitaires de France, 1958.
—. *La foi n'est pas un cri.* Foi et institution. Paris: Editions du Seuil, 1959.
—. *Bonaventure: Itinéraire de l'esprit vers Dieu.* Introduction, translation and notes. Paris: Vrin, 1960.
—. *Raison et religion dans la Philosophie de l'Action.* Paris: Editions du Seuil, 1963.
—. *The Problem of God.* Translation and introduction by Courney. Evanston, Illinois: Northwestern University Press, 1964.

*Articles*

Duméry, Henry, "De l'athéisme contemporain," *Nouvelle revue théologique,* No. 71 (Louvain), 1949, pp. 367-374.
—. "Pour une philosophie de la religion," *Etudes philosophiques* (Aix-Marseille), 1950, pp. 34-42.

—. "L'intellectualisme Blondélien," *Teoremi. Rivista di cultura filosofica*, No. 5 (Messina), 1950, pp. 54-66.
—. "L'Athéisme Sartrien," *Esprit*, No. 18 (Paris), 1950, pp. 240-252.
—. "Catholic Thought in France," *Philosophical Thought*, No. 15 (1950), pp. 219-248.
—. 'Blondel et la philosophie contemporaine," *Esprit*, No. 18 (Paris), 1950, pp. 457-477.
—. "La spiritualité Blondélienne," *Nouvelle revue théologique*, No. 72 (Louvain), 1950, pp. 704-714.
—. "Blondel et la philosophie contemporaine," *Etudes Blondéliennes*, Fasc. 2 (Paris), 1952, pp. 71-141.
—. "Blondel et la méthode réflexive," *Etudes philosophiques*, No. 7 (Aix-Marseille), 1952, pp. 390-395.
—. "Aspiration et réflexion," *Etudes philosophiques*, No. 9 (Aix-Marseille), 1954, pp. 420-427.
—. "Une philosophie de la religion est-elle possible?" *Actes du XI Congrès international de philosophie* (Paris), 1954, pp. 26-34.
—. "Critique et religion," *Revue de métaphysique et morale*, No. 59 (Paris), 1954, pp. 435-453.
—. "Le Senne et Blondel," *Giornale di Metafisica*, No. 10 (Turin), 1955, pp. 426-431.
—. "Les rapports mutuels de l'être et du connaître d'après Joseph Moreau," *Etudes philosophiques*, No. 13 (Aix-Marseille), 1958, pp. 245-259 and 525-532.
—. "Discussion avec Jean Mouroux," *Revue des sciences philosophiques et théologiques* (Le Saulchoir, Etiolles), 1960, pp. 89-97.
—. "Foi et connaissance," *Revue Thomiste* (O.P. de Saint Maximum, Paris), 1960, pp. 419-424.
—. "Le modernisme," *Les grands courants de la Pensée mondiale contemporaine*. Les tendances principales. Vol. I (Paris: Marzorati), 1961, pp. 123-158.
—. "Maurice Blondel," *Les grands courants de la Penseé mondiale contemporaine*. Portraits. Vol. I (Paris: Marzorati), 1961, pp. 153-182.

II. WORKS AND ARTICLES ON HENRY DUMERY

*Works*

Barthell, Pierre. *Interprétation du langage mythique et théologie biblique*. Leiden: E. F. Brill, 1963.
Ecole, Jean. *La philosophie de la religion selon Henry Duméry*. Sorbonne, Paris: Thèse de doctorat, 1961.
Malevez, L. *Transcendance de Dieu et création des valeurs. L'Absolu et l'homme dans la philosophie de Henry Duméry*. Paris-Louvain: Desclée-De Brouwer, 1958.
Van Riet, Georges. *Problèmes d'épistémologie*. Louvain: Nauwelaerts, 1960.

*Articles*

Brugger, Walter. "Henry Duméry und das Problem der Gotteserkenntnis," *Scholastik* (Frankfurt a. Main), 1959, pp. 232-239.

Danielou, Jean. "Phenomenology of Religion and Philosophy of Religion," *The History of Religions.* Essays in Methodology. (Chicago: University of Chicago Press, 1959), pp. 67-85.
Dejaifve, P. G. "La foi n'est pas un cri," *Nouvelle Revue théologique,* No. 80 (Louvain), 1958, pp. 468-494.
Leonard, Augustin. "La tentative de M. Henry Duméry," *Revue des sciences philosophiques et théologiques* (Le Saulchoir, Etiolles), 1959, pp. 283-300.
Malevez, L. "La connaissance de Dieu selon M. Henry Duméry," *Nouvelle Revue théologique* (Louvain), 1958, pp. 806-839.
Marlé, René. "La philosophie de la religion de Henry Duméry," *Recherches de science religieuse* (Paris), 1959, pp. 225-241.
Mouroux, Jean. "La tentative de M. Henry Duméry," *Revue des sciences philosophiques et théologiques,* (Le Saulchoir, Etiolles), 1959, pp. 95-102.
Nicolas, J. H. "La foi est plus qu'une visée. A propos de la réédition de 'La foi n'est pas un cri,' " *Revue Thomiste* (1959), pp. 719-737.
Paliard, Jacques. "L'essai d'Henry Duméry sur l'intellectualisme Blondélien," *Etudes philosophiques* (Aix-Marseille), No. 4, 1949, pp. 33-36.
Trouillard, Jean. "Compte rendu de Henry Duméry's 'Le problème de Dieu en philosophie de la religion,' " *Esprit* (Paris), 1957, pp. 458-464.
Van Riet, Georges. "Idéalisme et christianisme. A propos de la philosophie de la religion de M. Henry Duméry," *Revue philosophique de Louvain,* No. 56 (1958), pp. 361-428.
—. "Philosophie de la religion et théologie. A propos de 'La foi n'est pas un cri,' " *Revue philosophique de Louvain* (1959), pp. 415-437.
Widmer, Gabriel. "Synthèse et exigence critique. La philosophie de la religion selon Henry Duméry," *Revue de théologie et de philosophie* (Lausanne), 1958, pp. 203-217.

### III. VARIA

*Works*

Asveld, Paul. *La pensée religieuse du jeune Hegel.* Liberté et aliénation. Louvain: Desclée-De Brouwer, 1953.
Aubert, Roger. *Le problème de l'acte de foi.* Données traditionnelles et résultats des controverses récentes. 2e édition; Louvain: Desclée-De Brouwer, 1950.
Barthell, Pierre. *Psychologie complexe, Langage mythique. Théologie biblique.* Thèse présentée à la Faculté de théologie protestante de l'université de Strassbourg, 1962.
Beauvoir, Simone de. *Mémoires d'une jeune fille rangée.* Paris: Gallimard, 1958.
Bergson, Henri. *L'Evolution créatrice.* 102e édition; Paris: Presses Universitaires de France, 1962.
Blondel, Maurice. *Exigences philosophiques du Christianisme.* Paris: Presses Universitaires de France, 1950.
—. *L'Action.* Essai d'une critique de la vie et d'une science de la pratique. Paris: Presses Universitaires de France, 1950.

—. *Lettre sur les exigences de la pensée contemporaine en matière d'Apologétique. 1896. Histoire dogme.* Paris: Presses Universitaires de France, 1956.
—. *La philosophie et l'esprit chrétien.* I. Autonomie essentielle et connexion indéclinable. II. Conditions de la symbiose seule normale et salutaire. Paris: Presses Universitaires de France, 1961.
—. *Letter on Apologetics and History and Dogma.* Translated and introduced by Alexander Dru and Illtyd Trethowan. London: Harvill Press, 1964.
Bonhoeffer, Dietrich. *Letters and Papers from Prison.* New York: Macmillan, 1962.
Bouillard, Henry. *Blondel et le Christianisme.* Paris: Editions du Seuil, 1961.
Brantl, George. *The Religious Experience.* Edited with introductions by George Brantl. Vols. I and II. New York: George Braziller, 1964.
Buber, Martin. *Eclipse of God.* A critique of the key 20th century philosophies – Existentialism – Crisis theology – Jungian psychology. New York: Harper Torchbooks, 1957.
—. *I and Thou.* New York: Scribner, 1958.
Bultmann, Rudolf. *Kerygma and Myth.* New York: Harper Torchbooks, 1961.
Danielou, Jean. *The Dead Sea Scrolls and Primitive Christianity.* Translated by Salvador Attanasio. Baltimore: Helicon Press, 1958.
—. *The Lord of History.* 2nd printing; Chicago: Henry Regnery, 1964.
Desan, Wilfrid. *The Tragic Finale.* An essay on the philosophy of Jean-Paul Sartre. New York: Harper Torchbooks, 1960.
Dondeyne, Albert. *Foi chrétienne et pensée contemporaine.* 3e édition; Louvain: Desclée-De Brouwer, 1961.
Dupré, Louis. *Kierkegaard's Theologie of de dialectiek van het Christenworden.* Antwerpen: Het Spectrum, 1958.
Eckhart, Meister. *Meister Eckhart.* A modern translation by Bernard Blakney. New York: Harper Torchbooks, 1941.
Eliade, Mircea. *Le mythe de l'éternel retour.* Archétypes et répétition. Paris: Gallimard, 1949.
—. *Traité d'histoire des religions.* Paris: Payot, 1959.
Eliot, T. S. *The Complete Poems and Plays: 1909-1950.* New York: Harcourt, 1952.
Guenon, René. *Le règne de la quantité et les signes du temps.* 14e éd.; Paris: Gallimard, 1945.
Guitton, Jean. *Le problème de la connaissance et la pensée religieuse.* Paris: Aubier, 1939.
—. *Portrait de Monsieur Pouget.* Paris: Gallimard, 1945.
—. *Le problème de Jésus.* I. Les fondements du témoignage chrétien. II. Divinité et résurrection. Paris: Aubier, 1950 (I), 1953 (II).
—. *Dialogues avec Monsieur Pouget.* Paris: Grasset, 1954.
Hammerskjold, Dag. *Markings.* Translated by Leif Sjoberg and W. H. Auden. New York: Alfred A. Knopf, 1964.
Husserl, Edmund. *Idées directrices pour une Phénoménologie.* Traduit de l'Allemand par Paul Ricoeur. Paris: Gallimard, 1950.

—. *Ideas. General Introduction to a Pure Phenomenology.* Translated by W. R. Boyce Gibson. New York: Collier Books, 1962.
Huxley, Aldous. *The Perennial Philosophy.* Cleveland and New York: Meridian Books, 1962.
—. *Bhagavad Gita.* Translated by Swami Prabhavanada and Christopher Isherwood. Introduction by Aldous Huxley. 10th printing; New York: Mentor Religious Classics, 1963.
Kaufman, Walter. *Existentialism from Dostoevsky to Sartre.* The Basic Writings of Existentialism Selected and Introduced by Walter Kaufman. Ohio: The Word Publishing Company, 1964.
Kierkegaard, Soren. *Fear and Trembling. The Sickness Unto Death.* New York: Doubleday Anchor Books, 1954.
Lubac, Henri de. *The Discovery of God.* Translated by Alexander Dru. New York: Kennedy & Sons, 1960.
Luijpen, W. *Existentiële fenomenologie.* Utrecht-Antwerpen: Spectrum, 1959.
Lynch, William F. *Christ and Apollo.* The dimensions of the literary imagination. New York: Mentor Books, 1963.
Marcel, Gabriel. *Creative Fidelity.* Translated and introduced by Robert Rosthall. New York: Noonday Press, 1964.
Marlé, René. *Au coeur de la crise moderniste.* Le dossier inédit d'une controverse. Paris: Aubier, 1960.
Merleau-Ponty, Maurice. *Sens et non-sens.* Paris: Nagel, 1948.
—. *Phénoménologie de la perception.* Paris: Gallimard, 1955.
Muller, Herbert J. *Religion and Freedom in the Modern World.* Chicago: University of Chicago Press, 1963.
Pascal, Blaise. *Pensées.* Paris: Editions Garnier, 1957.
Pieper, Josef. *Leisure, the Basis of Culture.* Translated by Alexander Dru, with an introduction by T. S. Eliot 6th printing; New York: Pantheon Books, Inc., 1961.
Plotinus. *Enneads.* Translated by Stephen MacKenna. 3rd edition, revised by B. S. Page; New York: Pantheon Books, Inc.
Robinson, John A. T. *Honest to God.* Philadelphia: The Westminster Press, 1963.
Russell, Bertrand. *A History of Western Philosophy.* New York: Simon and Schuster, 1945.
Spiegelberg, H. *The Phenomenological Movement.* An Historical Introduction. Vols. I and II. The Hague: Martinus Nijhoff, 1960.
Sartre, Jean-Paul. *L'Etre et le Néant.* Paris: Gallimard, 1943.
—. *Le diable et le bon Dieu.* Paris: Gallimard, 1951.
—. *Being and Nothingness.* Translated with an introduction by Hazel E. Barnes. New York: Philosophical Library, 1956.
—. *The Devil and the Good Lord.* Translated by Kitty Black. New York: Random House, Inc., 1962.
—. *L'Existentialisme est un humainisme.* Paris: Editions Nagel, 1964.
Teresa of Avila, Saint. *Complete Works.* Vols. I, II, and III. Translated by E. Allison Peers. 5th printing; London: Sheed & Ward, 1957.
Tillich, Paul. *The Shaking of the Foundations.* New York: Scribner, 1948.

—. *The New Being.* New York: Scribner, 1955.

—. "The Lost Dimension in Religion," in *Adventures of the Mind.* Articles from the *Saturday Evening Post* edited by Richard Thruelsen and John Kobler. New York: Vintage Books, 1959, pp. 52-62.

—. *The Courage to Be.* New Haven and London: Yale University Press, 1963. 19th printing.

Tresmontant, Claude. *Essai sur la pensée hébraique.* 3e édition; Paris: Editions du Cerf, 1962.

—. *Introduction à la métaphysique de Maurice Blondel.* Paris: Editions du Seuil, 1963.

Trouillard, Jean. *La procession Plotinienne.* Paris: Presses Universitaires de France, 1955.

—. *La purification Plotinienne.* Paris: Presses Universitaires de France, 1955.

Underhill, Evelyn. *Mysticism.* A Study in the Nature and Development of Man's Spiritual Consciousness. New York: E. P. Dutton & Co., Inc., 1961.

—. *The Mystics in the Church.* New York: Schocken Books, 1964.

Vuillemin, Jules. *L'Héritage Kantien et la révolution Copernicienne.* Paris: Presses Universitaires de France, 1954.

Waelhens, Alphonse de. *La philosophie et les expériences naturelles.* La Haye: Martinus Nijhoff, 1961.

Weil, Simone. *Attente de Dieu.* Paris: La Colombe, 1950.

Whitehead, Alfred North. *Religion in the Making.* 2d printing; New York: Meridian Books, 1961.

*Articles*

Desanti, Jean. "Hegel est-il le père de l'existentialisme?" *Nouvelle Critique,* Nos. 56-57.

Lacroix, Jean. "Le sens de l'athéisme actuel," *Esprit* (Paris), 1954.

Moeller, Charles. 'Is It Possible in the 20th Century To Be a Man of the Bible?" in *The Liturgy and the Word of God.* Collegeville: Liturgical Press, 1959, pp. 119-156.

Van Riet, Georges. "Y a-t-il chez St. Thomas une philosophie de la religion?" *Revue philosophique de Louvain,* No. 61 (1963), pp. 44-81.